AF483605

THE TORCH OF LIFE

A PLAYBOOK FOR GENERATIONAL PROSPERITY

DAVID W. ROBBINS

Disclaimers

This book is for motivational and inspirational purposes only. It depicts events in my life as truthfully as recollection permits. Any reference to others, living or dead, is purely coincidental. The contents are based upon my personal experiences, perspective, and interpretation of the subject matter. I do not render financial, medical, legal, or any other professional advice to the reader. Readers should seek professional guidance before acting. Results will differ for every individual. I make no guarantees of any kind, express or implied. No liability is assumed for loss, harm, or damage due to suggestions or information contained in this book.

It's nothing graphic, but be advised this book does contain general references to death and mental health issues, including suicide.

Library of Congress Control Number: 2025927199
Published by David Robbins
Wesley Chapel, Florida
davidrobbinstol@gmail.com

First Edition, Printed in USA

Cover Design and Interior Formatting by:
Ebook Launch, 409 Noel Ave, Comox, BC, Canada

ISBN 979-8-9942158-0-7 (hardcover)
ISBN 979-8-9942158-1-4 (paperback)
ISBN 979-8-9942158-2-1 (e-book)

CONTENTS

INTRODUCTION

News flash – we're all gonna die! Whew, now that that's out of the way, let's start living! That's right, we're owed *nothing* in life, not even life itself. Think of the stillborn babies, infant mortality, childhood deaths, and many other instances of someone dying before their time. That thought saddens me. It also lights a fire under my butt to cherish every single moment that I have here on Earth. Remember, everybody dies but not everybody lives. I'm intent on living my best life possible and I hope you are, too. For me, that involves many things such as growing, learning, maturing, helping, loving, playing, and especially living out my personal mission(s) to the fullest before I die. I'm also a smaller part of something bigger and plan to leave a lasting legacy after I'm gone. That's where this book comes in. Part of my legacy and heartfelt obligation is to pass along more than a half century of life experience to the next generation, including *you*. That hand-off encapsulates decades of knowledge, education, training, personal experience, and many vast concepts that lead to a prosperous life. Therefore, this book's contents are big…very big. Far more than career, money, or fame, it's about *life*…and the generations that follow. If you'd like to live your own life of prosperity and pass the same along to subsequent generations, then read on!

The Torch of Life

First of all, you may ask, "What is a torch of life?" Good question. Most people have heard the idiom *pass the torch*, believed to have originated during the ancient Greek torch relays. Passing the torch is symbolic of turning something over from one person to the next, often a responsibility, knowledge, or position. A passing of the baton. For example, the outgoing U.S. President passes the torch to the incoming one. The outgoing CEO of a company passes the torch to the incoming CEO. You get the idea. In that regard, we all get to pass along our very own personal torch. What torch? The biggest torch of all…life! When our time is up and we're called to leave this Earth, we pass our torch to those who follow – the next generation. Yes, my life will soon be over but many others will follow. What will I pass along? Allow me to introduce you to *The Torch of Life*…

As a father and retired military veteran, I'm passing along my own personal torch of life to my two adult kids (and *you*). Like many parents, I've spent a lot of time *verbally* telling my kids how to succeed in life. They'd forget half of it by nightfall and I got tired of repeating myself, so I decided it would be simpler to write it down. The initial idea was to pass along a book on topics such as education, career, money, health, relationships, values, and more. In essence, how to be *successful* in key areas of life. This is good. Mission accomplished. **Well, countless books exist on those stand-alone subjects of** *individual success*.

So, why stop there? I wanted to *exceed* mission objectives, so I took it to the next level. This involves not only achieving success in those key areas but also connecting it across generations. In other words, mine to theirs, theirs to the next, and so on. It's a framework for continuity. Preserving that success would lead to what many would call *generational wealth*. This is very good. **I've seen some books on** *generational wealth*.

However, I went yet *another* level further. Here, I saw fit to connect all the puzzle pieces together, as they play out in real life. In other words, let's go beyond success and generational wealth. Let's step up our game and seek true *prosperity* in those areas and others. (And as I'll soon explain, there *is* a difference.) So, that adds systems and processes to the continuity framework. This is great! **I've yet to discover many (any?) books on** *individual prosperity*.

Then, just for the heck of it, I went *all out*. What's the connective tissue between all generations and humanity at large? Going beyond generational wealth and individual prosperity involves much deeper and more meaningful things such as personal values, core beliefs, relationships, parenting, emotions, and human spirituality. In short, the entirety of not only our lives here on Earth, but also into death and beyond. Full circle. All the way through. It's a continuity framework with integrated systems and repeatable processes aimed at achieving the total package. This is phenomenal! **I've found precisely zero books on achieving the holy grail –** *generational prosperity*.

I thought how wonderful it would be to pass along such a treasure trove of valuable knowledge to my children and others. So, I decided to capture all of it in a single book. *This* is that book. Let's call it a *playbook for generational prosperity*. **This is my attempt to add value.**

What is Generational Prosperity?

I define generational prosperity as having prosperity in key areas of your life and passing that along to the next generation. The two parts are linked; *prosperity in your life* and *passing that along to the next generation.* (Organizations and companies refer to this concept as succession planning.) Here, it applies to your life and the generations that follow. Let's look briefly at the first part.

In my opinion, too many people strive for success in life. Heck, I do too – why not, right? It's good to be successful, but I've grown to believe it's wiser to work towards prosperity. As I said, they are different. So, what's the difference? Well, without playing word games or splitting hairs over vocabulary, I make a fairly simplistic differentiation here. I don't squabble over the two terms and often use them interchangeably. However, I generally view *success* as more narrowly focused and specific. Here are just a few examples of what many people would call *success…*

- Accrue a certain net worth.
- Grow a business to a specific annual revenue.
- Achieve victory and medals in professional sports and other areas.
- Receive awards, trophies, and high acclaim in entertainment.
- Accumulate millions of followers and subscribers on social media.
- Earn an advanced academic degree.

All of the above (and many other things) would reasonably be called successful by most people and I would agree. Milestones. Goals. And transactional. All true. However, if you widen your perspective a notch or two and go much deeper, you'll reach what I call prosperity. Stretch your success, if you will. This provides a more rewarding, meaningful, and holistic perspective.

Here are just a few ways to be *prosperous*…

- Grow a rewarding career or business that fuels your passion, adds value, and changes lives for the better.
- Thrive in entertainment or professional sports with integrity and mentor others along the way as a positive role model.
- Build a strong, healthy, committed, and loving marriage.
- Apply your social influence to unite others, lend a hand up, and reshape entire communities for the better.
- Raise immature, curious, and aimless *kids* into respectful, caring, and purposeful *adults*.
- Live a life of meaning and purpose through a value system of integrity and service.

As you can see, success is grayscale; prosperity is color. Prosperity adds meaning and purpose. It's richer, deeper, and more meaningful. Success is *how*; prosperity is *why*. But remember, all of this is only part of the equation. So, don't stop there. In order to come full-circle, you must pass that along to the next generation – those who will follow you. That brings us to the second and final part.

Sadly, many people will achieve success in life only to have it die with them. A series of stand-alone lives and subsequent deaths. Someone lives and someone dies. Repeat. They're one and done – generationally, everything starts over from scratch. We've heard about too many folks who die broke. We've heard about the celebrities, professional athletes, business tycoons, or other rich people in the news who died without an estate plan. For every one of these sad stories, there are millions of similar ones that never make the news. These folks worked very hard for their success, only to see it all squandered away through enormous attorney fees, costly legal battles, broken relationships, and bitter in-fighting among heirs or surviving family members. Even worse, many generations never inherit a system of personal values or the benefits of higher education. Saddest of all, there aren't enough inheritances of parental structure, guidance, and love.

I believe a better way is to intentionally and systematically link prosperity from one generation to the next. Yes, individuals will die, but they can leave an interconnected and seamless legacy for the next generation.

As per the aforementioned individuals, a well-constructed estate plan could have turned their *individual success* into *generational wealth*.

More importantly, adding a foundational value system, a loving family, and proactive parenting could have ensured a strong and healthy hand-off of *generational prosperity*! A focus on the bigger picture could have preserved their legacy. In turn, each generation builds upon the one prior instead of starting over.

As you'll discover, this playbook will certainly show you how to succeed in many areas of life. It will also help you achieve generational wealth. But it doesn't stop there. The core concept of this book is to focus on the holistic big picture. So, money, career, home ownership, and other tangible things are all very important. Those can bring success. However, I suggest you go further…much further! Wait, what?! Yes, those things are important, but so are many other things. What do I mean? Well, sit back, get comfortable, and continue reading to learn more. We'll eventually get to growing wealth, but your mindset and perspective on true prosperity are even more important. That's why it's all included. So, why read this book?

Why Read *The Torch of Life*?

If I could recommend only *one* book to my kids (or anyone), this would be it. Many books are fun, informative, mysterious, or entertaining. However, only a rare few offer the potential to **revolutionize your entire life**. This is not about someone else's life, but rather *your* life. You are the focus. You may be a senior citizen, full-time student, retiree, corporate executive, pro athlete, single parent, entrepreneur, celebrity, or an 'average Joe'. Regardless of age, circumstance, or demographic, you can use this book to realize your fullest potential.

Sadly, there are far too many people struggling with poverty, crushing debt, food insecurity, dead-end jobs, stress, anxiety, addictions, broken homes, dysfunctional families, misguided values, and more. Some are simply stuck. Running but going nowhere fast. Or maybe they're somewhat successful but not truly prosperous. If you're looking for a better way, you've found it.

With much help along the way, I've managed to achieve a certain level of success in all areas of my life. I sincerely hope you do, too – that's why I hope you read this entire book. So, how about you? Are you on the path to wealth? Are your days fruitful? What are your hopes, dreams, and aspirations? Will you get married? Have kids? What's your purpose in life? Perhaps you've never really thought about those things. Well, today's your chance. Now's your time. This is your opportunity to quit going through the motions. It's time to wake up and start living like you mean it! Even if you already know what you want out of life, how well are you progressing towards your goals? Are you succeeding? You may know what you want, but are you actually getting it? How's your health? How are your finances? Are you happy in life? *In other words, if you're doing it your way…how's that working out for you?* Regardless, this book can help, but only if you let it.

You should read this book if you'd like to have a successful and prosperous life. If you'd like to go from ordinary to *extra*ordinary. Let's face it, no matter where you are in life, it's always nice to achieve that *next* level. The principles in this book can help you get there and can be applied at any age and across many areas of life. You should read to gain valuable knowledge and insight on how and why to achieve generational prosperity. You should also perform some self-reflection about your hopes, dreams, and your beliefs about life and beyond. Ideally, you'll live a fruitful and inspired life *and* leave a lasting legacy to the next generation.

I'm passing this torch (of life) to my adult children. I'm also passing it to anyone who wishes to benefit from it…including *you*. In turn, I hope you pass it along to *your* next generation. Of course, you don't need to have children to pass along helpful life principles. This same prosperity can be passed to a spouse, partner, cousin, niece, nephew, friend, co-worker, charity, or whoever else you wish to help. The torch can be passed to anyone at any time. In fact, you don't have to pass it along to anyone; you can use this book to simply live *your* best life possible. Think of it as a continuity book for life. Answers to the test. **Keys to living an inspired and fruitful life.** These keys can help you find your purpose in life, achieve your dreams, and enable the next generation to do the same. It puts **you** in charge.

You're the Head Coach!

Think of the head coach of a football team. He's the maestro – the master coordinator of his team. The coach doesn't just walk the team onto the field and wing it. He *could* do that, but I doubt the team would be very successful. No way. The coach has a playbook for the big game and uses it to guide his team to victory. A playbook doesn't guarantee a win, but it stacks the odds in the team's favor through a set of high-percentage plays. And they practice those plays over and over and over again. So, if the team doesn't wing it on game day, why would you wing it with your *life*? After all, isn't your life more important than a football game? I hope so. Wouldn't it be nice to have your own playbook? Well, look no further…here it is! Keep in mind, even football players are coached to excel in specific areas of the game. They have special coaches for offense, defense, and even for key positions within each. For example, running backs train together, quarterbacks receive in-depth coaching, receivers practice their routes, and so on. Those are all extremely valuable things to learn and execute if you want to win a football game.

Just as football players strive to master key positions of the game, many of us strive to master key positions of our *life*. This includes areas such as career, money, parenthood, marriage, education, and much, much more. We should work to excel at all of them. One way to do that is by reading. Books can offer an educational deep-dive into each of these areas. Please read as many of those books as possible.

However, *this* book does not dive into the weeds; it's not a *vertical* silo of any one specific area. **This book is for the head coach of your life – you!** As such, *The Torch of Life* oversees *all* major areas of your life and provides you with a *horizontal*, strategic, integrated, big-picture, head coach perspective of life. It stacks the odds in your favor – not for a football game, but rather for *generational prosperity*. This master playbook offers a path to true prosperity for you and your family. It should oversee and prioritize all other books in your library. Please use it to achieve *your* victory! As the table of contents suggests, there are a number of ways this book can help you *level up* your life, so allow me to elaborate a bit.

What's in this Playbook?

People often fail to prosper due to *lack of know-how, self-defeating beliefs,* and/or *inaction.* This book addresses all three reasons across three respective parts. It provides a framework (playbook) to follow. You should customize things to the personal circumstances of *your* life.

First, *Part I* focuses on *HOW* to achieve prosperity and is generally more *prescriptive.* It consists of principles that provide knowledge and foundational skills necessary to achieve success in many areas of life (the know-how). It also covers essential values and a proper mindset to facilitate your journey. These principles are very effective and fairly universal. But the more you read, I hope you'll also experience something much bigger – a deep-seated fire and passion for life and those you love.

That's where *Part II* comes in, which is generally more *descriptive.* These concepts are far more individualized and unique to each person. With each passing chapter, you'll learn progressively more about *WHY* you should do these things. Explore *why* you should live like you mean it. Living with purpose and meaning will benefit you, your family, and generations to follow. This part tugs at your heart and reminds us what life is really about.

Lastly, *Part III* will tie it all together and leave you with a call to *ACTION.* It's one thing to acquire knowledge, build a proper mindset, and adopt a set of values, but you must then execute (do the work)! By doing the work, you'll begin to forge your own personal path to the life you've always wanted.

Simply put, *The Torch of Life* is a collection of valuable concepts, principles, systems, lessons, models, and advice on achieving prosperity. Here's an appetizer of what to expect…

A Mini-Overview
(*Part I - How*)

Intentionality & Critical Thinking

- Understand why *intentionality* and *critical thinking* are foundational to success.

- Start with the end in mind; *intentionality* is consciously deciding what to do, *on purpose.*
- Determine how to get there; *critical thought* is the logic, rationale, and reasoning behind intent.

Lifelong Learning

- Uncover numerous methods to pursue lifelong learning and appreciate how it can *level up* many areas of your life.
- Learn many ways to earn a college degree, certifications, and other education *100% debt free.*

Grow a Career

- Transition from high school or college into a rewarding full-time profession.
- Ditch the J-O-B! Grow a rewarding career at the intersection of *passion* and *prosperity.*
- Instead of a 5-figure income, go ahead and *level up* to a 6-figure income (or more).
- Be an entrepreneur; *level up* from owning your own *job* to owning your own *business.*

Financial Wealth

- Choose to *level up* from millionaire to *multi*-millionaire and change your family tree.
- Become 100% debt free; *level up* your life from financial bondage to financial freedom.
- Experience the power of home ownership; increase your net worth by 6 or 7 figures.
- Retire with dignity; *level up* from relying on social *in*security to enjoying wealth and financial independence.

Health Wealth

- Learn to care for the *one* body that you have; physical and mental health are vital to prosperity.

- Health wealth includes your *total* health: physical, mental/emotional, intellectual, spiritual, and relational health.

Unplug (~~Virtual~~ Actual Reality)

- Undergo a digital detoxification; unplug from *virtual* reality and *level up* to *actual* reality.
- Discern how to *use* virtual reality and *live* in actual reality; it may revitalize your entire life.

Life Principles (Rules of the Road)

- Learn the many benefits of giving helpful hand-*ups* instead of hurtful hand-*outs*.
- Use different input to obtain different output; transform your entire life for the better.
- Decide to *level up* from a life of *chaos* to one of *order*; be blessed with more time and more money.

Personal Values (Who Are You?)

- Build character, conviction, and a strong set of personal values; walk your own path in life instead of following sheeple.
- Hand down the *most important legacy* possible – a solid value system.
- What you are matters; *who* you are matters more…far more.

The Power of Individualism

- Discover the power of *individualism* and how you can *level up* from victim to *victor*.
- Break free from allusions of sexism, racism, labeling, stereotyping, and a host of other self-limiting misperceptions.
- Shatter the mold of group-think and living in a box; live your own life, your own way.

A Mini-Overview
(*Part II - Why*)

Marriage (Lasting Love)

- Decide to *level up* your love life from a hot mess to a loving, healthy, and thriving relationship.
- Instead of infidelity, indifference, and abuse, you'll *level up* to support, love, and excitement.

Parenting (The Next Generation)

- Don't be a stagnant parent (the noun); *level up* and start to proactively parent (the *verb*) – your family will thrive.
- Raising kids into successful adults is a key component to achieving *generational* prosperity.

Life (Meaning & Purpose)

- Go deep into personal thought and self-reflection to answer, "What's the meaning of life?"
- Discover what (or who) gives you *purpose* in life and why it's vital to achieving prosperity.
- Enjoy the richness and beauty that life has to offer; laugh, love, and *live*…like you mean it!

Death (Acceptance & Anticipation)

- Explore how *acceptance* of death and *mental preparation* can actually lead to a richer life!
- Should we think about death with curious *anticipation*? If so, why? Read on to find out!

Beliefs (Spirituality & Beyond)

- Leverage perspective and thoughts on eternity, infinity, religion, spirituality, and life *beyond.*
- Is death inevitable? What is life as we know it? Remember when people *used to die*?!

Warning: some areas are counter-cultural and may reframe your entire way of thinking!

A Mini-Overview
(*Part III - What Now?*)

Part III contains a **convergent summary** of *Part I* and *Part II*. It wraps everything up, ties it all together, and then issues a **call to action!** Here, you'll formulate a **game plan** and then **execute**. You'll be on the way to living and leaving your own legacy.

That's just to whet your appetite; a mini glimpse into what you'll learn in this playbook and how you can achieve explosive success in many areas of life. There's much more to come! Like I said, the contents of this book are big.

As you'll discover, *The Torch of Life* is packed with valuable advice, principles, and actionable ways to achieve prosperity. That can mean many things so let's clarify what it's *not*.

This book is *not* a deep-dive into investing, tax laws, healthcare, estate planning, marriage counseling, legal advice, or therapy. For that, you must seek professional advice. Likewise, it does *not* make guarantees of any kind.

So, spoiler alert – there are no short-cuts and hard work *will* be necessary. I won't give away any secrets, but you'll discover just how simple things really are. Not easy, but simple. The value add is that you now have a one-stop-shop for prosperity in many areas of your life and for the generations that follow. You have a guiding framework, principles, and repeatable processes that can be passed down many generations.

Although this book does not guarantee success, it does stack the odds in your favor. Just like the football team's playbook does not guarantee their success. If they don't *execute*, they will not be very successful. The players must block, tackle, kick, throw, and catch; they must execute the plays. You too must execute. That's why I go even further still and demonstrate ways to do so. In order to help you execute, I do two things throughout this book...

First, I apply real-life examples.

I weave in real-life *application* of principles into each area so you can see things in action. I do this primarily through memoir-style highlights from my own personal life. By sharing true parts of my own story, I hope to show how these principles actually work in real life. Of course, this is only my first-hand experience and everyone's situation is different. However, the principles can be applied by any able-bodied person. So, this playbook isn't just a 'list of things' but also illustrates how to execute them. You can act or not, it's up to you. Remember, you must execute in order to succeed.

Second, I demonstrate dependency.

There's no silver bullet for success. No short cut. No easy button. The principles, concepts, and values that I include here are interconnected, interdependent, and supportive of each other; they're not simply a sequential checklist of things to do. For example, being a life-long learner can help grow your career which, in turn, can help you build wealth. Another example is how the power of individualism can help you break the victim mindset and remove self-limiting shackles that hold you back. Also, living by a set of personal values can help you succeed in *many* areas of life. So on and so on, exponentially. Therefore, as you read, don't simply focus on one area; that's old-school thinking. Use each area to support the others.

Like the gears of a well-oiled machine, they all work together; if one is missing, the machine is less effective and often breaks down altogether. For example, a football pass play is more effective if the linemen block, the quarterback throws, and the receiver catches; if even *one* player fails to execute, better luck next time. That means the more principles you follow, the more prosperous you'll be!

Remember, none of us can foresee the future. Many things will change in life. Out of the mountains of advice in this book, you'll adjust and customize things along your journey in order to best fit your circumstances.

Unpacking the Contents

[Note: It's nothing graphic, but this book does contain general references to death and mental health issues, including suicide.]

It should go without saying, but be advised this book does not contain all of the answers to life. Hardly. You can (and should) be a lifelong reader of many educational, motivational, and/or inspirational books. Seek to learn as much as possible in the areas that interest you. There are countless other books, educational programs, and professional certifications to accomplish just that. This book is not the small picture but the big picture. It's not comprised of short-cuts or hacks, but rather it takes an overarching and holistic approach. This is the head coach's book – *your* book. I've extracted hundreds of lessons from life, selected the most valuable ones, condensed them down, and packed them into a single book. So, the content is based upon a number of things.

This book's **input** is the culmination of knowledge and actions that lead to prosperity. It contains decades of life experience, advice, valuable lessons, and universal principles that can work for every able-bodied person. It's the lessons learned from my own stupid mistakes and that of others. Looking back, this is the book I wish I had many times during my life. My parents raised me well and taught me many things. However, at age 18, I left home for the military. I fell under the guidance of many different people in various organizations all over the world. A few decades later, I realized I had learned many things; some good and some not so good, but all in a haphazard, patchwork, and inconsistent manner. There was no structured continuity. Life has given me many teachers: my parents, school, the military, college, friends, family, co-workers, classmates, and more. One of the strictest teachers I had was the school of hard knocks (learning the hard way). This book is a compilation of all those teachings and lessons learned to date. Plus, plus, plus. It's the transfer of an enormous body of knowledge from one generation to another. It's a product of my mind's never-ending honing of strategic thought (a blessing and a curse). Over a half century of education, training, mentorship, critical thought, real-life experience, and results. The **output** is a playbook that has the potential to transform your entire life.

This book both *symbolically* passes along life knowledge and *literally* passes along a book to the next generation or anyone who's interested. I've written this book in such a way that it's timeless and can span many generations. Well, it's as timeless as possible; after all, the only constant is change and nothing lasts forever. It's my wish that if someone were to read this book 50 years from now, it would still be just as *true* and just as *valuable* as it is today. I won't be around then, but I hope my kids are — maybe you, too. If so, you'll see if my wish came true. But please don't wait 50 years…start today.

This book contains the plays for living a rewarding life. But mind you, it's *a* playbook, not *the* playbook. I don't consider my advice better than any other; it simply *is*. If you don't *want* my advice, don't take it. If you don't *like* my advice, don't follow it. This is my personal opinion and my own perspective. It's my beliefs and my walk. There are many ways to win in life; this happens to be *a* way that has worked for me and my family. It has worked well for us — very well. I am truly humbled and ever so grateful. I wish to share the principles that have enabled my success. I'll lend a hand to anyone but I won't do the work for them. Any able-bodied person can succeed if they execute. I hope *everyone* chooses to execute. This is the very book I'm leaving to my own two adult children. However, it's written for *anyone* and *everyone* who chooses to use it for their own benefit. Do so if you wish. I'd be honored if this book was helpful to you in some way. Likewise, my feelings won't be hurt if you choose not to follow my ideas. No worries. I've devoted time to writing this book not because it can help *me*, but because it can help my kids (and *you*). Trust me, I'll be fine either way. I've learned too many things the hard way. I'd like others to avoid the same stupid mistakes I've made. I want to lend a long-lasting *hand up* to others and help them succeed in any way possible. Who am I, you may ask.

Who Am I?

First, what I'm not. I'm not a Zen Master, genius, life guru, or mystic prophet. I make no promises or guarantees of any kind. If you're looking for a life hack, shortcut, or magic wand of some kind, please look elsewhere — I don't have it. I'm not a social media influencer, famous celebrity, or world leader. So, then who am I?

There's more about me in the back of the book and I'll expand upon my background in the pages that follow. I've also woven in examples of my life to help solidify particular principles where appropriate. All in all, I'm just a simple guy who lives a simple but wonderful life. A grateful and humble life. I tell my wife often that I could have died years ago with zero regrets, having achieved far more than I ever thought possible. I feel like I'm walking on clouds of prosperity. I'm convinced that I've already won! But I'm not finished just yet. Each and every day has been, and continues to be, icing on the cake. I savor every day with family and friends while serving my community along the way. I'm the guy who holds the door for you at the grocery store. I'm the guy who shakes your hand and looks you in the eye. The guy who says, "please and thank you." I mean what I say and say what I mean. I quietly make things happen and get things done, no credit required. I'm the guy you've never heard of – the man behind the curtain. *Shh*. In short, what I've done across more than a half century and around the world is worked hard, earned higher education, received countless training, gained much experience, and acquired many valuable life lessons along the way. Nothing fancy or paranormal; just decades of keeping on. Grinding. Learning and evolving. If I go, I go all in.

Adding to that is the enormous and invaluable help I've received from co-workers, mentors, classmates, friends, and family. Yes, I've been truly blessed. As a result, I've taken what I've learned and compiled it into this collection of life principles. Again, life advice that applies to everyone. It works if you do. Take it or leave it, completely up to you. My two adult kids are the main reason I wrote this book. When I'm dead and gone, they'll be the next generation to carry the torch. Perhaps one day my kids will have children of their own. If not, no worries, they can leave it to someone else. My wife will have a copy. Our family will have a copy. I hope *you* and your family each have copies. I sincerely hope this book helps *you* live the most inspired and fruitful life possible. It can, if you let it. Use *The Torch of Life* to live with fire. So, enough about me – what about you? Are you ready? If you'd like to *live* a legacy of prosperity and *leave* a legacy for the next generation, then read on.

PART I (HOW)

CHAPTER 1

INTENTIONALITY & CRITICAL THINKING

The foundation of success in nearly every area of my life is not clairvoyance, secrets, or magic – it's *intentionality* and *critical thinking*. These concepts took me the longest to refine. I'd argue they're the most difficult principles and the most critical to master, which is why I mention them here first. In order to succeed at nearly anything, you must be intentional about it. In other words, make a conscious decision about what you want to achieve and where you want to go. You don't get to anywhere worth going to by accident. Ask yourself...

- How can you become a millionaire if you don't *decide* you're going to do it? Set a goal.
- How can you have a stellar marriage if you don't *decide* that's what you want? Work at it.
- How will you lose 20 pounds without first *deciding* that's what you will do? Diet and exercise.

These things, and many others, don't happen by coincidence. They take time, effort, and intentionality. The more specific you are, the better your chances of succeeding. For example...

- You don't just wake up one day and receive a college degree in the mail – you *decide* to enroll in classes and complete the degree plan.
- Your boss doesn't suddenly double your pay – you *decide* to level-up your skillsets, boost productivity, and take on roles of increasing responsibility for a promotion.

This point **cannot** be overemphasized and must be internalized. Live on purpose! Too few do. Charting your own future is very rewarding. Play a life of chess, not checkers; think strategically, a move or two (or three) in advance. Intentionality is great as a stand-alone concept but it's even better when paired with its kissing cousin, which is the ability to think critically.

If *intentionality* is deciding what to do, on purpose, then *critical thought* is the logic, rationale, and reasoning behind that intent. Critical thinking helps to inform things such as why, how, when, and the specifics of your decisions. For example, you may decide you need a new vehicle. Who doesn't, right? The problem is that many people act impulsively when they see a shiny new vehicle at the dealer. Critical thought, however, applies a degree of logic and rationale. Let's use the need for a new vehicle to briefly walk through this principle…

The top-level decision: whether to buy a new vehicle. First of all, is it a need or a want? Let's be real, *need* versus *want* is relative, right? For our purposes, we'll define 'need' as your current vehicle's repair costs will exceed its after-repair value. You wouldn't spend $5K to fix a vehicle that would be worth less than $5K after the completed repairs. So, in our example, let's say you *need* a new vehicle.

Think it through. What kind of vehicle do you need and for what purpose? Perhaps you need a work vehicle to haul things (pickup truck). Maybe you need extra space and seating for a big family (van or SUV). Or you might just need basic transportation to putt around town (economy car). The point is, think about what you need. Then, establish a budget.

If you're debt-free and have the money, go buy your new vehicle (in cash)! When you have the money, buying a car you need (or want) is easy – that's why it's smart to follow the wealth principles in chapter 4.

However, if you have debt, it's wise to buy the cheapest and most reliable vehicle that you can afford (in cash). Beggars can't be choosers. Simple, right?

If it's so simple, then why are so many people going broke? Well, here are some common knee-jerk reactions to 'needing a new vehicle'…

> ➤ Go to the dealer and finance or lease a brand-new car (usually with a high interest loan). Now, you're under a smothering pile of debt.

> ➤ Trade-in your current vehicle at *wholesale* instead of selling it to a private party at *market* value. By selling at wholesale, you typically lose thousands of dollars.

> ➢ Trade *up* from a $5K vehicle to a $30K vehicle (after all, you deserve it). You impulsively spend far more than you had planned (or could afford).

As you can see, being intentional and thinking critically is simple but powerful. Contrast that with impulsive, irrational, immature, and illogical decisions. This small example alone can save you tens of thousands of dollars, buyer's remorse, and years of crushing debt! (You're welcome.) That said, this does not apply to every single detail of every single decision you make. No. As with most things in life, be sure to *balance* your critical thinking to avoid analysis paralysis (over-thinking it). For example, if you follow this playbook and become a multi-millionaire, then go buy any car you want. The point is to apply a degree of thinking to your life that's commensurate with the situation.

Typically, you'd only apply lots of time and brain power to significant decisions. I don't recall ever racking my brain on trivial matters in life and wouldn't recommend anyone else to either. For example, if you want a candy bar, then buy the darn thing and eat it. The principles of intentionality and critical thinking should be applied to significant areas of life: health, career, education, relationships, parenting, money, etc. When it comes to cost, the more time and money that's involved, the more thought I put into it. In other words, you'd invest more brain power into buying a house than you would a new laptop. You'd put more thought into planning a 3-week road trip than driving to the corner store. The beauty and power of intentionality is that *you* get to decide what's important in life. There's no book answer.

Intentionality is a universal principle that you can use in every area of life. So, as the old saying goes, "Be careful what you wish for." Why? Because the decisions are yours but so are the consequences. That's why critical thinking is so integral to intentionality. You *choose* to blow your money on eating out and material stuff because you "deserve it, life's too short, or you're living your best life." Then your car is repossessed, your house is foreclosed, and you live like a pauper in retirement because you blew all of your money. (I hope it was worth it.) Yes, you reap what you sow! Let me share a personal example of intentionality and critical thinking in my own life...

When our son started college, he was still living at home, commuting to and from. My wife and I stepped up our discussions with him regarding dating. We reminded him that he was now a young man, over 18 years old, independent, and free to date as he saw fit. Having personally lived through college and military dorm life and 'been there, done that' myself, life experience taught me that many teenagers allow hormones and experimentation to lead the way. If they're not *thoughtful*, the result is a life-long sexually transmitted disease and/or unplanned, life-changing pregnancy. I was lucky to avoid such outcomes but learned some valuable lessons. Below are two approaches my wife and I could have taken with our son. See if you can guess which approach we took…

Option 1: Have a mindset that he's 18 now and can do whatever he wants. Believe that "he's gonna do what he's gonna do" and that's just part of life. *Assume* he's capable of making fully mature decisions at only 18 years old. Either don't talk to him at all since it's his choice or tell him what *we* think he should do.

Option 2: Have an *intentional* and guided discussion with our son. Don't dictate his decision, but rather educate him on the consequences, both good and bad. Tell him to *critically think* things through and *intentionally* decide what kind of dating relationship *he* wants during college, if any at all. Remind him to live life and have fun, but to do so responsibly without regret.

Can you guess which route we took? By the way, I won't reveal our son's dating life, but I will tell you I have tears of pride over what a fine young man he's become. I wish I could say the same of myself when I was his age. Whatever he decided, we would have supported our son 100 percent, as long as he'd thought it through. Mind you (and we told him this), if he got a girl pregnant then *he's* a father…not us. We'd love him and support him, but we made it crystal clear what responsibilities fatherhood entails (for *him*). If he's man enough to have an intimate relationship, he's man enough to follow through with responsible actions. Yes, we chose option 2 <wink>.

Remember, this is only one small scenario from my own personal life. Together, with our hypothetical example of buying a new vehicle, they illustrate the concepts of intentionality and critical thinking. As basic as these examples are, it goes much beyond that. These are real life situations that happen every single day. Many situations are far more complex and consequential. People everywhere are deciding (or not) how to shape their lives. The careers they choose, the education they earn, the family they raise, and much, much more. My wife and kids will tell you about one of my favorite dad-inspired fictitious characters in life, the Bumbling Dumbledorf. Who is that, you may ask? This is who…

Me – "How much did you budget towards your debt this month?"

Bumbling Dumbledorf – "What's a budget?"

Me – "What certifications do you require to advance in your career?"

Bumbling Dumbledorf – "I'm not sure."

Me – "At what age do you plan to retire and how much money will you have?"

Bumbling Dumbledorf – "Retire? Who has money to save for retirement?"

Me – "What specifically have you done lately in order to build a strong and healthy marriage?"

Bumbling Dumbledorf – "Huh?"

Wow. Don't be a Bumbling Dumbledorf. Don't just bumble through life like an empty candy wrapper bouncing down the street on a windy day – dum-dee-dum-dee-doo. Be intentional. Get answers. Set a direction. Make things happen. If you jump in your car and just start driving with no destination, guess where you'll end up? Your guess is as good as mine – you'll most likely travel in circles. However, if you map a destination to Main Street and plan the route, just like magic you'll end up on Main Street! Please don't be mistaken, intentionality is **not** planning out every minute of your life. You're not going to get married on January 7th, have a baby on October 9th, work 40.2 hours a week at Company XYZ for 32 years, and die on your 75th birthday while eating strawberry cake. No. What it *does* mean is to cast a vision – the direction you're headed in life. Big picture. Allow that destination to be your north star; from it, you can set clear goals and milestones. Step up your game and take charge. Make your vision happen one step at a time. I'll share another personal example…

While preparing to write this book, my son was 22 years old and had been living on his own for about six months. He didn't know about the book idea but I asked him if he was allowed only *one* single question about *anything* in life, what would it be. After a month or two of thought, he was home for Thanksgiving weekend and I asked him what question he came up with. Here's what he asked…

Question: **"What gives you fulfillment in life?"**

Question, Part B: **"When did you find yourself? Or does it always change?"** (Essentially, if someone were to ask…who are you and what do you stand for.)

I almost fainted. He knew nothing at all about me writing this book, but the question was a direct bullseye for *why* I was writing it! He didn't ask a tactical, small-picture question that may be indicative of his young age such as how to get a promotion, buy a house, or invest money. No, he asked a strategic, big-picture question about life. As he framed his question, he was asking both in general terms and specifically about me personally. I told him he was light years ahead of most people simply because he was asking the question. When I was 22 years old, my head was ~~up my butt~~ in the clouds and focused on the fastest, coolest motorcycle I could buy. I shared with my son that fulfillment in life is unique to everyone and can change over time. It can be personal and/or professional. The idea is to try new things; follow what interests you and avoid what doesn't. Your *head* can lead you to fulfillment but your *heart* will tell you when you've found it. If you're purposeful (intentional) about following your passion, I believe you'll look up one day to realize that you've suddenly "found yourself" and have been doing what you love all along. People may find fulfillment the moment they marry their beautiful and amazing spouse. Parents may find fulfillment (and tears of joy) the day their child is born or adopted. You can find purpose and fulfillment through family, work, religion, volunteerism, or a million other avenues. And it doesn't always happen in an instant; you may slowly grow into your passion over time.

I used myself as an example while I continued talking with my son. Sadly, I was a Bumbling Dumbledorf for way too long in my younger years. It took me decades to realize my own purpose in life but today it provides me a laser focus and fills my heart with passion. I'd always been happy, but what deeply and truly *fulfilled* me in life had been right in front of my face all this time. I'd been living it for many years but wasn't clear-eyed (or intentional) enough to realize it. How stupid of me. Another lesson learned. But the more I matured and the more I learned in life, the clearer my purpose became. I felt so blessed and vowed to *never* again take it for granted. I decided to intentionally amp up my devotion to serving in the best way I could. Allow me to share what drives me today; my 3-part personal mission in life is listed below. In July of 2020, I had it etched onto an acrylic plaque that sits in my bedroom. As I was talking to my son that Thanksgiving weekend, I went to my bedroom, brought it out and showed him the plaque. What gives me fulfillment (who I am and what I stand for)…

My Personal Mission Statement

"As a *husband*, to love and support my wife with all my heart and ability."

"As a *father*, to love my children and raise them to be respectful, caring, and successful adults."

"As a *person*, to succeed through hard work, education, and teamwork & help others do the same."

I expand upon these roles in chapters 10 (marriage), 11 (parenting), and 12 (life), respectively. My mission statement is nothing Earth shattering, profound, or overly complex. Like me, it's simple and to the point (and intentional). I find simplicity usually works better and is far more powerful than trying to get overly fancy. The fundamental act of writing down my personal mission statement reminds me to reflect on who I am and where my focus is. I see it every day. *Where you focus, you prosper.* And I have full intentions to prosper in marriage, parenthood, and life! Yes, I have other goals in life such as financial milestones, building a new house, maintaining my health, and more. However, those goals support my mission above…they *fuel* my mission in life. All guns are pointed in a single direction.

I set financial and life insurance goals that support my wife to ensure she's taken care of if I pass away before her.

I maintain an estate plan to make things easier for my wife and kids not if, but *when* I pass away (or become incapacitated).

I improve my diet and exercise which not only helps me personally but sets a better example for my children.

I continue to learn and grow so I can better mentor my kids, family and friends, or anyone else who may be interested in succeeding in key areas of life.

Note that it's an on-going, lifelong process; I'm never *done* as long as I have another breath in my body. The process and the journey are what matter. This focus drives my daily actions. Try it for yourself. Intentionally decide on your mission in life and write it down. What excites you and/or fills your heart? It may not crystalize today, tomorrow, or even this year, but it will eventually. And again, please write it down. Eat it, sleep it, breathe it, and live it. It probably won't be easy, but it will be worth it! Speaking of *easy*...

Once you become intentional about things in life (mission, meaning, purpose, goals), you'll discover this – **nothing worth doing is easy**. In fact, it's usually quite hard. Wake up. Be intentional. Set a direction in your life and create some worthy goals. Here are just a few ideas...

- Raise kids into successful adults.
- Build a strong, long-lasting, and loving marriage.
- Grow a rewarding career.
- Become a world-class professional (at anything).
- Own a home.
- Become wealthy.
- Earn a college degree.
- Serve honorably in the military.

Those are just a few stepping stones of success that lead to true prosperity. I'm sure you can think of many others. I call those things hard but worth it! I also struggle to think of a single thing that's *easy* to do that's also worth very much. It's easy to be fat, dumb, and lazy (no offense to anyone; I may have been all three at some point in life). It's easy to *be* broke, but ironically, it's not easy *being* broke! It's easy to be an absent parent. It's easy to be a Bumbling Dumbledorf. No thanks! What did President John F. Kennedy say on Sep 12, 1962? He emphatically stated, "We choose to go to the moon in this decade and do the other things, not because they are easy, but *because they are hard...*" Amen.

You may decide to become the 'first' in your family. The first college graduate. Or perhaps the first to quit smoking (my mother quit at age 71...cold turkey!). The first to buy a house. The first doctor, astronaut, business owner, pro athlete, scientist, or military veteran. Be the first to leave gang life or the first to avoid prison. Be the first to enforce the law instead of break it. Be the first to give instead of take. Be the first to serve others. Yes, it's up to you. People may say it's too tough, but stand up tall and exclaim, "Watch me!"

So, my challenge to you is to do things that may not be easy, but in fact may be hard. Do so intentionally. Do them because they're worth it. Do them because *you're* worth it. Parent like you mean it. Love like you mean it. Work like you mean it. And above all, live like you mean it!

Here are some final thoughts about intentionality in particular. First, don't be fooled into thinking that intentionality guarantees success – it does not. Simply deciding to do something does not mean it will happen. However, **not** being intentional almost certainly guarantees failure. **If your destination is to nowhere, that's exactly where you'll go!** It bears repeating, things don't happen simply because you decide to do them. The work must always follow. Action will get you *some*where but intentionality determines *precisely* where. The rat in the wheel is full of action but where is it going? So...what will YOU be intentional about? Where are YOU going? Add intentionality and critical thought to your life – you won't regret it.

CHAPTER 2

LIFELONG LEARNING

So, you can see how intentionality and critical thinking are foundational in life. A natural extension that follows is the principle of lifelong learning. If your mind was a garden, what would it look like? Not what you'd *want* it to look like, but what it would *actually* look like. Seriously, what would it *really* look like? Have you been tending the garden of your mind? Have you been planting weeds or seeds? Remember, we reap what we sow. Therefore, if you've sown *weeds*, your mind is a patchy and scrubby garden. But if you've been sowing *seeds*, your mind is likely a rich and beautiful garden of bounty. If you've sown *nothing*…well. So, where do we begin our educational journey of lifelong learning?

For most of us, the public school system provides the basic foundation of our education. This education typically starts in pre-kindergarten and culminates in high school graduation. For perspective, if you go back far enough in time, there were no schools or formal education systems. School simply didn't exist. As time progressed, schools started to form but were usually reserved for the select few that could afford to attend. Many folks didn't have time or money for school. The entire family was farming or breaking their backs in some way just to survive. Much of this work was labor intensive. For most, school was a luxury or a privilege. In fact, it sadly still is for many people in the world today. The educated few typically earned more money and were key decision makers within their government and society.

However, as fortune would have it, the school system evolved and slowly became available to more common folks. Today, instead of toiling at the factory or digging ditches, there's an avenue for people to get educated and progress in various careers. Modern day schools teach critical thinking skills and introduce children to a variety of subjects, allowing them to explore their passions beyond unskilled labor jobs. As a result, public education has opened all kinds of doors to the masses. Keep in mind, *uneducated* people rarely prosper.

As you'll soon see in an upcoming chart, a high school graduate's median salary is at least **25% higher** than a non-graduate. A high school graduate's unemployment rate is 4.2% versus 6.2% for a non-graduate. Remember, you don't *have* to go to school, you *get* to go to school!

Now, let's assume you've graduated high school. Is that the extent of your life knowledge? What have you done since to feed the garden of your mind? What other seeds have you planted? Be objective, not defensive. Take a moment to *write down* what you've done. Here are a few examples from my own list…

- ✓ Graduated from 3 schools of professional military education.
- ✓ Earned a bachelor's degree in information systems management.
- ✓ Earned a master's degree in management.
- ✓ Earned multiple gold-standard professional certifications.

There's a wee bit more to my list, but this is not a competition or a brag-a-thon; heck, some people even hold multiple PhDs. That's not the point. Nor is the act of learning something that you *finish* – it's not a one-and-done. Rather, the point is simply to illustrate the value of lifelong learning. Always be learning in some manner. So, what's on your list? What's the latest significant thing that you've learned? Remember, if you're not tending the garden of your mind, it will wither away and die. Imagine a garden that's not watered, fertilized, or weeded. You wouldn't have much of a garden but rather a scratchy plot of dust, cobwebs, and tumbleweeds. You want the garden of your mind to flourish. To blossom. Feed your mind until the day you die. How so?

Well, think about the content that you consume on a daily basis. Reflect on the list you just wrote. Do you mindlessly scroll through junk on 'social' media? Do you get your life advice from a 2-minute short-form video? Many people spend more time streaming the latest mini-series than budgeting their own finances. They know more about some pro athlete's career stats than their own career development. They care more about who's dating who on some 'reality' show than their own intellectual growth. All *weeds*. Junk food for your mind. But mindlessly consuming digital content is easy, you say. Yes, it is, just as growing a scratchy plot of dust and tumbleweeds is easy. Growing a lush garden is hard, but it's worth it! (See how it all ties together?) So, what's the alternative?

Sow something in your mind worth reaping. What can you learn this month? Perhaps you can learn a new skill to enhance your career. I continue to study and learn other languages; can you guess which ones? It really doesn't matter what *I'm* learning; pick what *you* want to learn and go for it! Learn to build better habits. Learn techniques to better manage your time, so you'll have more of it. Learn how to budget and invest your money, so you'll have more of that, too. Learn a new skill: painting, sewing, cooking, or crafting. Explode your talents – the options are endless. There are countless ways to enrich your mind and learn new things that will help you thrive in life. How to start? Below are just a few examples.

Reading

My wife is a reading maniac! Some years, she's read close to 50 books. She has me beat but I'm an avid reader as well. I've read dozens and dozens of non-fiction books, mostly on topics that improve my life in some way. I also enjoy a good fiction book from time to time. Some of my favorites are thrillers and mystery novels. Be intentional about what you read. Ideally, it should feed your mind and lift your soul. Reflect on your own personal library. They say you are what you eat; you are also what you read! So, what have you been reading? Books are a great way to learn. If you want to learn something specific, consider formalizing your knowledge by earning a certification.

Certifications

Nowadays, it seems like you can get certified in a gazillion things! There are online classes just a few clicks away that provide training and certification on many things. These courses have become very prevalent in career development. In fact, many professions even *require* some level of certifications in order to maintain licensing and operating credentials. Some can be acquired with just a few hours of training and may even save someone's life one day; for example, cardiopulmonary resuscitation (CPR). My daughter was certified in CPR as a teenager, which fit in nicely with her path towards medical school. My son has completed a number of certifications in computer programming on his path towards software engineering. Other certifications, such as project management professional, are more involved and can require years of experience and formal testing. Certifications demonstrate that you've achieved a baseline knowledge and/or competency in a certain area; examples include computer programming, emergency management, electrical, supply chain, human resources, healthcare, mechanic, beautician, and much more. Even sports such as martial arts provide certifications of sorts. For example, you can start as a white belt and work your way up to black belt! Do your research. Find the certifications applicable not only to your current job or hobby, but ones that will advance you in your career and overall life. Certify yourself as a professional and get paid accordingly …cha ching!

College Education

Many years ago, my wife earned a master of business administration (MBA) degree. I think it's fair to say that wasn't *easy*. Let me tell you something about my wife (with her permission). She immigrated to the U.S. when she was 14 years old and unable to speak English. She fast-tracked herself through public schools, studying day and night. She read books non-stop and immersed herself in anything she could that would help her learn English. (Today, she probably has better grammar than I do.) After high school, she wanted to further her education. College was too expensive and she didn't want crushing student loan debt. So, she gave up, right? Wrong. She enlisted in the U.S. Army, in part for the educational benefits. She fought through culture shock, boot camp, and an accent that terrified her when speaking in public. While serving on active duty, she worked 40+ hours a week, performed field exercises, rotated overseas, and battled severe health issues. As you'd imagine, she was too busy for college, right? Wrong. Many long nights and weekends followed. Studies, homework, research, and testing. Step by step. Class by class. Yes, nine years after joining the Army, she received her MBA degree. Debt free. Don't tell *her* about easy. Yet, right here in our very own country we have U.S. citizens (born here) who are dropping out of school left and right. We have kids too busy committing crime to be bothered with school. It's too hard, they say. It's not their fault, they say. There are systemic issues in society, they say. Blame the rich, the politicians, or the man, they say. Hmm. Believe that if you like. Just don't talk to my wife about that. Don't you dare try to tell her that. Yes, I love my wife.

There's no shortage of ~~excuses~~ reasons for not going to college. Trust me, I've heard it all…

- ❖ "It doesn't prove that you know what you're doing."
- ❖ "I don't have time."
- ❖ "I don't want student loans."
- ❖ "It's not necessary to be successful."
- ❖ "It's not really going to help me in my job."
- ❖ "School is not for me."
- ❖ "My big toe hurts."

I'm sure you've heard plenty of other excuses for not getting a college education. Perhaps you've made a few yourself? Listen, college doesn't make you *better* than anyone. It's also not *required* for you to be successful. All true. In fact, certain trade professionals can be quite successful without any college. Many even go on to become millionaires, often through some version of apprenticeships and/or small business ownership. I'll talk more about apprenticeships soon, but a college degree can help your career (and life) more than you know.

First of all, some jobs *require* a degree, period. In that instance, getting a degree is not optional if you wish to pursue that job. For example, if you wish to be a brain surgeon, you must (thankfully) get a medical degree. Likewise, becoming an attorney obviously requires a law degree. And there are many other jobs besides brain surgeon or attorney that require a college degree.

Second, there are jobs that don't require a degree but having one is *preferred* and beneficial. Why? Because you learn valuable skills through education. By having a degree applicable to the job, all things equal, you increase your chances of getting that job. Your degree will enable you to stand out from non-degreed applicants. It also shows your commitment to the profession.

Lastly, is the data. A college degree is statistically shown to increase your lifetime earnings. Hey, who doesn't want to earn more money? Below is an eye-opener from the U.S. Bureau of Labor Statistics (www.bls.gov). At the risk of dated statistics, these numbers are so powerful that I felt compelled to include them here. It's okay because this general correlation between education and earnings has held true for decades, if not longer. Earnings for the holder of a professional or doctoral degree are more than *double* those for someone with a high school diploma. Even the earnings for a bachelor's degree are over *50% higher* than a high school diploma. Also, take note of the unemployment rates. Boom!

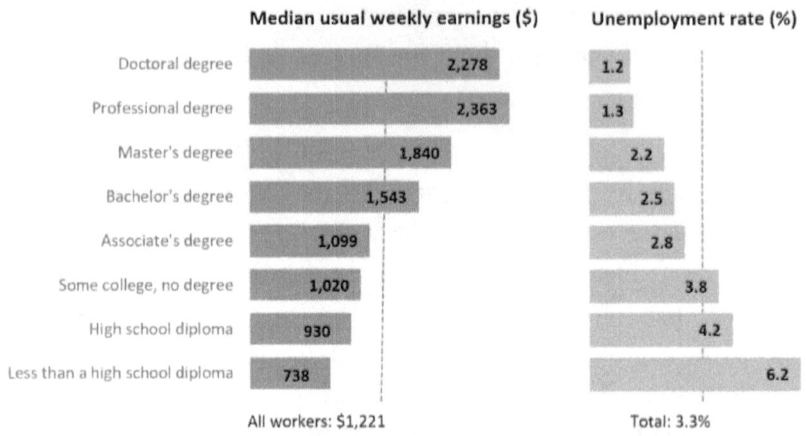

Earnings and Unemployment Rates by Educational Attainment, 2024

Keep in mind, if you choose to get a degree to advance your career, ensure the degree aligns with your profession. For example, a degree in microbiology may be great but it won't help you very much in structural engineering jobs. Likewise, a law degree can be valuable but probably won't help in the field of nursing. In other words, your degree should provide knowledge applicable to your profession. By the way, I've never heard of anyone doing a *worse* job because they went to college. I doubt anyone ever made *less* money or got *demoted* once their boss heard about their degree. Even if you're self-employed, the right college education can help advance your earnings. How so?

A degree in finance or business can provide enormous value to an entrepreneur or small business owner. Remember, the paper degree itself means nothing; it's the *knowledge* and *skills* that you gain earning said degree that matters. By learning about advertising, accounting, human resources, and other core business functions, an entrepreneur can really grow their business! Therefore, even if you don't earn a full degree, taking a handful of classes that are relevant to your business or career can help immeasurably. You may even double (or triple) your income!

One final note – **college can be helpful for more than just your job.** Depending on the field of study, it can be extremely helpful for your *life*. In my college studies, I've learned critical skills around team building, public speaking, effective writing, ethics, human motivation, and much more than simply doing my job. My college education has elevated my career performance by a lot; it has enhanced my *life* even more! So, to zoom out a bit, college is part of lifelong learning, not just a prelude to a job. While college can certainly accelerate any career, it can also enhance many other areas of your life. A quality education can help you parent better, marry better, invest better, vote better, and simply live better. So, don't get blinders on and think the only reason you should go to college is to get a job. Some people go to college for reasons outside of their career. Their passion may be making music, so they get a music degree. Perhaps they love history, so they get a history degree. Or maybe they find education more meaningful than binge watching the latest episode of who's cheating on who. Weeds or seeds. Regardless of motivation, a college education can only help you. If you put in the work, it will be worth it! There are also other learning alternatives to college.

Apprenticeships

Whereas college is generally a more *holistic* and white-collar model, apprenticeships are generally more *focused* and aimed at technical blue-collar professions. They exist mainly to develop skills and knowledge to learn a specific profession. These valuable professions, by and large, are commonly referred to as "the trades" and are usually very hands-on. This can include electricians, welders, roofers, heating and air technicians, plumbers, mechanics, artists, beauticians, and a whole lot more. The main reason for enrolling in an apprenticeship is to learn a specific skilled trade (profession). The beauty is you'll get paid while you learn. It also contributes to lifelong learning. You can gain extremely valuable skills through an apprenticeship. Some are less formal and managed by a company to give you the requisite training and experience. Others are more formal and managed through an academy or school. You may want to get sponsored by an employer or an association in your desired field of study. Do your research. Either way, the main idea is to gain the knowledge and experience necessary for a successful career in a particular trade/profession. As I mentioned, apprenticeships can be the starting point to a lucrative and fulfilling career in the trades. However, you'll want to keep some things in mind.

Each of the trades have their own equivalent levels of training, commensurate with their specific career requirements. The apprenticeship itself may have pre-requisite entry criteria and is only the beginning stage of a career path. Many of these professionals (if they are professional) will complete ongoing, specific education to maintain their licenses and credentials. This can entail hours and hours of continuous learning, licensing, testing, and hands-on practice. All of that added up is essentially the time and work equivalent to getting a college degree. Mistakenly, some people think the trades are a "short cut" compared to college. Not true. They both demonstrate a baseline level of knowledge and/or experience. One results in an accredited degree, the other in a professional certification. Six of one, half-dozen of another. Either way, you'll put in the time and you'll do the work. Remember, the work must always follow. So, you're not proving anything by being successful without a degree – it happens often. Just know the truth; apprenticeships can take just as much work, often times *more* overall work than college in order to achieve that success. I repeat, neither is *better* than the other. They are simply different paths. I suggest you choose the path that interests you and lights a fire within you. Either way, don't ever adopt the mindset of doing nothing. Never do nothing. Another way to learn that's not quite as formal or intensive as college and apprenticeships is to become an intern.

Internships

An internship is a type of job program used to gain experience. In fact, the online dictionary (dictionary.com) defines internship as "any official or formal program to provide practical experience for beginners in an occupation or profession." Some internships are paid and some are unpaid, so do your research before applying. Why work for free, you may ask? Well, many internships exist to provide 'this for that'; in other words, you provide work and they provide an opportunity to gain experience, mentorship, recommendation letters, or potential future employment. I use the word "work" loosely because you're usually an intern for a reason. You're generally a novice, just starting out and learning the job. You'll most likely be given a level of work reflective of your fledgling skill sets. My two kids have experienced internships first-hand …

During one summer in college, my son took a paid internship to develop his skills and gain experience as a software engineer. That experience taught him useful and marketable skills that ultimately helped him land a full-time job after college.

Likewise, as a college senior, my daughter worked a paid internship as a registered behavior technician. Under the supervision of a board-certified behavior analyst, she helped implement behavior intervention plans to teach communication and life skills to autistic children. The training and experience she received was extremely valuable in her overall career development towards becoming a future healthcare provider.

In short, internships are a stepping stone to bigger and better things. Similar to apprenticeships, it's common to apply for an internship for the purpose of furthering your career in some manner. I wouldn't imagine too many people getting an internship just for fun or as a hobby, but you never know.

Shadowing

Shadow programs are another great way to learn. You get the opportunity to follow (shadow) an experienced professional in a workplace setting. Shadowing allows you to walk a "day in the life" of a particular profession. As a pre-med student, my daughter has shadowed multiple doctors in various clinical settings as part of her healthcare education. This has provided her with exposure to standard medical terminology, clinical protocols, bedside manner, and much more. Shadowing is very common for pre-med students. In fact, it's expected and virtually *required* in order to be competitive for acceptance into medical school.

When I was in the military, as a form of reward, some organizations would provide top performing workers the opportunity to shadow the commanding officer for a day. They would accompany the commander through every meeting, inspection, or other function scheduled for that day. This was a great way to learn about leadership and decision making up close and personal. It also helped the worker to better understand the bigger picture of the organization's mission. Shadow programs can be a fun way to learn and are usually less formal, structured, or demanding than internships. If you're interested, research one that works for you.

So, reading, certifications, college, trade apprenticeships, internships, and shadow programs are all great ways to not only learn, but also to enhance your career and your life. Look into them. I talk more about careers later, but here the emphasis is on becoming a lifelong learner. Case in point, I'm currently on hiatus from a traditional career but I certainly continue to learn all sorts of things. The above are simply more formalized methods of learning. That said, there are countless other ways to learn. There are more than just book smarts. Therefore, lifelong learning does **not** mean we sit around the library seven days a week and read encyclopedias. It does **not** mean we are career students who attend college for 30 years and never get a job. No. Okay, so how else do we learn?

There are many ways to learn new things but one of the most common is simply by *doing* – classrooms, books, and teachers not required! In 2008, I attended about a month-long instructor course through Air University in the U.S. Air Force. The course covered teaching methods, curriculum and instructional design, assessment and evaluation, classroom management, and other related competencies essential to instructing. Coincidentally, my college classes also included some of the same material on teaching and learning. This training included lots of brainiac academia concepts such as pedagogy, learning styles, domains of learning, and much more. However, what was my big takeaway? The class reinforced the notion that 'doing' is a core component of learning – not just thinking, discussing, reading books, or taking tests. Don't get me wrong, academic and intellectual learning is extremely valuable. My point here is to stress that it's not the *only* way to learn (nor should it be). While academic learning is great and enhances learning, it's certainly not required…just start *doing*. You can learn a new artistic talent such as pottery, painting, or drawing. Master a sport. Learn to play an instrument. The list is endless. In fact, a great thing to learn nowadays is practical life skills; this includes cooking, budgeting, minor car and house repairs, gardening, and other things that can save us time and money. These valuable life skills seem to be dying on the vine; after all, many people can't pull themselves away from their phone long enough to learn anything new. One caveat here, be sure to *think* before you jump headfirst into something new. For example, taking up scuba diving, motorcycle racing, or other dangerous activity without proper training can get you killed! Investing money into assets that you don't understand can make you broke! Some things can even land you in legal hot water! So, keep learning but do so safely and responsibly. My kids each have a hobby they're learning...

Upon graduating from college and landing his first job, my son moved into his own apartment. His new bachelor pad inspired him to take up baking. He'll look up a recipe and through trial and error, practice baking various things. Every so often, he sends my wife and I some pictures of his latest creations: pizza, donuts, brownies, etc. By that, you'd probably guess he eats lots of junk food. You'd guess wrong. He's quite a healthy eater and very much into fitness and exercise. Most of his recipes are healthy versions (low sugar, gluten free, fat-free, etc). He made us gluten-free, low-fat pizza one time and it was very good! The point is, I'm proud of him for safely experimenting and learning a new skill.

My daughter is the artistic one of the family. She's great at painting and enjoys it very much. I think every one of our extended family members has one of our daughter's canvas paintings hanging on a wall in their home. My wife and I fan the flames of her artistic talent by encouraging her to paint more. However, our daughter's schedule is quite hectic in this season of life; she's busy with college classes, shadowing, interning, volunteering, preparing for medical school, and other stuff. I hope she resumes painting when things slow down because she's very artistic and could learn to become a great painter.

I love to see my kids learning new things. Learning is a great muscle to build. I hope you learn new things, too – even if it's not easy, it should be fun. Up to this point, I've covered many formalized learning methods and also emphasized that simply *doing* is another great way to learn new skills. As if that's not enough, there are countless online training academies that offer various classes from the convenience of your own home. Most are reasonably priced and some are even free! Please, do **not** go into debt for education. Sometimes, cost can be an ~~excuse~~ reason why some people don't attend college, technical schools, trade schools, and other classes. You may ask, "How can I afford college?" I'm glad you asked. Let's apply *intentionality* and *critical thought* to lifelong learning using my own children in a real-life example...

Both of my kids attended high school while living in Florida. During that timeframe, Florida had a program called the *Florida Bright Futures Scholarship*. It still exists as of this writing and may exist for many years to come, but who knows. The eligibility criteria have changed over time, but the core idea was to offer merit-based college scholarships to graduating high school students. The three main criteria were high school GPA, community volunteer hours, and SAT score. Simple. First, my kids worked hard and achieved the required GPA. Second, they volunteered the required hours in their community. Lastly, they studied hard and scored high enough on the SAT. (All of which they should do *anyway*.) And presto, they each earned a merit-based full-tuition scholarship to any public college in Florida! They both chose to attend the University of South Florida (USF) since they could commute from home, thus saving money on room and board expenses. In addition, their GPA and SAT scores earned them the USF Directors Award, which was *another* merit-based scholarship from USF itself. Since their tuition was already covered by the *Florida Bright Futures Scholarship*, they got to pocket the money from the USF scholarship – $12K! Thus, they were getting *paid* to go to school. Yes, 100% debt free.

Now, you may be thinking how lucky my kids were to live in Florida and have a program such as that. Well, that's true. But let me ask you, how many other kids in Florida had the same exact program available to them, but chose not to work for it? Sadly, too many. Some didn't even know about the program! (Shame on their parents.) My kids didn't have any backstage, secret handshake, golden ticket access to college. They simply worked hard for the programs that were available to them. They were *intentional*, had a plan, *thought out* a course of action, and *did the work*. Those actions paid off! My kids' real-life example is just one of many, many ways that people can (and do) graduate from college *debt free*. Let's dig a little deeper.

Believe it or not, Florida is not the only state that has some kind of scholarship or other program to pay for college, professional certifications, and/or trade schools. Far from it. Have you looked? Do your research. Check on programs offered in *your* state. Some are merit based while others may provide money based upon your income or other demographic factors. Learn the eligibility criteria and take advantage of the programs that apply to you and/or your children. These programs are in place for a reason; use them to further your (or your kids') education. While we're on the topic of *debt-free* education, let's dig even deeper still.

There are many other ways to avoid taking on educational debt. I just described how my two kids personally paid for college tuition by using a state sponsored, merit-based scholarship program. Another thing that parents can do is plan ahead for their kids' college fund (i.e. 529 plan). After all, *The Torch of Life* is a playbook for generational prosperity, so let's take a step towards changing the trajectory of our family tree. If you don't have kids, perhaps you have other family that you'd like to help: younger siblings, nieces, nephews, etc. Talk to their parents and offer to contribute money towards their college fund. If they don't have a college fund, encourage them to start one. Invest in their future, they'll thank you later. If you simply invest $100 per month at 10% annual growth over 18 years, your child's college fund will be about $60K! Yes, just $100 per month. Chapter 4 covers more on investing for college. Okay, so maybe you don't have kids or maybe it's too late for a college fund. In that case, here's another suggestion for avoiding debt. Hint…it's arguably the biggest thing you can do.

That's right, if you want to avoid student loans, the biggest thing you can do is <gasp> attend a school you can actually afford! Crazy, right? As I said, my two kids chose to attend USF, which is consistently ranked a *very* good school by many sources. The annual tuition at USF is a mere *fraction* of some other nearby schools (public and/or private). So, even if they didn't have scholarships, their school of choice was quite affordable compared to other alternatives. Don't buy a mansion if you can only afford a bungalow. If you have the money and want to attend a pricey school, go for it. But why in the world would you rack up tens or hundreds of thousands of dollars in debt when it's totally unnecessary? Many community colleges are quite affordable and allow you to transfer your credits to other universities. Do your homework. After all, we should be *smart* about paying for *education* (pun intended). What school you attend matters very little in the big scope of life – especially if it means going broke! You go to school to learn, so start by learning how to avoid debt! Remember, folks…apply *critical thinking* to your intentions. We're on a roll here – there are even more things you can do to avoid student loans.

I already mentioned state-sponsored scholarship programs, but also get out there and search for other scholarships. When my wife and I guided our kids through researching scholarships, we couldn't believe how many we found! There are scholarships sponsored by non-profits, corporations, schools, hospitals and many other organizations. Some are merit based, while others involve volunteering. Some are based upon your demographics, specific field of study, or income levels. Our daughter earned $100 by submitting an essay for the Veterans of Foreign Wars' *Voice of Democracy Scholarship*. (If I remember correctly, the overall winner of that particular program earned a $30K scholarship!) In addition, our daughter also earned another $1K by volunteering at a local hospital. In other words, there are many, many scholarships out there. Seek and ye shall find. Still not enough? Ok, let's dig deeper still.

Yet another way to avoid college debt is to take advantage of company-sponsored tuition reimbursement programs. That's right, many companies offer tuition reimbursement to their employees. Essentially, you take classes and they reimburse you for the tuition. Talk to your boss or human resources department to see if your company offers any such benefits. If they do, jump on it! It's a great way to earn a free education. By the way, if you're open to working for Uncle Sam, I have even *more* good news for you.

Serving in the military is how my wife and I received our debt-free educations. We did it the old-fashioned way…we earned it. Having personally served for over 21 years, I may be biased towards the benefits (and personal fulfillment) of military service but for good reason. Look, I get it – military service is not for everyone. It can be very demanding and rough on family life. I personally found it hard at times, but worth it! If the idea of joining the military interests you, please know there are countless benefits and education is surely one of them! Things change over time but when I served, tuition was fully reimbursed provided you earned a minimum grade in class. They didn't pay for failing grades. I took college classes at nights and on my days off, while working 40-60 hours per week. That's how I earned my bachelor's and master's degrees. As if that wasn't enough, I *also* have the GI Bill. In short, the GI Bill pays for college tuition and professional certifications after my military service. For many reasons, I decided to pass my GI Bill benefits to my kids when I retired. Since neither of my kids needed it for their bachelor's degree, I plan on using the benefits to pay for my daughter's medical school. My wife and I plan for her to graduate **medical school**…debt free! Yes, intentionality works, but only if you do. If not for my GI Bill, we'd use the other methods I've described to pay for it. And finally, I propose one more way to avoid student debt. Drum roll, please…

Another suggestion to avoid student loans is a 4-letter word. W-O-R-K. I know, crazy again, right? Believe it or not, people all across the country *work* to pay for things, including their education. My wife did it. I did it. Clearly, not everyone does though; many are unnecessarily racking up thousands in debt. As of this writing, total student loan debt nationwide is approaching nearly *two trillion dollars*! Good grief. Which route will you take? Decide. You can work full-time and school part-time or vice versa. Heck, high school kids have a head start; they can work part-time and during their summer breaks to pile up thousands of dollars before they even start college. They can then continue working part-time while enrolled in college. Again, I worked more than full-time *and* schooled full-time…both at the *same* time! And I'm still alive. Hustle. Grind.

In my day, I was stuck physically driving to and from class. Depending on where I was stationed at the time, my school commute was up to one hour each way. Forget driving – for a full year in South Korea, I *walked* to my classes after work, often carrying an umbrella in the rain and/or sweltering heat. Yes, summer in South Korea is brutally hot and humid! Anyway, enough of my ~~explaining~~ whining. The point is, going to school has become much easier.

Today, learning is offered on a silver platter. The massive availability of online learning brings school right to you, wherever you are. The ability to take classes from the comfort of home opens the door to dual working parents, single parents, shift workers, people living far from campus, and more. You can also take classes while traveling, as long as there's an Internet connection. If necessary, you can even use the computers in a public library (usually for free). Get it done.

Folks, this is crazy. I just gave you not 1, not 2, not 3, not 4, 5, or 6…but *seven* (7) ways to avoid taking on debt for an education! In case you weren't counting, here's a quick recap…

1. State-sponsored scholarships.
2. College fund (529, educational savings account, etc).

3. Attend an *affordable* school (one that you can cash-flow).
4. Other sponsored scholarships (non-profits, corporations, schools, hospitals, etc).
5. Employer tuition reimbursement programs.
6. Military service (Army, Navy, Air Force, Marines, Coast Guard).
7. Employment (aka work); pay for tuition as you go.

Just for fun, I'll throw in an eighth (8th)! That's right, *another* option to pay off student loan debt is the Public Service Loan Forgiveness (PSLF) Program. To those who qualify, the PSLF essentially provides a way to have your student loans forgiven by working a number of years in public service. Admittedly, this doesn't *avoid* debt but it eliminates it. The PSLF is 'second best' to the other seven options, but under certain circumstances it's far better than a life of student loans. If you're interested, research the program's eligibility criteria and the specifics of how to apply. Programs change all the time. Do the work.

So, there you have it; sooo many ways to get a debt-free education. And I'm sure you can think of even more. I just shared with you how not one, but *both* of my kids went to college debt free (and got *paid* to do so). I also shared how my wife and I *both* went to school debt free. You can do this! You have many options. As you can see, when people state they *can't* go to school without debt, it's not true — it's a *choice*. Please…spread the word. Pass *The Torch of Life* to everyone you know. There's no excuse to be drowning in student loan debt.

In aggregate, our country is saddled with soul-crushing student loan debt. In years past, some of our "leaders" in Washington D.C. have falsely promised to "forgive" the evil student loans. Is the debt forgiven? Magically erased? Or is it moved to the backs of the taxpayers? The same taxpayers who chose not take out loans? The same taxpayers who chose the other eight options I just laid out? Or worse yet, the same taxpayers who didn't even go to college but would have to pay for those who did? Hmm. Something to think about. I guess people love paying higher taxes and seeing less in their paychecks. Yet, the government *still* continued making even *more* of said student loans?! Unreal. I believe some of our politicians need a course in critical thinking. Folks, there are no shortcuts. I hope *you* know better. That aside, you now know the importance of education and many ways to pay for it. Take control of your life. Don't wait on

Washington. Don't rack up debt. (*Pssst…*if you've already racked up debt, just wait until chapter 4.) Ok, let's shift gears a bit.

So, as we know, there are many ways that people learn in life. The mostly formal methods of learning outlined above are a relatively small part of our life. For example, to a young person in their late teens or early twenties, getting a 4-year college degree may feel like eternity. But relative to 70-80 years of life (or more), it's really nothing. Not only that, but even while you're enrolled in formal learning, you don't stop living. While I attended school full time, my life didn't stop. I still learned on-the-job. I still read other books and still took other technical training. And we also learn through good old-fashioned experience (by *doing)*.

All of that to say, as you pursue lifelong learning, you should use a model or system to make things easier for yourself. By the way, I also use models and systems for other areas of my life (which I'll cover later), but let's start right here, right now. A model or system is nothing more than a structured process or way of doing something. Allow me to share one system that has served our family well thus far.

Learn How to Learn

As our kids went through school, especially when they entered high school, we taught them about learning how to learn. Some people think learning just happens by magic; sadly, it does not. Learning is a *skill* like public speaking, teaching, juggling, construction, and many other things. By learning how to learn, you get better at it.

So, my wife and I taught our kids to *learn how to learn*. Mind you, there was nothing highly sophisticated here. Mostly, common sense. The idea was more about habit, consistency, and intentionality than anything else. It was building the muscle to learn. *Anyone* can use this system to be a better learner…

First, be proactive. Know the class syllabus and lesson objectives. Understand specifically what it is that you're trying to learn. Read ahead and ask questions about class expectations. Take notes. Raise your hand and speak up when you have questions. Stay after class if necessary.

Second, complete the learning cycle. When our kids scored poorly on a test, their normal reaction was, "That stinks. Oh well, on to the next assignment." Over time, we helped them to go back and analyze *what* they got wrong and *why* they got it wrong. In other words, we helped them complete the learning cycle. Any time they were unsure, my wife and I told them to ask the teacher for clarification – "I don't know" was never an acceptable response. At first, mom and dad were simply nags who didn't understand. Just "let it go", mom and dad. But we persisted and over time, it caught on. They became better at performing an 'academic autopsy' to figure out what went wrong and how to correct it from happening again.

Third, finally, and most important by far was writing down grades. This part was so simple but so amazingly effective, it should be bottled and sold! It was almost magical. When our kids got home from school, the very first thing they did was write down their current numerical grade for each class as of that day. They transcribed their grades from the school's online portal to their notebook and then showed the grades to me or my wife. For example, science (85), math (92), history (91), etc. To write the grades down for all six classes took about a minute or two at most.

They brought their notebooks to me or my wife and we quickly reviewed their grades; 90s and above, great! Anything less involved a discussion about what was being done to fix it. Again, they didn't write down grades to individual tests, quizzes, or assignments – only their current *overall* grade in each class. The kicker was our kids' motivation. So, if any overall grade dipped to 79 or below, they were not allowed to use their electronic devices until it went back to 80 or higher. That meant no TV, phones, tablets, or gaming consoles of any kind unless it was required for school work. If they had time for that stuff, then they had time to focus harder on school work. They knew their priorities and the system worked well.

We even tried an experiment with our son during one semester of high school. We told him he didn't have to write his grades down if he didn't want to – just to see what happened. After all, his grades were already online in his student account portal, so why write them down, right? Well, he chose not to write them down. Sure enough, when we spot checked his grades a few weeks later, they had dropped like a rock. He went back to writing his grades down again and they went right back up! It may sound silly or trivial, but the simple power of *writing down* their grades forced the kids to *focus* on them. *Where you focus, you prosper.* Not to mention, they knew they'd have to show the grades to us, their parents, and already knew what we'd say. This built a muscle, a habit, and an automatic reflex into their daily study routine.

My wife and I preached these habits to both kids. It took some active parenting, but by the time they were high school seniors, they were on auto-pilot. I know, common sense. But alas, common sense is quite uncommon. It worked out well for everyone...

By building these basic learning habits, our kids both maintained excellent grades (4.0+ GPAs). However, more importantly, they were eventually able to do this independently, without us prodding them. They were now academically independent...yay! **Score one for mom & dad.**

If our son got a poor grade on a test, we'd simply ask, "What's your plan?" He explained all the things he'd do to analyze what went wrong and how he'd get back on track. Sure enough, he fixed it! **Score two for our son.**

By the way, our daughter also learned from her older brother's experience, so she learned the process even faster. She overheard plenty of household conversations about schoolwork between me or my wife and our son. She'd come home and say "Mom, dad, I didn't do so hot on today's test. Here's what I think I did wrong, we're going over it in class tomorrow, and here's what I'm doing to fix my grades." **Score three for our daughter.**

I give our kids credit – they both learned fast, worked hard, and made us very proud. They kept kicking butt all the way through high school and college. Their hard work paid off big time. Most importantly, they built mental callouses, a work ethic, and study habits that will last a *lifetime*. All because they were intentional about lifelong learning. All because they followed a *system* of learning how to learn; small, common-sense repeatable processes that make learning easier. Anyone can do the same. It's a choice. I'll share another system (principles) that we use for building wealth in chapter 4. Until then, what's the big takeaway from lifelong learning?

Learning is great, but here's the big reveal – *apply* it! We learn in order to apply what we've learned. Frankly, who cares if I earned a certification in project management? I should apply the concepts at work to cut costs or keep the project on schedule. I can apply my new found knowledge to improve productivity. As a result, I am now a more valuable employee. I can then get a raise, a promotion, or take a new job making more money. Contrast that with employees who are doing the same job they did last year, but picketing for more money. What have they done to *earn* that raise? Have they upskilled? Have they increased productivity? Too many snowflakes think they're entitled to a raise simply for showing up.

Likewise, this applies to many areas of life. We can learn about budgeting *in order to* become debt free. Learn about investing *in order to* grow wealth. Learn about parenting *in order to* raise kids into successful adults. We can apply learning to achieve a strong marriage, a great career, or better health. You get the idea. The list is endless. **Learn in order to apply.** Just like work follows intentionality, application follows learning. It's a one-two punch! I'll share more examples of applied learning throughout the book.

In closing, this entire chapter showcased many ways to be a lifelong learner…all debt free. There are many other ways, so seek them out. It also highlighted the value of using a learning system or model to provide consistent and repeatable processes for more effective learning. And remember, the real reason for learning is to *apply* what you've learned. So, what are you waiting for? Plant seeds, not weeds. Always be learning. Learning is growing. Crank up the volume and learn like you mean it!

Secret Sauce:

Don't focus on getting good grades. Rather, focus on the *underlying behaviors* that lead to good grades; take notes, do the work, study hard, and learn how to learn. Then repeat. Good grades will follow.

Chapter 3

Grow a Career

Alert, alert! Interns and new hires are anxious, nervous, and uncertain. Executives, career professionals, and seasoned employees are stressed out, burned out, or even unaware of their unhealthy work-life imbalance. Is that you or a loved one? How about someone you know? Perhaps you should consider a new approach to your career. It's time to shift into high gear and grow a career that you love! This journey should be combined with principles in chapters 2 (lifelong learning), 5 (health wealth), 7 (life principles), and 8 (personal values) for a healthy and prosperous work-life balance.

You'll find a rewarding career at the intersection of *passion* and *prosperity*. A key component to living an inspired and fruitful life is having a career. But alas, not just an ordinary career. I'm talking about an extraordinary one! If you haven't noticed, the difference between ordinary and extraordinary is the little *extra*. An extraordinary career can provide the foundation of your financial success. It can also be the heartbeat of your entire life and provide you with meaning and a sense of purpose. The average person spends many decades working over their lifetime, yet very few find true meaning in a rich and rewarding career. To some, their work is drudgery. Building an extraordinary career is tough. But remember, nothing worth doing is easy. You want to pursue your **passion** doing what you love. However, you must also earn enough money to be **prosperous** and avoid poverty. Your goal is to pursue passion *and* prosperity.

If you're going to spend most of your adult life working, shouldn't you put some thought and effort into it? A certain level of intentionality? A degree of focus and energy? I think so. Sadly, too many people don't. If you're reading this book, I must assume you want to achieve a high level of success in your life, to include your career. Perhaps you already have a great career. If so, I believe you can take it to the next level! Maybe you're still trying to figure out "what you want to do with your life" and haven't started a career yet. Or maybe you've been working various dead-end jobs with no potential for growth. Either way, there are certain things you can do to grow a career that you love…starting right now. I know not only from my training and education but most importantly from first-hand experience.

So, it doesn't matter where you are in your career, or if you even have one at the moment. What *does* matter is deciding what you'd like to do in life. First, you must practice *intentionality* and *critical thinking* (remember those?). If you set a course to nowhere, that's exactly where you'll end up! What are you passionate about? What gets you out of bed in the morning? What fires you up?! Woooo!! I repeat, it doesn't matter what you're currently doing; that can always change. And by the way, you're never "too old" to change careers or even start a side hustle doing something that you truly love. If you trudge to work every day like a down-trodden donkey, you *might* want to find another job. Your job is to find and live your passion while getting paid to do it. Gallop to work like a stallion! Don't think about this weekend; ask yourself where you want to be 5 or 10 years from now and beyond. Admittedly, it's tough to answer that. In fact, it's tougher to figure out *what* to do than *how* to do the thing you love. I offer plenty of suggestions on the latter, but you alone must determine the former. It takes some soul searching.

The good news is, if you struggle with finding a career you love, there are tools to help. Some people just seem born to do certain work. Would you like an office environment or prefer to work outdoors? Do you like working with your hands or your mind? Do you thrive on working with others or do you prefer to work alone? Do you enjoy being creative or dotting i's and crossing t's? Aligning your passions with a career can be its own book. However, there are plenty of career assessments and 'know thyself' personality instruments available to help you narrow down some options. I've taken a number of them. I've also taught them to senior leaders in the military. I don't recommend any specific assessments, but if you simply search online for "career assessments" or "personality assessments", you'll find plenty to choose from. If you're open minded and view the results objectively, some of these assessments are really good at helping to identify your interests. Why not give it a shot? It's not wise to invest time, energy, and money into starting a career that you may hate. Test the waters and do some research *first*. Dream a little. Once you've locked in on something, then dive in full speed ahead. Remember, you can always adjust course.

As a parent, I've applied this advice within my own family. My wife and I have walked this walk not only in our own careers, but also by mentoring our kids. By helping our kids discover their individual interests, we guided them in choosing their own career paths. They didn't require the use of career assessments, but we helped them narrow down their interests over the years. After all, like most parents, we know our kids pretty well. Allow me to share the process we used…

Our kids had no aspirations to be in the sports or entertainment industry. My wife and I were not self-employed and didn't have our own business. Therefore, although they could have, our kids never gave the business route much thought either. For many reasons, we guided our kids to consider three main roads towards a career. In no particular order, we educated them on options for the military, the trades, or college. Either route is an on-ramp to many professions. Since my wife and I both served in the military, I bet you think we pushed that route on them. Nope. The kids will tell you we objectively informed them of the pros and cons of all three routes and forced them to think through their decision. *Their* decision. Mind you, this happened over many years, not over a weekend. There's no need to get into the weeds of each option (military, trades, or college) here for our purposes. Suffice it to say, my wife and I provided a summary of each route to our kids and what it would take to be successful in each. All the while, we emphasized they had a clean slate and could do *anything* they wanted to do in life. Yes, even if they chose sports or business ownership, we would have supported them – they simply never showed any interest in that.

Our son was focused on engineering ever since grade school. His first thought was mechanical engineer, then electrical engineer, onto robotics engineer, and then he finally decided on becoming a software engineer. He chose college. So, after a degree in computer science (the forest) and multiple certifications (the trees), he landed a job as an associate software engineer. I believe he hit the bulls-eye because he's always been into computers, video games, and programming. He's also the quiet, thoughtful, analytical one – very logical and process oriented. He has the capacity for a stellar career in engineering!

Our daughter always wanted to be a doctor of some kind. She has a big heart and loves babies and animals. First, it was a veterinarian, then a dentist, and then some type of surgeon. However, she soon discovered that becoming a surgeon was not a good idea. Why not? Because she gets extremely light-headed around blood, needles, and other "icky" things. So…psychiatrist it is! It's funny because I think she too hit the bulls-eye. Our daughter is the more animated and 'bubbly' of our two kids; a regular comedian when she wants to be. She's also extremely aware of others in her surroundings and has a very high social intelligence. She picks up on the smallest of human behaviors, habits, and non-verbal cues very quickly. She's currently a pre-med college student and on track to become a fantastic psychiatrist!

If you hadn't noticed, the common theme for our kids deciding on their career paths was once again, intentionality and you guessed it…critical thought. They didn't throw darts or draw random careers out of a hat. They didn't burn bridges by getting poor grades in school or wait until high school graduation to figure out what they wanted to do for a living. Their path to a career was many years in the making. Of course, as parents, we helped guide them (more on parenting in chapter 11). However, our kids each made *their* own career choices. That's why I purposely didn't get into the weeds on those three career path choices I mentioned. Because it really doesn't matter. I also didn't want the three routes of military, trades, or college to influence *your* decision. Perhaps you want a career in sports or entertainment. Perhaps you want to work in the family business, or start one of your own. Maybe you want to be the next great author (like myself…cough, cough). Just like my own kids – you, too can be *anything* you want to be. The point is for *you* to figure that part out.

This book isn't meant to help you with that part, except to suggest that you consider using the aforementioned career and personality assessments. Although not necessary, those tools *can* help guide you in your decision making. By the way, if you're a parent, you can also use this advice to help your kid(s) work through the same process. Once you critically think through and intentionally decide on your career path, then it's time to jump in. It's time to dive in and grow your career!

Action Rules to Fuel Your Career!

At this point you may expect to read about writing resumes, dressing for success, or how to land the interview. No, those things will be tailored to specific jobs. Some jobs will require a formal application. Other jobs, especially in the trades, may entail word-of-mouth referral. Some may require you to be within the geographical vicinity of the job (skilled trades, actors, athletes, etc). Whereas, you may be able to work other jobs remotely from anywhere (computer programming, accounting, digital marketing, etc). So, job searches and job preparation take research and practice.

Yes, you should learn such day-to-day skills to better navigate job searches and applications. How to *land* a job is certainly important, but it's the small picture. My goal is to provide universal advice that can be applied *strategically* (big picture) to nearly all professions. Whether you pursue professional sports, engineering, politics, healthcare, entrepreneurship, information technology, or any other profession, the following principles apply to you. I've taken enormous amounts of experience, education, principles, and lessons learned and boiled them down to **three simple rules**. Here's a brief overview…

Rule 1.

Once you've decided on a career path, *servant leadership* helps you establish a *service-oriented mindset*. Contrary to common thought, work is not simply about me, me, me and how much I get paid. It's about the value you add and service you provide. While it's true that you should be justly compensated for your service, rule one reminds you to follow your passion, add value, and provide exceptional service. The money will follow.

Rule 2.

Complementing your service-oriented mindset, *rule 2* guides your *career actions* towards results. Remember, the work must always follow;

the *doing* of the work. However, instead of being a rat in a wheel, your actions should be precisely aimed at *productivity* and continually *applying lifelong learning*. Those actions will keep you sharp, qualified, and highly desirable in your career, not to mention highly compensated…cha ching!

Rule 3.

Lastly, *rule 3* helps you *cast a vision* for your future. You'll pan back far enough to see the forest and not remain lost in the trees. Rather than flitting from job to job and running in all directions like a Bumbling Dumbledorf, you'll lift your head up, survey the horizon, and set a *strategic direction* for your career.

If followed, these rules (actions) will certainly help with aforementioned interviews, resumes, job applications, and other *tactical* things. However, the real benefit of the rules is to help you *strategically* grow a rewarding career. The rules are simple but not easy. Hmm, why can't anything be easy? Carry on.

I believe these rules will lead to a lucrative and long-lasting career. They can be applied to nearly every single profession. These are the rules that have worked for both me and my wife and the same rules that we preach to our kids. As you read through the details of each rule below, be sure to reflect on your own current (or desired) career. Again, be honest and objective, not defensive.

Rule 1 – Servant Leadership Mindset

This rule is primarily about *mindset*. So, what the heck is servant leadership anyway? The concept grew on me while serving in the military. I'm aware that it may not be a commonly used phrase and I'm sure many variant definitions exist. To me, servant leadership is simply **a leadership style that serves others or a cause greater than yourself in a proactive way.** Broadly speaking, certain professions may come to mind: healthcare workers, first responders, educators, and military veterans. However, there are countless professions that exemplify servant leadership – most, if not all should. In fact, it's not the profession but the *individual* that matters. (More on individualism in chapter 9.) There are good apples and bad apples in any profession. Many individuals display servant leadership regardless of their profession. Think of the quarterback, team captain, or other leader on a professional football team. Think of a commander or senior leader in the military. Think of a night-shift manager, plumber, truck driver, general contractor, head nurse, or anyone desiring to provide world-class service within their profession. The mindset is to provide value to others by serving. Heck, even our elected officials are supposedly public *servants*, ideally with *our* best interest in mind. How's that working out, by the way? More about politicians later. Anyway, it's amazing how powerful and energetic people can be when they adopt a mindset of service and selflessness. It's almost as if their work is no longer *work*; it truly becomes their passion! So, let's look at three ways that you can be a servant leader in your career. Again, the same advice I've followed and lived in my own career. The same advice I give to my own kids.

First, serve your *customer*. This obviously entails knowing your customer. The customer *is* your business – no customer, no business. While in the military, I served my customers, the American people, including *you*. I served my customers by doing my part to protect their lives and freedoms 24/7. I protected the lives of healthcare workers, teachers, politicians, athletes, actors, trades professionals, business owners, hospitality staff, the young, the old, and every American living at home or abroad. This granted people the freedom, safety, and opportunity to pursue their own individual dreams.

So, who is *your* customer? A customer is not only a person buying widgets from a store. Your customer may be a patient, a homeowner, a student, a client, or a taxpaying citizen. For example, if you work as a receptionist, your job is to 'receive' and help your customers, regardless of what industry you're working. This could mean checking them in, answering questions, or providing information. Serving does *not* mean checking your phone, filing your nails, and gossiping with others while the customer stands there waiting for help. It does *not* mean the customer is a bothersome nuisance or an annoyance – they *are* your job! Be grateful they exist. Without customers, there's no reason for your job to exist; serve them well. Stand up, smile, and look your customers in the eye. Ask them if they have any questions or if they need any help. By the way, this is true in sports and entertainment also. Your *fans* are why you exist, so don't forget to act accordingly and treat them as such! No fans, no pay.

No fans, no stardom. Your fans shouldn't worship you; you should worship them! I know it sounds crazy, but it works and it speaks volumes about *you*. Yes, we all have more than one customer that we serve, commonly referred to as stakeholders. There are also internal and external stakeholders (customers). However, my purpose here is to keep it simple and focused. Deliver world-class excellence to your customers. Go above and beyond. You must know your customers; whoever they are, serve them well. If you don't, someone else will.

Second, serve your *team*. Your team is the group of people you work with – your workplace peers. These are people who help you get the job done. While serving in the military, my team was my fellow Airmen, Soldiers, Sailors, Marines, Guardians, Allied Forces, civilians, and contractor employees. Yes, your team can also be your customer but again, keep it simple. A good analogy is a sports team. Your team consists of fellow players, trainers, and coaches. Be a team player; pass the ball, block, defend, and assist your teammates. Don't be a ball hog or a glory hound. You and your teammates have a singular goal or mission – beat the other team.

In your case, serving the customer is your team's common goal or mission. That entails involving the entire team for maximum effectiveness. In some jobs, this could mean assistants, suppliers, co-workers, advisors, or anyone else who helps you get the job done. Be quick to praise your team when warranted. Often times this means giving credit where it's due. Don't take credit for other's work. If a co-worker helps you on a project, be sure to thank them, ideally in front of others. Likewise, don't cast blame. If you mess up, take responsibility, apologize to your team, and take corrective action. Don't throw your co-workers under the bus. Don't talk about them behind their back. If they need help, be there to help. When they do something well, don't be jealous, praise them – again, especially in front of others. Many hands make light work. Serve your team well.

Third, serve as a *leader*. Yes, a leader is part of a team. However, a coach is not a player and is tasked with the unique responsibility of *leading* the team. You may say, "Well, I'm not a team leader or manager, so this doesn't apply to me." You'd be wrong. Hear me out.

There are formal leaders and informal leaders in any organization. Basically, a *formal* leader gets their authority from their position; it may be government authority, military authority, corporate authority, business authority, legal authority, or something similar. Alternately, an *informal* leader earns their authority through character and performance (leading by example). How can you lead as an informal leader, you may ask.

Many **informal** leaders are actually far more proficient and competent than formal ones. After all, look at some of our politicians…good grief. Simply put, be and act like someone that people want to follow. Sounds crazy, right? One way to serve as an informal leader is by doing things without being told. Don't follow lazy sheeple or half-hearted workers – you're better than that. Do more than the bare minimum. Much more. It may seem trivial, but if you see a mess, clean it up. If you see something out of place, fix it. Set the tone. You can also do things even though they're not in your job description. Do this within limits, of course. You would not perform a job that you're unqualified for or one that's prohibited for some reason. Perform your work in an exceptional manner. Informal leaders also look out for others. If a team member is struggling, lend a hand. Ask the team what they need in order to do their job better. Exude positivity at work, not negativity. Smile. Perhaps you're a seasoned employee who's been with the company for a few years. Take time to mentor and provide career advice for newer team members; show them a clear path to career progression. Walk with them and help them assimilate as they learn the job. Challenge them to work at full potential and provide them with appropriate guidance. Share information. Being a good informal leader is good practice for when you become a formal leader.

Again, **formal** leaders get their authority from their position. That doesn't mean you throw your character and values out the window when you're promoted into a formal position. You shouldn't suddenly transform into a tyrant, dictator, or lazy bum. To the contrary, it's time to step up your game! All of the behaviors you exhibited as an informal leader are a *starting point* to be used in a formal position. A leader should work *harder* than anyone else. Lead from the front; be the first one in and the last one out.

The most powerful advice I can give on being a good servant leader for your team is to remember this – they don't work for you; *you work for them*! I don't mean that in a literal sense. Of course, they're obligated to follow legal rules and instructions from you, the formal leader. Here, I'm referring to the mindset that it's *your* job to ensure your team members are trained, qualified, and informed. You are the lead locomotive for your team – plow full-steam ahead! It's *your* job to remove any impediments or roadblocks to them serving the customer. It's *your* job to build work ethic, culture, and set expectations. It's *your* job to motivate your team. Do your job. You must train and equip your workers, help them, reward them, and yes, if required…discipline or fire them. Praise in public; punish in private. Entire books are written on leadership, counseling, and motivation – read some. Occasionally, things will get tough – sometimes *very* tough. That's when the leader gets off their butt, rolls up their sleeves, pitches in and gets their hands dirty. Step on the bleeping gas. Don't push – *pull* the load! Get the job done. As they say, "With great power comes great responsibility." Take ownership. *That* is servant leadership. You serve your team; your team serves your customers. That's the hallmark of a professional organization. Everyone firing on all cylinders. The success or failure of an organization ultimately rests on the shoulders of its leadership!

I hope you get the point – leadership matters. Servant leaders keep the best interest of *others* in mind, even though *they* are in charge. This is true when things are inconvenient, difficult, dangerous, or sometimes even life threatening. They must also have the experience and qualifications necessary for the job.

My son has only just started his career in software engineering. If he hopes to grow into leadership, my advice to him has been to first be a good follower. Also, he must perform his very best at each task he's given. Anything worth doing is worth doing right. He knows if he can't be trusted with the small stuff, he can't be trusted with the big stuff.

The same holds true for my daughter as she progresses towards becoming a doctor. During the transition from college to medical school, she'll work and volunteer in many jobs. Those jobs are opportunities to serve and lead with a mindset to add value. It's my hope that she never forgets to put the 'care' in healthcare.

This same career rule holds true for *you* and anyone else who strives to become a leader. So, rule 1 is a service-oriented leadership mindset whereas rule 2 is rooted in results-oriented *action*.

Rule 2 – Career Actions
(Be Productive & Apply Lifelong Learning)

This rule is about action-oriented *results*. Some people can have a decent career without the proper mindset of servant leadership. However, I don't know anyone who's had what I'd call a truly successful career without actionable *results*. This is the doing of the work. Your actions must be effective. The two actions I've applied to my career that have consistently led to success are **productivity** and **lifelong learning.** I've worked alongside many others who have done the same…world-class professionals at what they do. Absolutely world-class.

First, please note that *productivity* is not the same as work. Many people work hard – very hard. However, so does the rat in the wheel. But alas, it never gets anywhere. It's true that you should work hard, but ensure you are productive! Don't spin your tires in the mud. Get traction. Get results.

Secondly, with regard to lifelong learning, I've covered that principle in chapter 2 and will not repeat it here. However, I must remind you that learning extends to every area of your life, not just your career. That said, you'll see frequent references to it throughout this book. The same is true of other principles. Here, it's pertinent to explain how best to apply lifelong learning towards growing your career. This is *why* you learned what you did (college, apprenticeship, internship, etc).

Also remember that most of the principles covered in this book interrelate and overlap in many areas of life. They're not a sequential series of 'things to do', but rather an intricate web of principles and concepts that support one another. Together, productivity and lifelong learning are vital to growing your career. They are the high-octane fuel for your career! Let's start by exploring how to be productive.

Be Productive. It sounds more sophisticated than 'work', right? It's true that hard work is involved in productivity but there's more to it than that. We all have the same 24 hours in each day. As stated earlier, most of us (including the rat) work hard every day. However, *results* can vary greatly from one person to another. Imagine everyone was given one acre of land to grow corn. Some people may produce 150 bushels of corn from that one acre. Others may produce 160, 170, or even 180 bushels from their acre. In other words, they may be more *productive* at growing corn. If a company hires three auto mechanics, it's quite likely that one will be more productive than the other two. Perhaps it takes two of the mechanics one hour to replace an engine part. The third mechanic may replace that same part in 45 minutes because they're more productive. This holds true in most any profession. Some people are simply more productive than others. It's one thing to say "be productive", but how can you do so? Below are a few ways to increase your productivity…

Work while you're at work.

Serve the customer and serve your team. After all, didn't you *apply* for your job? Show them who they hired. Blow their doors off! Unless it's work related, get off your stupid phone and hustle. Work ethic plays a big part in productivity – it's a reflection of *you*. If it's that horrible, quit! Otherwise, do your job.

Be flexible.

Some employees are so rigid and set in their ways, they're unable to adapt to new ways of working, using new equipment, or following a different process. Remember, change is the only constant – embrace it. Always be learning new and better ways. The more flexible you are at your job, the more productive (and valuable) you are.

Be dependable.

This includes completing assigned work and showing up on time, every time. If you don't show up to work on time, others must cover for you. If there's nobody to cover for you, the customer suffers. Obviously, your lack of courtesy and respect for others reduces productivity. If you're scheduled to be somewhere, be there. If you sell a product, ensure it's delivered. If you're hired to perform a job, get it done. Focus efforts on the *critical path* of a process and completing *essential* work. Deal in results, not excuses!

Go above and beyond.

This is where you can really shine because too many people do the bare minimum. Don't do ordinary. Get to work early. Stay late. Work like a stallion! Volunteer for overtime if it's available. Ask for increased responsibility and tasks that nobody wants or likes to do. Don't eke out the *least* you can do, but rather the *most* you can do!

Leverage technology.

By smartly implementing the proper technology, you can greatly improve your organization's productivity. This could entail installing new hardware or software. It could also mean simply adjusting the equipment that you're already using. A word of caution here – improper use of technology can be counter-productive!

For example, installing an idiotic phone tree that delays and frustrates customers will cause you to *lose* customers. Trying to get cute with stupid chat-bots instead of smart and professional human beings nearly always backfires! Use *actual* intelligence instead of artificial intelligence. Likewise, upgrading a software system incorrectly can bring operations to a screeching halt. Technology is great, but it must be implemented wisely. It's imperative that your IT professionals are well trained and seasoned experts in your specific industry. It's even *more* important that leadership and business owners exercise critical thought and common sense on when and how to implement technology.

Build professional relationships through networking.

As you'll discover in chapter 5, relational health is vital to strong relationships. Just as strong *personal* relationships can make your *life* more rewarding, building strong *professional* relationships can make your *career* more successful. The better your professional relationships are, the more productive you are. This means two things…

First, you should learn who does what within your organization. Know that Joe works in the IT department and can help you resolve computer problems. Know that Jane works in the county permitting department – the same department your company relies on to start a new construction job. *People* get things done; know and help other people.

Second, you should build a network of professional connections across your industry. Keep in touch with previous classmates, professors, trainers, managers, and co-workers. This network is a *web* of professionals, all supporting each other. You can reach out to your network for job changes and upward mobility opportunities. Likewise, they may reach out to you. You should communicate relevant information with each other: upcoming conferences, trade shows, association meetings, industry best practices and innovations, hiring trends, job fairs, training opportunities, and other professional events. The stronger your network, the stronger your career!

Get more training on your job.

More on this shortly.

So, increasing your productivity will set you apart from the typical worker. I've listed a few ways to do so and I'm sure you can think of many more. Even doing *half* of the above things will probably put you in the top 10 percent of your peer group. That's your opportunity to work like a beast and pull ahead of the pack. But don't stop there – you're going from ordinary to *extra*ordinary. It's time to step it up *another* level!

Apply Lifelong Learning. This is where you get to showcase your education and all the skills you've been learning. You *have* been learning, haven't you? But remember, don't just learn for the sake of learning; the *application* of lifelong learning is a one-two punch! When it comes specifically to your career, here are some ways to accomplish that…

On-the-job training (OJT).

Most organizations provide some type of OJT. Your obligation is to listen, learn, ask questions, and *apply* the training. You must know the organization's mission, customers, policies, processes, and procedures. Training is a two-way activity. The information cannot be poured into your head – you must actively participate. This is also where volunteering for tasks and working overtime can pay off. The more you work, the faster you'll master your job. If I ever encountered a slow period at work, I would often seek out opportunities to help others with their work. That gave me more time to learn.

Another way to learn on the job is through a 'lessons learned meeting', an 'after action report', or something similar. Although one is a meeting and the other is a written report, the purpose of both is to educate workers on how to do better. If you make a mistake, damage equipment, or cause a problem, take the time to analyze what went wrong and why; that's the purpose of an after-action analysis (meeting or report). It's a feedback loop of continuous process improvement.

The goal of all this OJT is to continually enhance performance and productivity, regardless of your job. Whether you're a senior military instructor, an engineer, barber, mechanic, doctor, or anything else, always strive to be better at your job; OJT helps you do that.

Cross-pollination.

Just as bees transfer pollen from flower to flower, so too can workers transfer knowledge and skills from job to job. The idea is to learn as much as possible about the core job functions that are vital to your organization and serving the customer. For instance, a cashier can learn something about warehousing. A computer programmer can learn the purchase order process. A plumber or electrician can learn about marketing and branding. So on and so on. By learning something about an adjacent position in your company, you make yourself more valuable.

As you might imagine, military readiness can be the difference between mission success or mission failure. The difference between life or death. Many of the organizations where I worked operated 24 hours a day, 7 days a week. Every position (job) had a primary and an alternate person assigned to it. Each person was tasked with becoming qualified in that particular position. Therefore, if the primary person was unavailable due to sickness, injury, deployment, or leave, the alternate person could step right in without missing a beat. Similarly, it was also common to ensure key leaders had someone qualified to step in during their absence (commander, first sergeant, director, etc).

So, whether it's a military, corporate, private, public, small business, or non-profit position, it's wise to ensure continuity of operations through cross-pollination of skills. *Shadow* your boss and become familiar with his or her responsibilities. Volunteer to learn about other positions within your organization. *Apprentice* under a seasoned employee to learn another skill.

(See how it ties together?) Yes, this makes you more marketable and valuable over the span of your career. It also helps to strengthen your organization and better serve your customers.

Certifications.

As previously mentioned, certifications are part of lifelong learning. Seek out professional certifications that apply to your job specifically and your profession more broadly. For example, if you're a project manager, you may earn a Project Management Professional (PMP) certification. By the way, PMP skills can be applied across many professions (cross pollination). PMP certification entails learning resource management, scheduling, organizing, planning, and many other valuable skills. Those skills can be used in healthcare, IT, engineering, small business, general contracting, hospitality, manufacturing, and countless other professions. Many professionals (if they are professional) can benefit from various certifications. In fact, many *require* certification to meet licensing, legal, and/or operating requirements. Others are simply a smart way to level-up your skillsets. Your job is to research what certifications can help advance your career and enable you to better serve.

Also, be sure to think a step or two ahead. In other words, a particular certification may not benefit your current job, but it may open doors to a new/better job with a higher salary. For example, in IT, I've worked positions where PMP was beneficial. However, another job demanded a certification in IT security, which is why I also earned my Certified Information Systems Security Professional (CISSP) credentials. Possessing both PMP and CISSP allowed me to better *serve* my customers and my team. Due to a hiatus from work, I've let my certifications go inactive, but they were very valuable to my career and made me more productive. However, I still use some of those skills today in my everyday life. There are many certifications that can be valuable across many industries – seek them out. Research ones that are best suited for your line of work. Bottom line, get certified and apply your newly acquired skills to your job (and your life).

College, apprenticeships, and internships.

Being components of lifelong learning, I've grouped these three together here since I've already discussed them in chapter 2. You can choose to *apply* any of these learning avenues to your career. Some people fail to recognize the benefits and miss out on enormous amounts of money. For example, a small business owner may not realize that a college degree in business or marketing may help them to *double* their profits! Perhaps you like working with your hands in the trades (carpenter, plumber, welder, etc). That can be hard work, but remember, even the rat works hard. By *formalizing* your skills through an apprenticeship, you gain considerable experience, valuable skills, *and* build the foundation to a six-figure (or more) lucrative career! Then your hard work turns into *productivity*; you gain *traction* and start advancing in a professional career. I challenge you to cast a vision to *double* your salary within the next 3 years!

Rule 3 – Cast a Career Vision

This final rule is primarily about a strategic *career vision*. Work today; prosper tomorrow. It's very easy to get lost in the mundane, every day shuffle of work – loving Fridays and dreading Mondays. You know the drill; countless emails, endless phone calls, pointless meetings, aching feet, sore back, and busy, busy, busy. I repeat, many people work hard and they should be proud of that! In fact, working today is what you *should* do. Don't ever "mail it in" or work in some half-hearted, lazy, snowflake manner. That's disrespecting your company, your teammates, your customers, your community, and *yourself.* If you're unhappy at your current job, then have the courtesy and the backbone to leave. Until then, work the job you're at – you know, the one you *applied* for! However, don't stop there.

Remember to follow your passion. Do work that you love and gets you out of bed in the morning. Who knows, you may even start loving Mondays again! That's right, I encourage you to look up from your feet and gaze out into the horizon. (Intentionality rears its head again.) What you're doing today is not what you'll be doing 10 or 15 years from now. You may be in the same line of work, but it will surely change in some way. Take control of the direction of that change. Don't let life happen to you; you happen to it. Periodically look to your north star. Where's your career headed? Have you made any progress? If not, what are you waiting for?! I challenge you to formulate some career goals and milestones and yes, write them down. It's hard to follow a career roadmap if you don't even have one! Remember to think critically; if you're not getting to where you want to be, ask yourself why. Be objective, not defensive. Your goal is results, not excuses. Don't be a Bumbling Dumbledorf. Here are just a few things you can challenge yourself to accomplish...

- ✓ Increase your income by 10 percent (or more) this year. Repeat it again next year.
- ✓ Earn a professional certification within the next 6 months. Then earn another.
- ✓ Grow your customer base by 20 percent next calendar year. Hire help if required.
- ✓ Ask your boss, "What's the *one* thing I can do to earn advancement and/or more pay?" Then go do it and repeat the process again. And again. And again.

Those are simple starter ideas. I'm sure you can devise your own career goals, but do so and then *act* on them! Then, as you move further into your career, you'll want to consider transition and/or exit strategies, as applicable. Very rarely do careers happen in a straight line. Although you can chart a roadmap, you'll often encounter zigs and zags along the way. There may even be major detours and huge potholes to navigate. How do I know? Been there, done that. My 25+ years of combined military and civilian service were certainly a twisty-turny career adventure. Here's a personal example of me and my wife casting a career vision...

While serving on active duty, I lived in 13 different homes across many different countries and states; 21 homes if you include additional stays of about 1-4 months each. Each one of my assignments brought about its own unique and demanding responsibilities. However, my head was always *up* and my eyes always *forward*. I gave each job 100 percent but always knew there would be the *next*. As I approached eligibility for military retirement, our daughter was nearly 5 years old. My wife had been staying at home to care for the kids and was now eager to resume her career. We made the joint decision for me to retire so she could have job stability. That decision left me with a transition from military work to civilian work. I polished up my resume and accelerated my certifications in preparation for a new job. Before I could blink, I was retired from the military and working a new civilian career in the federal government. However, that was only the first major transition.

About 2-3 years after my military retirement, my wife's career was in full bloom as a contract specialist for the federal government. I was then working as an IT Specialist. It was during that time that her persistent health issues got extremely bad. She was forced to leave the workforce and focus exclusively on her health. We moved yet again, this time to be closer to family. After less than one year of that, her health was so bad that I voluntarily resigned from my own career to support her and our two kids while she battled through her health issues. In short, this led to about a decade of practically living in hospitals and managing a gazillion medications. We had a virtual revolving door to the emergency room; I could almost drive there blindfolded. Our kids spent nights in the hospital waiting room doing their homework on their computer tablets. We kept blankets and pillows in the car for when they got tired. All of this was essential to my wife's health and life and we would do it all over again if required. Yet, we continued to move forward one day at a time – each hospital visit was a win. Each positive medical test was a win. Each day alive was a win. We kept our head *up* and our eyes *forward* and still do today.

Things have leveled out a bit over the years, but I resist the urge to digress. Here, my focus is on the effect these events had on our careers so that it can be a valuable lesson learned for everyone. You simply never know when you'll be unable to work – for many unforeseen reasons. We've incurred about $2M in combined lost incomes over those years of career hiatus. Thankfully, my military pension and our combined Veterans Affairs medical and disability benefits have kept us afloat. Time will reveal how my wife's health progresses and in turn, the resumption of her career. Until then, we'll keep planning and casting a vision.

Currently, the next shoe has yet to drop on my own career. Besides writing, I have yet to finalize a decision on my next step forward. Back to IT? Career change? Writing full time? Perhaps a $B startup company? Origami (paper folding)? Counting tooth picks? Who knows, but I'll continue thinking it through and will act when the time is right. Until then, my wife and I keep on keeping on. Her health is top priority. All of that said to stress the importance of a long-term vision for *your* career and *your* future prosperity. Don't stall. Don't stagnate. Drive hard and fast, but know where the exits and rest areas are. That leads me to one final tip for casting a vision for your career.

You can (and should) prepare for career hiccups and challenges like my wife and I faced. It's wise to formulate transition and exit strategies (i.e. Plan B's). What do I mean? Well, like it or not, you won't work your job forever. One day you may even change careers. You may retire. You may resign and volunteer full time. You may become disabled. You may… (get the idea)? There are many possible reasons why, but you *will* leave your job one day.

One key way to 'plan for the unplanned' is to ensure you have **long-term disability insurance**. I talk more about this as it relates to financial planning in chapter 4, but here it's *very* important to have long-term disability insurance as part of your overall career planning. It's often (but not always) provided as a workplace benefit so check with your employer. Your income is the engine of your wealth building. If your income stops, you're in trouble. In a nutshell, this insurance provides you with a monthly income if you become physically or mentally unable to work. It's super important. My wife and I were fortunate to have earned military veteran's benefits. Had we not been in the military, we surely would have purchased long-term disability plans and good healthcare insurance.

When our son landed his first job, the salary and other benefits sounded great, but I practically ignored them all and told him one thing. I emphasized, "Make sure you have long-term disability insurance." My wife's career journey and subsequent health scares have been forever seared into my soul. If you become unable to work without this coverage, it can be a financial catastrophe! I think it was Benjamin Franklin who said, "If you fail to plan, you're planning to fail!" Don't fail to plan.

So, there you have three action-oriented rules that can take you from a J-O-B to a rewarding and prosperous career. Be a servant leader, be productive and apply lifelong learning, and cast a vision. Those rules alone go a long way to a phenomenal career, but I'd like to add some cherries on top. Here are a few career bonus tips…

Tip 1 – Work-Life Balance

This tip stems from my daughter. I asked her if she was allowed only *one* single question about *anything* in life, what would it be? The first thing she did was ask me *two* questions. (She's an over-achiever.) The first question was about finding happiness in life versus just settling. I address that question in chapter 8, under the value of *contentment* (happiness).

However, her second question was related to education and career. As a hard-working college student, aspiring to attend medical school, and planning a career in psychiatry, she also asked me, "**How do you find work-life balance?**" Wow, these kids ask tough questions! Little did she realize, but 'balance' is a key principle that spans many areas of life, not just a career. As luck would have it, I talk more broadly about balance as its own principle in chapter 7. Here, I retain focus on balance as it relates specifically to *work-life balance* (her question).

Like many things, including work, there are two extremes and everything in between. First, you may know people who don't work at all. Maybe they're independently wealthy. Perhaps they're medically disabled. Maybe they're on career hiatus. They might even be fully retired. Perhaps they're just plain lazy. Who knows. There are many reasons. Then, to the other extreme are the people who seem to work 24/7; you wonder if they ever sleep, eat, or have a life at all. It's my opinion that neither of these extremes are healthy *or* productive over the long-term. My advice is to fall somewhere in the middle – with a caveat.

The caveat is that work-life balance is rarely a static steady-state rhythm. You won't work precisely the same hours and the same exact days of the week for decades and decades. More often, your work-life balance flows in waves (or seasons). There may be periods when you work 12-hour days (or more). You might do this while learning a new, demanding job – think residency for doctors or newly hired investment bankers at large Wall Street firms. You may even have a backlog of product to deliver. For example, it's possible you manufactured toilet paper during the COVID-19 pandemic. (If you're too young, just know toilet paper was scarce for a while.) A new parent may take time off to be home with the baby. As the baby grows, the parent may then transition back to full-time work. My own personal career has been a case in point for such balance…

There were times (before I had a family) that I worked *relentlessly* to get stuff done. It may have been a high workload, completing my degree, military deployment, working out, or all of it occurring at the same time. Occasionally, I'd temporarily forgo sleeping and eating in order to get things done. No excuses. I certainly don't recommend this to anyone, but it's done and I'm still alive. During one deployment to the middle-east I worked a *minimum* of 6 days a week, 12-13 hours a day for 4 months. However, upon returning stateside, I transitioned back to a steady-state rhythm of 40+ hours a week. Things were often hectic even with family life.

When my wife and I were working full time, we both balanced careers and parenthood. Our kids may remember us sitting in the daycare parking lot at 6:30am waiting for the doors to open so mom or dad could make it to work on time. We did that for years. Now, make no mistake, there have been *plenty* of years of relaxation, downtime, and goofing off as well. As you can imagine, there are many other scenarios where your work-life balance will ebb and flow.

So, fittingly, the key to work-life balance is…balance. I'd argue that if you work like a sloth and never accomplish anything, you'll struggle to be very prosperous. Work builds character and resiliency. The effort itself is often the intrinsic reward. However, if you run yourself into the ground, endanger your health, and sacrifice life, you miss the point of working in the first place. Know when to hit the gas and when to tap the brakes. So, on the occasion that work-life *imbalance* is necessary, it should only last for a *season*. It should be both *necessary* and *temporary*.

Lastly, from a broader perspective, the phrase 'work-life balance' contains both work *and* life. As you'll discover in *Part II*, I don't live to work, but rather **I work to live!** That's a bold statement from someone who believes in hard work – very hard work. You *should* work hard…no doubt. After all, being a human mushroom is a waste of precious life. Work should provide a sense of fulfillment and purpose. That's exactly the point; so, what is your purpose? Ask yourself *why* you work. To keep busy? To earn money? For me, it's *in order to* have a rich, meaningful, and prosperous *life*, which includes serving, loving, and supporting my wife, my kids, and the world around me. I enjoy adding value. I love helping others. Work…like education, personal finance, and many other things is certainly important to life. But it's *part* of life, not life itself. If I was handed $50B dollars, I would still do some kind of work. However, in order to truly prosper, you must have *balance* and a higher purpose (why) for working. For me, I've found that purpose as I shared in my personal mission statement (chapter 1). That means I work hard not only to serve my customers, but also to support myself, my wife, my children, my family, and my community. I wrote this book to add value and help others in life. In fact, the reason I'm currently on temporary hiatus from a 'traditional' career is to provide support and caregiving to my wife. I value her life over work. Under ideal circumstances, we can (and should) balance both work *and* life. However, it's only when you're *forced* to choose does it become clear which is more important. Let's hope only a rare few of us are ever forced to choose. And even then, let's hope it's only for a season of life. More on the principle of balance in chapter 7.

Tip 2 – Small Business

I've never owned a small business, so it's best to seek out experts who have succeeded in that area. However, when viewing a small business objectively from the outside, I often see one glaring problem for many self-employed people. The problem is they think they own a *business* when in reality they own their *job*. What's the difference? A business is an entity; it can have intellectual property, a book of business, assets such as real estate or machinery, branding, a legal corporate structure, employees, and a whole lot more. In short, if you went on permanent vacation, a true business would still operate and produce income. You could also sell a business to an absentee owner, meaning they would not work the business themself, but rather hire a manager to do so.

So, do you own a business or are you self-employed (own your job)? If you remove yourself from the job (quit working), will you have sustainable income? If not, you own your job. While it's common to *start* as self-employed, if you truly wish to create a self-sustaining business, you must do the things necessary to build one. That's where education, books, mentorship, and advice on growing a small business can be extremely valuable! Just remember the difference between owning a business and owning your job.

Tip 3 – Brand Yourself

Like it or not, we all work for ourselves. We're all self-employed in some manner. Oh sure, we may be employed by a big company, non-profit, or the federal government, but make no mistake, we agree to do X work in return for Y compensation. That agreement can be severed at any moment for many reasons by employer or employee. Be postured and prepared to find new employment at all times. The trick is to make yourself as valuable as possible in the market place. You want to be, as they say, in high demand! The way to do that is to brand yourself professionally. Here are a few ways to do so…

- ➤ First and foremost, be valuable. In short, know your job and broader profession. This comes from ongoing education, training, and experience. The more valuable you are, the more employable you are…and the more you can earn!

- ➤ Build a reputation for being dependable, honest, hard-working, respectful, and helpful. Yes, values matter.

- ➤ Sharpen your communication skills. Be a polished speaker and an effective writer.

- ➤ Maintain a strong *professional* network and online presence. A single careless and unprofessional comment has the potential to ruin your career.

- ➤ Have a current resume handy at all times. Always be adding to your resume: education, training, certifications, experience, industry skills, and anything that can help you stand out.

- ➤ Practice your interview skills. You'll likely have many interviews over the course of your life. Preparation may mean the difference between getting hired or not.

- ➤ Dress for success. Depending on your work environment, this can mean many things to many people. To me, it means you should stand out in a good way and always present a professional image.

- ➤ Lastly, work *every* day as if it's your first (dress sharp, work hard, continue learning, and act professionally). Pretend your job is on the line…because it is.

Tip 4 – Policy, Process, and Procedure (PPP)

There's an entire business ecosystem involving organizational structure, software safeguards, business rules, governance, workflow, and much more…all of which are beyond the scope of this book. However, if you want to enhance your value and productivity at work, focus on three basic business items: policy, process, and procedure. This will not only increase your productivity, but it will also enable you to better serve your customers. These items, of course, will vary from profession to profession and job to job. However, the below example paints a simple picture – adjust accordingly. The hypothetical business is a grocery retailer.

Policy – conduct (re)stocking operations outside store hours. This is for logistical efficiency, customer convenience, liability, and safety (employees and customers).

Process – stock or re-stock shelves and displays.

Procedures – use approved hand carts to transfer goods from warehouse and storage-room areas to (re)stock customer facing shelves and displays.

Although this is a very basic example, you should ask yourself what the business policy is regarding the work you perform. Keep in mind, a business usually has many *policies*. You must also understand their *processes* and what part of the process you perform. In some instances, you may perform the entire process from start to finish. Lastly, through training and experience, you'll master the step-by-step *procedures* for completing the process while complying with policy. Some PPP will be general in nature, whereas some will be highly detailed and complex.

There you have four **bonus tips** for a strong career. All in all, I hope you're inspired and energized to grow a rewarding career. Please don't trudge along in a j-o-b. I sincerely wish you a phenomenal career of passion and prosperity! If you follow the three rules that I've outlined, I believe you can. You must. Life is too short to do something you hate. It's too short to be ordinary.

So, whether you're a CEO or a worker bee, an actor or athlete, a president or doctor, a senator or mechanic, these career rules apply to you and nearly every other profession. If followed, you're likely to be far more valuable to your organization than they are to you. Strive to be the best in the world at what you do. Take your career to world-class and work like you mean it!

Secret Sauce:

Don't focus on finding a rewarding career. Rather, focus on the *underlying behaviors* that lead to a rewarding career. Follow the 3 rules (service mindset, career actions, and career vision) and the 4 career bonus tips (work-life balance, small business, brand yourself, and PPP). A rewarding career will follow.

Chapter 4

Financial Wealth

[**Wealth**. What does it mean to you? A certain income? A specific net worth? Something else? There are countless definitions. Think about it. Reflect on it.]

You have an idea of what wealth means to you. As do I. My views have evolved over time. By the end of this chapter (and book), I sincerely hope I've influenced your views on wealth. Ideally, for the better in some way. You be the judge.

Yes, this chapter outlines a path towards building financial wealth. I also go much further. I elaborate on wealth through three main views: mindset, blueprint, and behaviors. In doing so, we go from big picture to small picture.

- **Mindset** is essentially *policy*, philosophy, high-level concepts, and views on wealth.
- **Blueprint** is more akin to a path or a *process* – it's a system of repeatable principles that lead to wealth over time.
- **Behaviors** are the day-to-day *procedures* for following the path to wealth.

Together, these three areas provide a holistic view of wealth. They show *how* to build it and reveal deeper insight into *why* you should. I'll elaborate further on each. (Coincidentally, you may note the parallel to policy, process, and procedure (PPP) from chapter 3, career tip 4.) Let's begin with an ever-so important mindset.

Wealth Mindset

Wealth should start with your mindset. My mindset around wealth is rather unusual in some ways. Let me ease into it with the help of three friends. What do my friends the ant, the tortoise, and the third little pig know about wealth?

First, I think most of us have heard the children's fable about the ant and the grasshopper. You may recall how the ant worked diligently all summer long, storing away food for the winter while the grasshopper lazily played music and goofed off all day. When winter inevitably struck, the ant was warm and well fed while the grasshopper was starving out in the cold.

Second, remember how the slow and steady tortoise beat the speedy hare when they raced. The hare would speed ahead and get so confident that he lazily took a nap midway through the race. The tortoise kept a steady pace, persevered, and eventually passed the napping rabbit and won the race.

Lastly, we have the three little pigs. They each built a house — the first of straw, the second of sticks, and the third of brick. We know which of these little pigs was the safest when the big bad wolf came huffing and puffing to blow their house down and eat them. Yes, it was the third little pig who worked tirelessly to build a house of brick!

So, a few children's fable characters can teach us about the values necessary for building wealth — diligence, perseverance, and work ethic are but a few. It's about slow and steady, not get rich quick. Moving forward, reflect on the *diligent* ant, the *steady* tortoise, and the *industrious* pig as you build not only your own wealth, but that of subsequent generations. However, let's first ask ourselves what exactly *is* wealth?

What amount of money defines wealth? It depends. So, if we calculate wealth by net worth, it's a simple equation:

[ASSETS – LIABILITIES = NET WORTH]

- Assets are what you *own*.
- Liabilities are what you *owe* (debt).

<u>Example Assets:</u>

- Home value ($400K)
- Car value ($20K)
- Savings ($25K)
- Retirement account ($80K)

Total Assets = $525K

<u>Example Liabilities:</u>

- Mortgage balance ($150K)
- Car loan ($15K)
- Student loans ($10K)
- Credit cards ($5K)

Total Liabilities = $180K

<u>Example Net Worth:</u>

$525K - $180K = $345K Net Worth

Therefore, if we use net worth as the official gauge, then everyone falls somewhere on a sliding scale of wealth. To the far left is a negative net worth (you're broke). To the far right is a positive net worth (you're a multi-billionaire). All the rest of us fall somewhere in between. The big question is, where do *you* fall? What's *your* net worth? If you wish to be wealthy, you should know. *Where you focus, you prosper.*

By definition, a *millionaire* is someone with a net worth of $1M or more. So, is a millionaire considered wealthy? What if you have $25M, $50M, or $100M? Perhaps $1B is what it takes. As you can see, although net worth is a concrete number, *wealth* is not. Wealth is relative.

So, we can use net worth to help measure wealth. I believe it certainly is a factor. However, let's not stop there. I told you my mindset here is a bit unusual. I don't put a specific number on wealth. A raw number can certainly define goals, milestones, and *success* (millionaire or billionaire). All very true. All transactional. But it takes something more meaningful to achieve *wealth*. And I believe *individual* wealth should feed into *generational* wealth...

To me, *individual* wealth is much deeper than a simple net worth equation. It's almost a feeling. Being wealthy means you have more freedom and options. It means you feel financially safe, secure, and comfortable in your life. You have a sense of peace and calm. Being wealthy means you live an enjoyable, meaningful life and can pursue your passions. Most importantly, wealth allows you to be generous and lend a hand up to others. And while individual wealth is aspirational and awesome…sadly, it dies with the individual. However, if wisely tended to, the roots of individual wealth will bear the fruits of generational wealth.

Generational wealth survives the individual and carries on to nourish the next. It's the *financial* component to generational prosperity. In this book, you'll discover there are many other components as well. This entails a systematic and repeatable process of passing along wealth, primarily through inheritance and estate planning. However, it also includes the character, values, and behaviors necessary to sustain that wealth. It's a package deal. This is a journey, not a destination. How so? Generational wealth is not a one-and-done process. There's no finish line. Rather, each generation *builds upon the one prior* and *contributes to the one after.* The process continues in perpetuity, amassing exponential family wealth over time. Mind you, this is not a greedy or selfish endeavor. Quite to the contrary.

A core requirement to generational wealth (and subsequent prosperity) is **selflessness**. Think about it. A *selfish* person who spends every penny will never have anything to pass along. Thus, like a broken record, the next generation will continue to struggle…to struggle…to struggle. (For those who remember record players.)

However, a *selfless* person has a bigger mindset. A generous mindset. A selfless person sees not only today, but also tomorrow. They think of others. In our case, my wife and I have our family in mind – specifically, our kids. As such, we've grown a selfless mindset of systematically building wealth, starting with us. As you'll see, money (and wealth) should not be worshipped but rather used for good and helping others. Wealthy people can (and should) help far more people than poor people can.

Lastly, as it pertains to mindset, I view wealth in a positive light. If your astrological sign is doom & gloom, it's time for an intervention. Do you…

- View wealthy people as trust-fund babies, lottery winners, or somehow *lucky*?
- Bemoan, "The rich get richer and the poor get poorer"?
- Demonize the evil millionaires, billionaires, and 1-percenters?

If this is you, I suggest you stay broke! Why? Because if wealthy people are so evil or spoiled, why would you want to be wealthy? Hmm. Something to ponder. Don't criticize or hate wealthy people – congratulate and emulate them. Follow their lead. If that's not enough, I have one final point about the positivity of wealth.

In times of need, would you rather have *less* money or *more* money? Trust me, this is a silly (not silly) question. Here are just a few scenarios that come to mind…

- Natural disasters (flood, tornado, hurricane, blizzard, fire, etc).
- Loss of income (layoff, firing, government shutdown, disability, etc).
- Major accident (home, auto, boat, plane, etc).
- Catastrophic medical expenses.

It seems when tragedy strikes, there's a desperate cry for money. People who say they don't care much about money suddenly seem to care very much. Having *less* money leads to compounding the tragedy. (Tragedy on top of tragedy.) You'll see fund raisers, telethons, donation requests, 401(k) loans, title loans, payday loans, and much more. The result is often enormous stress and a huge pile of soul-crushing debt on the other side of recovery. Yes, as chapter 9 will show, some people are their own worst enemy – even when it comes to managing money. They simply don't learn.

However, having *more* money turns mountains into molehills (financially speaking). Clearly, none of this alleviates human tragedy (sickness, death, etc), but rather the financial component. It's easier to write a check and move on. Money should *already* exist in the form of an emergency fund, savings, and investments. The rainy-day mindset is to make hay when the sun shines. Granted, we can't prepare for *everything*. And granted, money isn't a cure-all, but neither is being broke. That's why my mindset is to have *more*, not less – not for greedy purposes, but rather for humanitarian, helpful, restorative, and *selfless* purposes!

All of this mindset forms the basis of the wealth blueprint. Onward and upward if you wish to build wealth.

Wealth Blueprint

Bear in mind, I'm not a hedge fund manager, tax professional, investment advisor, economist, or insurance professional of any kind. I simply share what I've learned and what has worked for me. You should consult licensed professionals in a few key areas as you work towards building wealth…

- ❖ A certified financial planner (CFP).
- ❖ A certified tax professional.
- ❖ An estate planning attorney.
- ❖ A certified insurance professional.

The blueprint I suggest for building wealth is simple and straightforward. My advice is not filled with tales of get rich quick schemes, crafty tax shelters, financial leverage, or complex financial formulas. Some might even call it boring. There are no guarantees, no automatic millionaires, and surely no promises of easy wealth. This approach is not perfect, foolproof, or "better than" the myriads of others out there, but it has worked quite well for me and my family.

The approach taken is not just a specific micro-focus on money, but rather a holistic macro-view of your entire financial house. In other words, it's about more than just budgeting, investing, or paying off debt. You'll discover that building a strong financial house of brick also involves your career path, estate plan, insurance needs, retirement, personal values, and more.

Additionally, I don't get down in the weeds. The path I lay out is a universal one that can span generations. For example, there are many budgeting apps and tools available and they change all the time. Also, there are thousands of investable assets; they too change all the time. Examples include precious metals, commodities, cryptocurrencies, private equity, real estate, and more. Some people worship this fund or that fund. Search for ones that work for you and certainly with the help of an expert in those areas. Remember, this is a *playbook for generational prosperity*. Therefore, do not make this the only book you read about personal finance, investing, or wealth building. If you follow the advice in this book, you'll do additional research on investing and learn how to continually fine-tune your financial picture. So, where to start? Just as I outlined a learning model in chapter 2, here too I present another model…this one a set of financial principles.

Spoiler alert, this path to wealth is slow and simple. There are no gimmicks, tricks, or short-cuts. The principles are not flashy, fancy, or mind-blowing. Any able-bodied person can build wealth, but you must first *choose* to do so, and then you must *execute* (do the work).

Here's where to start. Below are six repeatable principles to follow. Write these on an index card and follow them – done.

Wealth Building Principles (follow in order):

1. Follow a Written Budget.
2. Always Grow Your Income.
3. Live Debt Free.
4. Keep a 6-Month Emergency Fund.
5. Invest 15% into Retirement.
6. Own Your Home.

There you have it – is your mind blown yet? See how simple it is to become wealthy over time? Ok, I explain more below, but not much. The problem is that very few people actually *do* these things. Do you…?

Note:

You may wonder why I call these *principles*, even though I advise to follow them in order. There's an order you should follow, but the principles are never truly *complete*. For example, once you're debt free, you must remain debt free. Once you have an emergency fund, you must maintain it. Once you own your home, you must remain free of a mortgage, home equity line of credit, or debt of *any* kind. I explain more under each principle. So, these are principles to follow ongoing (in order). The logic becomes clearer as you read on.

Principle 1 (Follow a Written Budget)

In my opinion, the single biggest reason why people have money problems is not following a written monthly budget!

Have you ever wondered where all your money goes? A budget is nothing more than a *written plan on how to spend your income.* That's it. It's not living on peanut butter and jelly sandwiches or squeezing pennies until they bleed. I list this as the first principle because it will provide insight into all other areas. Begin your financial journey with a written budget. In fact, do one tonight! Why do a written budget? Here's a better question – why would you *not*? Hmm. How can you strive to be wealthy if you can't even do a simple budget? It holds you accountable. There are many ways to do a budget, but two common methods are a budgeting app or a spreadsheet. I don't recommend any specific apps, but there are plenty to choose from. I'm old fashioned and I like to keep things simple. Plus, having worked in IT for 25 years, I minimize putting my personal and financial information 'out there' online any more than is necessary. Yes, that's why I use a spreadsheet. How to make a budget, you may ask.

Whether using an app or spreadsheet, your budget should list your total household **income** and total household **expenses**…

Total household **income** means from all sources. This includes all jobs, side hustles, incoming alimony or child support, social security, rental income, etc. If you're married, include incomes here from *both* spouses. (If you're not married, it's best to keep your finances separate.) Either way, you'll end up with one single number – your total, bottom line household net (take-home) income.

Then, list all of your household **expenses**. Include *everything*: utilities, groceries, rent or mortgage, taxes, insurance, outgoing alimony or child support, fuel, entertainment, subscriptions, lattes, pet expenses, etc. It's very likely that you'll miss a few things if you've never budgeted before. Don't worry, you'll get better with each passing month. Again, if you're not married this can get messy and it's best to keep your finances separate. The end result is one single number – your total, bottom line household expenses.

The **total income** and **total expenses** form the foundation of your monthly budget. It's possible that your income varies from month to month. In that case, simply adjust your budget using both historical averages and current projections. Make a new budget every month – a clean slate. List out *exactly* what you plan to spend for the upcoming month and stick to it! Remember to list everything and account for every single dollar. You work too hard for your money to waste it! The last thing to include in your budget is any debt you may have.

There's no right or wrong way to track **debt** on your budget, but I'd recommend a separate list. Here, you'll track any debt you have by the remaining *balances*. For example, you may have a car payment of $400 per month. If so, that's one of the monthly *expenses* in your budget. However, what's the remaining loan *balance*? If you owe $10K, you'd want to list that balance (debt) on a separate page or spreadsheet. This applies to credit cards, student loans, and any other debt you have. Of course, you'll also update the loan balances every month. Tracking your debt (if any) is vital to eliminating it (when you get to principle 3).

My golden rule when budgeting is **total expenses < total income**. This means your *total expenses* must be **less than** your *total income*.

[**Tip:** Any withheld federal or state income taxes will affect your take-home pay. Ideally, you should not receive *or* owe significant money when you file your taxes. If you *owe* a large sum every year, *increase* your tax withholdings to offset what you owe. If you *receive* a large tax return every year, *decrease* your tax withholdings to offset what you receive. Your employer and tax professional can help you do this.]

If you find your total monthly expenses are higher than your total monthly income, that's a problem! There are two ways to correct that. You can do one or both…

- **Increase your income.** Work more hours, get extra job(s), sell stuff, etc.
- **Lower your expenses.** Trim any fat from your budget. Sell stuff. Downsize in vehicle. Downsize in home (lower rent, mortgage, and upkeep). Get a roommate (or two). If you're

investing into retirement, stop for now. You'll resume retirement investing later (principle 5), but not while you're struggling to pay for food, rent, utilities, and life necessities.

That's it, there are no shortcuts. This part is critical. If you spend more than you make, it's nearly impossible to build wealth. Agreed? Agreed! If you earn $1M and spend $2M, you're known as *broke*! By following the other principles in this book, you should be able to significantly increase your income. However, you must make tough choices and slash expenses to the bone! At least for now. Remember, all of this cost-cutting is *temporary*. You're in the financial emergency room until you get your finances healthy. Stay the course. As your income starts to rise and your expenses start to fall, the financial urgency will dissipate. You'll eventually reach a balanced rhythm of financial stability. As you advance to principles 2-6, you'll adjust your budget accordingly. Your budget has many benefits.

A budget is your financial dashboard. It displays your total income, expenses, and debt. You'll see (possibly for the first time) exactly how much 'extra' money you have every month. Or…you'll see exactly how much you're in the hole every month. Yikes! Either way, it's usually eye opening. I suggest you also add your net worth to your budget. Track everything in one spot! Most importantly, a budget is an overall focus on your financial priorities.

Where you focus, you prosper. If you focus on money, you'll actually have some. A budget is intentionality for your money. Perhaps now you can see why the budget is principle 1. All other things rely on it. You can also see why it's a principle and never *done*. A budget provides order for your money…and your life! That's ironic because it's so easy to do – grade school math. All in, a typical monthly budget should only take about 30 minutes once you get the hang of it. If you're not currently doing a written budget, do one this month. If you're new to budgeting, don't get discouraged – practice makes perfect. Consider reading books that provide in-depth budgeting advice. As you fine-tune your budget, focus on growing your income.

Principle 2 (Always Grow Your Income)

Are you happy with your income? Your budget is the tool that tracks your income. Always grow your income is principle 2. At least annually, your income should increase in some manner: cost-of-living adjustment, pay raise, bonus, overtime, promotion, etc. At a minimum, you must keep up with inflation. For example, if annual inflation is 3% and you get a 3% raise, you're only breaking even. If your raise is less than inflation, you're falling behind!

Your income is the *engine* of wealth building. It feeds into and accelerates other principles. Your income gets filtered through your budget and funnels down principles 3-6 in order.

The primary way to earn income is through your career. This book highlights many ways to grow your career and thus your income. (Especially chapters 2 and 3.) All things equal, the higher your income, the greater your wealth. If you don't grow your income, then don't complain about not building wealth. Unlike a budget, which is easy, growing your income is hard – that's why they call it work. Besides your career, there are many ways to grow income…

- Side hustles.
- Real estate.
- Royalties (books, music, patents, etc).
- Investments (mutual funds, stocks, bonds, etc).
- Paid sponsorships.
- Ad revenue.
- Affiliate marketing.

Wise investments will generate income even when you're sleeping! By now, it should be clear how these principles all work together, hand in hand. Growing your income should become habit, just like brushing your teeth. You must grow your income (and/or slash expenses) until your total monthly expenses are lower than your total monthly income. Until that happens, you're stuck on principle 2. **Do not move to principle 3 or beyond until total expenses < total income.**

Principle 3 (Live Debt Free)

First, pick your tears! The ones that happen when you cry…

Option 1 – Tears of stress, anxiety, and sadness. These tears come when you get *into* debt.

Option 2 – Tears of joy, relief, and pride! These tears come when you get *out* of debt.

When it comes to debt, you'll hear about good debt, bad debt, leverage, and everything in between. Yes, you'll even hear about using "other people's money" to get rich. All of that is for other books. Or perhaps social media videos and late-night infomercials. I love only one kind of debt – no debt! If you have no debt, then simply keep budgeting, growing your income, and living debt free. Then move to principle 4 (emergency fund).

However, if you do have debt, read on. If you're on principle 3, it means your **total monthly expenses are less than your total monthly income**. It also means you now have margin (extra money) above your living necessities to pay off your debt. If you have a mortgage, hold that thought until principle 6. Here in principle 3, you'll pay off *all* of your debt (except your mortgage, if you have one). This includes IRS debt, vehicle loans, student loans, personal loans, medical debt, credit cards, phones, and any other debt you may have. How do you pay off debt?

Paying off debt requires intentionality and determination. Getting into debt is easy; getting out of debt is hard. You can coast into debt but you can't coast out – it requires horsepower! Don't try to be tricky or cute with debt consolidation, debt refinancing, or juggling your debt (from one credit card to another). There may be a situation where that's minimally helpful, and you may save a few points in interest, but the debt is still there. It's best to simply get rid of the debt! Pay. It. Off.

Before proceeding, temporarily stop any retirement investing; that will restart in principle 5. This frees up every available dollar to first pay off debt! Since you now have a budget, you know exactly how much debt you have (if any). List your debts in order, from smallest balance on top to largest balance on bottom. Think of a pyramid; smallest blocks on top and largest blocks on bottom. Ignore the interest rates of your debt and list them only by their current *balance*. The interest rate is the small picture; the debt balance is the big picture. You're lining up your debts to be disintegrated, one at a time. Remember, don't include your mortgage here (if you have one). Now comes the fun part.

Once you've listed your debts from smallest to largest by balance, you start disintegrating the first (smallest) one! After paying all *minimum* essential monthly expenses, take every available extra dollar that you have in your budget and fire it at that smallest debt until it's gone. (Extra dollars are any dollars above *essential* living expenses and all other *minimum* payments on any other debt.)

Example

Let's assume your smallest debt is a credit card with a $500 balance. Take all extra money and pay it towards the $500 credit card. If possible, use every available dollar to pay it off in *full!* If not, pay whatever you have and repeat that process each month until it's paid off. Don't tap dance around with minimum payments on this smallest debt – pay it off completely. Once your hypothetical $500 credit card is gone, pay off the *next* smallest debt and so on. (Notice that you'll have incrementally more 'extra' dollars every month as each individual debt is paid off.) Continue this process until you've paid off every single debt in full, from smallest to largest.

How long will this process take? Answer: it depends on how much debt and how much extra income you have. It's easy to get lost in the weeds, so pan back and look at big numbers. Suppose you have $20K in total debt (except a mortgage). If you throw $10K a year at it, the debt's gone in two years. That's only about $833 per month. You can make that mowing lawns, waiting tables, driving ride shares, or delivering pizza at a part-time job. Who knows, maybe you'll earn an extra $20K and pay off your debt in *one* year! Another option is to sell stuff – think of old furniture, gently used clothing, extra vehicles, collectibles, jewelry, unused tools, or anything (legal) that can bring quick cash. Clearly, the more debt you have, the harder you must work to pay it off. That's why you always grow your income – you'll pay off debt faster! The more serious you are, the faster you'll become debt free.

Remember, you must *temporarily* stop any non-essential spending until you're fully debt free. Do not invest. Do not eat out. Do not go to the movies. Do not blink (ok, I'm kidding). In all seriousness, cut out any frivolous spending until you're fully debt free. As you eliminate each debt, remember to update your budget. Remember, you dug yourself into this mess, you must dig yourself out. You can't bail out a leaky boat while it still has a hole in the bottom! Patch the hole(s) and **stop** borrowing money! Here are four tips for avoiding debt…

Tip 1 – Don't co-sign a loan for *anyone*! There's a reason they can't get a loan on their own. By co-signing their loan, you're taking on debt and will be on the hook if that person doesn't pay. Co-signing isn't being nice, it's being stupid. Don't do it.

Tip 2 – Don't *loan* money. If you have it and you're willing to, then *give* it – never loan it. You're unnecessarily putting a negative (loss) on your finances, which may never get paid back. More importantly, loaning money leads to ruined relationships and big problems. Don't do it!

Tip 3 – Don't take out a payday or title loan! This is digging the hole deeper. Adding fuel to the fire, these loans typically have astronomical interest rates and fees. Avoid these loans like the plague.

Tip 4 – Don't borrow from your home equity (HELOC) or your retirement account! With rare exception, it's a bad idea. You're borrowing from your future to pay for today. I like to say, "Pretend you couldn't – what would you do then?"

If possible, go nuclear!

[If you have any **non-retirement** money, use it to obliterate your debt! This could be extra money in a checking or savings account, money market, certificate of deposit, crypto-currency, bonds, gold, or any **non-retirement** money you may have. For example, it's silly to have $10K in debt and $10K in a savings account. Just don't pull money from a retirement account – you'll be penalized and taxed.]

Once you pay off all of your debt, this principle reminds you to live debt free for the rest of your life! One way to help yourself do that is to follow principle 4, have an emergency fund. **Do not move to principle**

4 until you're 100% debt free (except a mortgage, if you have one).

Principle 4 (Keep a 6-Month Emergency Fund)

Be the ant, not the grasshopper. The ant spent some time preparing for bad weather. He controlled the controllables. The ant built up a store of food for the winter. In other words, he built up an *emergency fund*. So should you. An emergency fund is there for ~~if~~ *when* bad weather arrives. Some call it a rainy day fund. Without an emergency fund, everything's an emergency (flat tire, water heater, medical bill, layoff, etc). Just like in principle 3, you should not spend *any* non-essential money until you've built a full emergency fund. Likewise, you should not invest into retirement until you have a full emergency fund.

Many life events can lead to **loss of income**. People lose their jobs for many reasons (layoffs, firings, illness, injury, budget cuts, downsizing, etc). I'm sure you can think of many reasons you might lose your income. How would you eat? How would you pay bills? Oh, you'd borrow money? Ok, you failed…go back and read principle 3 again (twice)!

Also, you may get hit with an **unexpected expense**. Most of us do. It's not a matter of if, but when. The list is seemingly endless: medical or dental bills, car or home repairs, unexpected death in the family, and much more. How will you cover those expenses? That's why this principle is so important.

If you don't have emergency savings when financial disaster strikes, you'll be tempted to go into debt. Going into debt is going *backwards* and is detrimental to building wealth. So, let's be clear on what makes an emergency fund.

Your budget lists your total monthly expenses. It helps you to easily calculate your emergency fund. (Gotta love that budget.) I suggest you keep six months of expenses in a separate savings account. I repeat, six months of *expenses*, not income. No, six months is not a rule, law, or scientific equation. It's merely a guideline for how much you should have in savings should a financial emergency occur. Six months is a great baseline, but if your job is super stable, a 3- or 4-month emergency fund may be sufficient. But why risk it? The idea is to have enough money for *essential* living expenses until the emergency is over.

Remember, a credit card is **not** an emergency fund. Neither is a home equity line of credit. Your emergency fund is **not** an investment. Keep the money in a savings account, separate from all other money and savings. It will stay warm and dry and always be available in case you need it.

Once you've built an emergency fund, this principle reminds you to maintain it. Also, be careful how you define an emergency. Buying a $40K new car because your current $8K one got wrecked is **not** an emergency. Installing $30K of new windows in your home because the current ones are drafty is **not** an emergency. And if you ever dip into your fund for a true emergency, your task is to build it back up again as fast as possible. You guessed it, rebuilding your emergency fund is an emergency! Once the foundation has been laid, it's time to get serious about building wealth. **Do not move to principle 5 until you have a full emergency fund.**

Principle 5 (Invest 15% into Retirement)

Be the tortoise, not the hare. Investing is a marathon, not a sprint. If you're debt free and have a full emergency fund, it's time to begin investing for retirement. Let's immediately dispel any myths or preconceived notions about investing. There's no magic involved. There are no sure-fire guarantees. *Investing carries risk. You can lose money.* In fact, you can even lose money by *not* investing (due to inflation). There are many ways to invest. As always, you should consult with a certified financial planner (CFP) to determine what's best for you.

By following this principle, you invest 15% of your gross earned income into a retirement account.

Example (adjust for your salary):

- $100K salary.
- Invest 15%, which is $15K/year ($100,000 x .15).
- Equals $1,250/month.

If you're married, both you and your spouse will *each* invest 15% of your own gross income. It's possible that one spouse doesn't have earned income. As such, there are IRS spousal rules for non-working spouses, so consult a tax professional for advice.

The idea is to invest over the span of your career (or as long as possible). As you'll discover in the coming pages, this can make you a multi-millionaire!

So, why not invest 5%, 40%, or some other random number into retirement? Well, 15% is not absolute or mandatory. It's certainly possible to grow wealth with 10-12%. In fact, you can invest whatever you like (within IRS limits). Retirement accounts have annual contribution limits per IRS rules and the limits can change over time due to varying legislation. However, keep some things in mind. If you invest *too little*, you won't have much of a nest egg at retirement. If you invest *too much*, you'll struggle to live comfortably in life. You'll also want to hit other financial goals during your life.

For example, if you have kids, you may want to invest in their college funds here in principle 5. College investing is not its own universal principle because not everyone has children. Also, I've shown you many ways to pay for college in chapter 2, so depending on your circumstances, you may not even *need* a college fund. (This was true for me, my wife, and both of our kids.) Remember, any college investing is *above and separate* from what you invest in retirement. If you choose to invest for your kid's college, contact a CFP and ask to open a 529 College Savings Plan which allows your money to grow tax advantaged. You'd be surprised how quickly it adds up over 18 years. Your child can use the money for qualified education – tax free. Like I mentioned in chapter 2, if you invest a mere $100 per month for 18 years at 10% average annual growth, your child will have about $60K in their college fund!

Another reason not to invest much above 15% into retirement is so you can pay off your home extra fast. By paying extra on your mortgage, you'll discover the power of home ownership and why it's so beneficial to growing wealth. More on home ownership in principle 6 ahead.

Finally, people may invest more or less than 15% due to extreme incomes. For example, high-income earners may find it quite easy to invest 15% of their income. Conversely, people earning at or near minimum wage may struggle to invest even 10%. (That's just one more reason to always grow your income and follow chapters 2 and 3, in particular.) Outside of extreme circumstances, investing 15% is a great baseline. It's a principle, not a rule of law. Plus, as you'll soon see, the math works.

Either way, remember to **update your budget** to reflect your new take-home pay after deducting retirement and/or college fund investing.

Invest in What?

As mentioned earlier, there are countless ways to invest. Over time, you may learn to invest in real estate, bonds, commodities, private equity, and more. However, I believe the simplest way for most people to invest is through a diversified portfolio of **mutual funds**. It's what my wife and I do and what we recommend to our own adult children. Why do we invest in mutual funds? Read on to find out. But let's first break down mutual funds a bit further. Again, this is not a course on investing, so I speak in very general terms.

A **mutual fund** is a basket of stocks. There are thousands of mutual funds to choose from. However, let's focus on just one for illustration purposes. You may have heard of the S&P 500, which stands for Standard & Poor's 500. It's an index of the 500 largest U.S. companies. So, think of the S&P 500 as a basket (index) of 500 different company stocks. If you invest in an S&P 500 mutual fund, you'd own a small share of the 500 biggest U.S. companies – pretty cool, right? The S&P 500 is considered by many to be the benchmark by which many funds' performance is measured. Some funds perform better and some funds perform worse. The S&P 500 is a popular mutual fund but there are thousands of others to choose from. Many people also invest in 'total market' funds. Such funds typically contain thousands of stocks in either U.S. and/or international companies. The idea is to gain *diversification*. Here, I simply use the S&P 500 as a reference for discussion. If you're unsure how to invest, consult a CFP. Regardless of which mutual funds you invest in, you should do so in a retirement account. Investing in a retirement account must normally come from earned income.

A **retirement account** is nothing more than a way to grow your investments tax advantaged. Think of it as an umbrella that shields your investments from taxes. In this case, either tax *deferred* or tax *free*. You can invest in many things within a retirement account, but for our purposes, we'll stick to mutual funds. There are two main types of retirement accounts that you can invest in: Traditional and Roth.

A *Traditional* retirement account is pre-tax investing. You invest money *before* any taxes are taken from your income and the money grows tax *deferred*. A tax-deferred account means you pay taxes when you withdraw the money.

A *Roth* retirement account is after-tax investing. You invest money *after* taxes are taken from your income and the investments then grow tax *free*. A tax-free account means you don't pay any taxes when you withdraw the money.

There are exceptions and caveats to both Traditional and Roth retirement accounts and their tax rules, so be sure to learn the details. There are also other differences between the two besides taxes. Contact a CFP or tax professional for advice on which is best for you, including detailed tax implications and how to roll Traditional investments into Roth investments. In either case, you should invest 15% of your household earned gross income into retirement.

So, why do we invest in mutual funds? For starters, the process is fairly straight forward. More specifically, we choose mutual funds for simplicity, diversification, ease of automatic monthly investing, and the *underlying assets* (income-producing companies).

But aren't they risky? Can't you lose money? It's true that mutual funds can be risky and yes, you can lose money. That's why it's important to select well diversified funds. It's also important to have a long-term investment horizon. The markets (and by extension, mutual funds) will go up and they will go down. They don't just go up or down in a straight line. By giving your money time to grow, you can weather the ups and downs of market volatility. Don't try timing the market. Be the tortoise and invest consistently each and every month.

A general rule is not to invest your money unless you plan to leave it alone for a minimum of 5 years. Ideally, you'll let it grow for decades. As of this writing, you normally can't withdraw money from a retirement account until age 59 1/2 without paying a penalty (and applicable taxes). There are qualified exceptions, so consult a tax professional. Why not invest in something safe and guaranteed like a high-yield savings account or certificate of deposit (CD)? Because that's *saving*, not investing and you must account for inflation.

You must factor inflation into your investments. If you put money into a 'safe' CD or savings account at a hypothetical 4% interest rate and inflation was at 3%, then you're effectively earning a paltry 1% on your money (before taxes). That won't cut it. Worse yet, if inflation were to spike, as it does on occasion, you could actually *lose* money (i.e. 5% inflation against a 4% locked-in CD rate). Technically, you're not losing the principal, but rather the purchasing power of that money. Therefore, your safe investment isn't so safe after all. That's why it's best to be diversified and invest for the long term. Although markets go up and down over time, the historical track record for the S&P 500 is about a 10-11% average annual return. Remember, historical performance does not guarantee future results. That said, here's a short but important note on risk.

Although mutual funds are the bulk of our investments, my wife and I do use savings in CDs as the concrete slab. This metaphorical slab provides us a safe foundation of savings to build our investments upon. While it's easy to get excited over 10% historical returns, remember that markets will occasionally face significant downturns.

For example, the S&P 500 was down about 18% in 2022. It also dropped about 36-37% in 2008 during the great financial crisis. It was down about 9-22% a year for *three years* in a row following the dot-com bubble (2000-2002). Mind you, the market has recovered each time, but you should avoid having too many eggs in one basket and be mindful of recovery time.

It's easy to ride out market downturns if you have other income, savings, or investments. However, if your retirement account is your *only* source of income in your retirement years, that could pose a big problem during significant market drops. (Not everyone has a pension or Social Security and if they do, it's not always significant.) This is where advice from a CFP can be valuable.

I'm certainly not a 'dooms-day prepper', but it's never a thing until it's a thing. Although unlikely, beware major risks: recession, depression, economic collapse, market crash, historical firsts, war, contagion/pandemic, and so on. While others may diversify into things such as gold, commodities, cryptocurrencies, and other financial assets, I do not. If you wish to do so, consult an expert in those areas.

How to Invest?

Ok, *how* do you invest into mutual funds in a retirement account? There are many ways, but start with your employer (typically the HR department). Many retirement plans exist but the 401(k) is perhaps the most commonly known. Some other plans are listed below in the discussion points. Ask what retirement plan your employer offers and how to setup automatic payroll investing. Money will automatically deduct from your paycheck and go directly into your retirement account. Some employers offer *matching contributions*, usually up to a certain percentage. That's free money! If you need guidance on fund selections and how matching contributions work, contact a CFP for advice.

If your employer does not offer a retirement plan, contact a CFP to open an individual retirement account and ask how best to fund it. Before you invest one penny, make sure you *understand* the process and what you're investing in. I've given you some valuable starter questions below. Ask as many questions as it takes. Don't be afraid to interview more than one CFP in order to find one that you're comfortable with.

If you're self-employed, contact a CFP for guidance on setting up your own retirement account. It's very important to set things up properly. Taxes can get messy.

Mini-Recap

So, to recap principle 5, invest 15% of your gross earned income into diversified growth mutual funds within a retirement account. I've explained *why* I suggest doing so and *how* to do it. That said, this is not a book on detailed investing or tax strategies. I present a strategic view and leave room for individual specifics. You should consult a CFP and read other books on investing. There are countless ways to invest and things can get complicated if you let them. Keep it simple. Also, you should be very mindful of the complex tax rules. Don't ever invest simply because you read that you should. Understand *why* you should invest; this book helps with that. Also, be sure to understand *what* you're investing in; a CFP can help with that. Here are some valuable discussion points to have with a CFP and/or tax professional *before* investing...

- Benefits of Traditional vs. Roth retirement accounts (what's best for you).
- How to conduct Roth conversions and backdoor Roths.
- IRS annual contribution limits to retirement accounts.
- IRS retirement account spousal rules for non-working spouses.

- Eligible retirement plans: 401(k), 403(b), 457, Thrift Savings Plan, etc.
- Employer matching contributions.
- Mutual fund turnover rate and tax implications.
- Mutual fund fees, loads, and expense ratios.
- How the CFP and/or tax professional gets paid.
- Differences between mutual funds, index funds, and exchange traded funds.
- Minimum retirement age and required minimum distributions.
- Differences between capital gains and ordinary income tax brackets.
- Best mix of mutual funds to invest in (balancing growth & diversification).

The discussion points above provide a great start to understanding your investment options. **If you don't understand it, don't invest in it!** Until then, here are some numbers to consider.

Dream a Little! (Fun with Numbers)

What follows are some basic illustrations on where retirement investing can lead. Many factors can affect your returns. These hypothetical examples are simply meant to inspire you to learn more about investing…

The S&P 500 Index has averaged about 10-11% annually for over 50 years. Some years were higher and some years were lower, thus the annual *average*. For simplicity, I'll round that down to a 10% average annual return. Below are some fun hypothetical investment scenarios based upon a 10% average annual return. Plug your own numbers into an online investment calculator and dream a little…

From age 22 to 65:

$200/month = about $1.7M
$500/month = about $4.3M
$1K/month = about $8.5M

Let this sink in:

From age 18-60, mow someone's lawn for $35/week ($140/month).

$140/month = about $1M

Get a late start in life?

<u>From age 45 to 65:</u>

$2K/month = about $1.5M
Without adding another dime after age 65, that $1.5M will be nearly $3M by age 72.

Get an even later start?

<u>From age 60 to 72:</u>

$2K/month = about $500K
(Go from broke to half-a-million!)

Ok, so now…let's use a standard scenario that invests 15% of your gross income over a typical career. (Adjust the numbers for your salary.) We'll use a hypothetical 10% average annual return, from age 25 to 65…

<u>Salary = $50K</u>

15% = $625/month ($7,500/annual)

Total in retirement = nearly $4M!

<u>Salary = $80K</u>

15% = $1K/month ($12K/annual)

Total in retirement = about $6.3M!

Even if you achieve HALF that, you're still a multi-millionaire! And that's if you don't get a pay raise in *40 years!* That would not only be a shame, but it would be a *double* shame because it means you weren't following principle 2 (always grow your income). And those numbers are also for a single income household – just imagine your spouse also worked! What are you waiting for, folks?!?!

I don't know about you but becoming a millionaire seems pretty simple to me. Yes, it takes time. No, it won't happen overnight. It may not be easy, but the sooner you start, the easier it is. Just imagine if you start *today*. Just imagine if you follow this playbook and earn and/or invest even *more*! Run your own numbers. Dream a little. Dream a lot! How wealthy do you want to be?

By the way, we haven't even gotten to the power of home ownership yet...just wait, it gets even better! Once your retirement investing is on track, you'll eliminate one last debt. That's right, this is where you turn your attention to your home.

Principle 6 (Own Your Home)

The first two little pigs built their houses from straw and sticks by having a mortgage. That left them with financial risk. You want to be the third little pig who built a financial house of *brick*, which means your house is fully paid off (no mortgage)! A paid off home will not be foreclosed on if you should lose your income and fall behind on payments. Why? Because there are no payments. Home ownership is a part of building wealth.

Think about it, if you rent for your entire life, guess what? You'll pay rent for the rest of your life *and* the rent will go up nearly every single year...a double loss! Whereas if you own your home, you'll eventually pay it off (no payment) *and* the house will appreciate in value...a double win! Cha-ching, cha-ching!

By the way, a home can be a townhouse, duplex, or condo; it doesn't have to be a detached single-family home with a white picket fence and rose bushes. You want to buy something that appreciates in value over time. Compared to renting, home ownership can easily increase your net worth by six or seven figures over a lifetime! That's why it's an integral part of wealth building. However, there are a few things to consider about home ownership.

Mind you, not everyone is financially ready to own a home. If you follow these principles, you'll notice home ownership is principle 6. To recap, this means you...

- Follow a written budget (principle 1).
- Always grow your income (principle 2).
- Are 100% debt free (principle 3).

- Have a 6-month emergency fund (principle 4).
- Consistently invest 15% into retirement (principle 5).

First of all, if you can pay cash for a house, then do so! However, most people don't have that much money available to them. In that instance, take out the smallest mortgage possible once you've reached principle 6 and are ready to buy a home. Once you have the extra money in your budget, it's time to save for a down payment. Consider these suggestions before buying…

> Take a 15-year fixed rate mortgage (at most). This helps avoid buying 'too much house' by trying to spread it out over 30 years. The interest rate is also lower than a 30-year mortgage. Plus, you'll be out of debt *15 years* sooner!

> Your house payment (including taxes & insurance) should be no more than 25% of your net household income (after taxes). Plus or minus a few dollars is okay, but you don't want to be house rich and cash poor. The more you spend as a monthly percentage of your income, the tighter your budget becomes and the more stressed *you* become.

> Put down at least 20% or you risk the added expense of private mortgage insurance (PMI). PMI protects the lender's financial interest if you default on your mortgage. In other words, you're wasting *your* money to protect *theirs*!

> Plan on living in the home for at least 3-5 years. If not, you could lose money due to realtor fees, market downturns, moving expenses, and/or closing costs. If you plan on living there for only a year or two, it usually makes better financial sense to rent.

Once you're ready to buy, now is another time to use a professional. When buying a home, you should consult a licensed, highly experienced real estate professional to guide you through the process. Why? Because a home is probably the most expensive thing most people will buy. Remember, the more money something costs, the more *critical thought* you should apply. A professional realtor is vital to helping you navigate this process. I know because I've bought and sold several houses using a realtor. I don't play do-it-yourself (DIY) realtor because there's too much at stake! Here are some valuable discussion points to have with your realtor *before* making any offers on a property...

- What flood zone is the house in? Discuss the implications & cost of flood insurance.
- Is there a condo or homeowner's association? If so, what's the monthly fee?
    - Get a copy of the covenants and restrictions.
    - Ensure there are no short-falls or issues with the association's budget.
- How much are property taxes? (and are they current)
- Cost of homeowner's insurance? (shop around)
- What utilities are available (water/well, sewer/septic, gas, Internet, phone, etc)?
- Do any special zoning restrictions or easements apply to the property?
- Do full mineral & other rights convey with the property?
- Are there any environmental issues (wetlands, protected waterways, etc)?
- Scheduling a property appraisal.
- Scheduling a home inspection.
- Scheduling a termite inspection.
- Estimated closing costs?
- Age of mechanicals (heating, cooling, water heater, etc)?
- Age of roof?
- Age of home? (lead paint, asbestos, old wiring/plumbing, mold, other concerns)
- Have all permits been approved & closed (if applicable)?
- Are there any liens on the property?
- Home warranty?

These questions will help protect your investment. Lots of money demands lots of questions and answers. A good realtor will discuss this list with you and guide you along the way. If they don't, find another realtor *before* signing anything with them. You want to buy the house of your dreams, not a nightmare! Properly addressing these issues can save you tens (or hundreds) of thousands of dollars. (You're welcome.)

Once you buy a home, it's time to re-examine your budget. Trust me, there will be many changes in your monthly expenses. You may have to pay for a new water heater, a new roof, plumbing repairs, or any number of issues that your landlord was responsible for when you were a renter. It's advisable to have a "house repair" fund of a few thousand dollars set aside because you *will* need it. This prevents you from dipping into your emergency fund for an "unexpected" repair.

Depending on your income and expenses, you should pay extra on your mortgage every month. Doing so will accelerate paying off your mortgage *and*…save you thousands in interest – yet *another* double win! It may take a few years but when you pay off your house, watch out (in a good way)! Here's what it will look like…

By owning your home free and clear, you'll have eliminated what was probably your largest monthly expense. When your mortgage is gone, remember to remove that line-item expense from your budget. Now, I want you to look closely at your budget; take a deep breath in and slowly exhale out. Soak it all in. Notice where the mortgage payment *used to be* is now a big fat zero. You no longer *owe* on your home…you *own* your home! Once your home is paid off, *never* get a mortgage (or any debt of any kind) ever again! When you're done basking in the glow of being 100% debt free, I want you to reflect on the wealth building principles we've covered so far. Without a mortgage payment, you now have more money and thus more options. Let's pretend your old mortgage payment was $1,500 a month. There are two main options for that extra money…

First, you can add it back into your budget and use it for other financial goals: upgrade in car, new furniture, parties, vacations, home renovation, etc. That new found money may be tempting. You may see dollar signs in your eyes. Whatever you do, save up and pay cash! Remember, no more debt…ever!

A second option is to put your foot on the throat of poverty and generational struggle once and for all. It's time to accelerate building wealth! You may consider *adding* some (or all) of that old mortgage payment to your current investing plan. By following principle 5, you've already been investing 15% of your gross household income. Now is the time to increase it!

If you've followed these principles from an early age, it's possible you purchased a modestly priced house around age 30. (My kids are on track to do exactly that.) You would have also paid it off by age 45 (remember, a 15-year mortgage). Let's say your mortgage payment was $1,500 a month and you decide to invest that until age 65 at our hypothetical 10% average annual return…

$1,500/month (your old payment) from age 45 to 65 = about $1.1M.

And remember, if you *also* invested a mere $500/month from age 22 to 65 into your retirement account (principle 5), guess what? That's right, *another* $4.3M! ($1.1M + $4.3M = **about $5.4M total**). Who knows, maybe you invested even *more* into retirement…?! After all, $500/month is not much once your career is growing (principle 2). And don't forget – you *also* have a paid off home which contributes to your net worth!

One caveat: remember, there are IRS maximum amounts that you're allowed to invest into a **retirement** account. However, once you hit that maximum, you can continue investing into a **non-retirement** account (without limit). Your **non-retirement** account is taxable, but it's better to make money and pay taxes on it than to not make money and pay no taxes! Talk to a CFP or tax professional for advice on how to invest in a tax-efficient manner.

Now, let's have even *more* fun. Suppose you follow this playbook and are then able to leave an inheritance of "just" $1M upon your death. That could be a retirement account, insurance policy, real estate, or any combination thereof. If your heirs also follow this playbook, that money will be icing on their cake. They'll have their own money and won't even need the inheritance.

Therefore, if they left that $1M alone for 40 years at 10% growth, they'd have over **$53M!** (If it's a Roth account, it's all TAX-FREE, with certain caveats.) That's just *one* generation. If the second generation did the same thing with that $53M, they'd have about **$2B!** (Unless my calculator just overheated.) **Talk about generational wealth!** (You're welcome.)

Of course, this is all hypothetical and many factors are at play across two generations. The exact dollar amount is not the point. The point is, every generation should do better than the one prior. So, quit perpetuating *poverty* and start perpetuating *prosperity*! And even if these numbers are off by *half*...that's still not bad <wink>.

As you can see, the wealth building just gets better and better! This *Torch of Life* stuff is pretty sweet...a playbook for generational prosperity, for sure. Wow. Again, these are simply example scenarios. Everyone's financial picture is different and these principles provide plenty of flexibility. You may not see the need to invest extra money in order to hit your retirement goals. You may simply enjoy life and spread the love through generosity (giving). Who knows, your career may take off and your increased earnings may *double* or even *triple* these estimates. After all, if you follow principle 2, you'll *always* grow your income (and by extension, your retirement investing). Go for it! Excuses or results.

So, the power of home ownership wraps up the amazing six principles to building wealth. Pretty simple, right? However, the blueprint to wealth contains a few more things that are necessary to solidify and protect your prosperity. After all, you want to build a financial house of solid brick!

Insurance

[Here's another time to consult a licensed professional – one who specializes in the area of insurance you're considering.]

I think of insurance as the roof over my financial brick house. It's a vital part of wealth building that helps protect us from life's financial storms. Don't buy insurance blindly and willy-nilly. Each person has their own unique circumstances. Each insurance product serves a specific purpose. **Insurance should be purchased as needed, when needed. It has nothing to do with the order of aforementioned principles.**

I've listed some common types of insurance below. Discuss each with an insurance broker. Any insurance (or lack of) can be financially life changing.

Common Insurance to Consider:

- Health Insurance (basically, a must-have).
- Auto Insurance (typically required by state law).
- Homeowners Insurance (vital if you own a home).
- Umbrella Insurance (consider as you build wealth).
- Renters Insurance (covers your belongings and minimizes liability).
- Dental Insurance (comparison shop).

Also, I've found certain insurance is often overlooked by many people. I've seen up close and personal how this can impact families in a big way. Below are some examples and thoughts based upon my experiences.

Long-Term Disability Insurance.

I briefly mentioned the importance of this in chapter 3 (rule 3 – cast a career vision). This insurance provides income if you become physically or mentally unable to work. Without it, you're pretty much stuck with Social Security Disability, which is very minimal and nearly impossible to survive on. You can become disabled on any given day for thousands of reasons, many outside your control. Do you want to risk not having an income? I don't.

I know from first-hand experience how my wife's health issues affected (and still affect) our collective household income. In recent years, our career earnings were devastated but at least my military pension and my wife's long-term VA/federal disability benefits helped provide us with partial income. If you're single, this is even *more* important because you don't have a spouse's income to help sustain your living expenses. People usually purchase long-term disability insurance through their employer or shop an agency who sells these policies.

Ask about premiums, definition of disability, limitations, income factors, benefit & elimination periods, payout periods & maximums, and more. Do your research, but if you work, get it!

Long-Term Care (LTC) Insurance.

This insurance helps to cover expenses related to long-term care for people who are unable to care for themselves. Unlike long-term disability insurance, which provides an income if you become disabled, long-term *care* insurance helps cover the cost of your *care*, commonly in old age. Depending on the policy, this care may include daily living activities (bathing, dressing, mobility, etc), various therapies (physical, speech, occupational, etc), and light housekeeping chores (laundry, meal prep, etc). It can also cover stays in rehabilitation facilities, nursing homes, or in-home care. Some people mistakenly think healthcare insurance covers long-term care, but it generally does not.

One option is to cash flow your care, which is extremely expensive. If you can, great. A full-time nursing home can exceed six-figures annually. I wish I knew about this insurance decades ago because I would have *insisted* that my parents get it! At some point, your age and/or poor health can make you uninsurable. My father got lucky in his last few years to have been approved for in-home hospice care. It certainly did not cover all of his care, but it helped. My brother and I also helped him manage the out-of-pocket expenses of in-home caregivers. We wished he had LTC insurance.

Another option is to apply for Medicaid, which has its own eligibility criteria and financial implications. I don't know about you, but that's my last resort.

That's where long-term care insurance comes in. Generally, people start to research and shop this insurance in their mid-to-late 50's, depending on their health. However, everyone's situation is different so do your homework. If you anticipate the need for LTC insurance, do your research and consider getting it (before you're uninsurable or rates become unaffordable).

Ask about premiums (fixed or variable), care provided (and whether in-home or in-facility), inflation protection, maximum coverage, benefit period, deductibles, policy renewal, covered conditions, and more.

Term Life Insurance.

There are different types of life insurance (whole life, universal, hybrid, variable, etc). In my younger and dumber years, I was talked into some stupid whole life or universal policy. I don't recall the details, but once I realized the high fees and fine print, I quickly canceled it. Nowadays, I only suggest *term* life insurance. It's simple. You buy it for a certain term (10 years, 20 years, etc). You'll also have a fixed death benefit ($100K, 200K, etc) at a fixed premium (monthly payment). This insurance pays your designated beneficiary with money upon your death. You should get it if someone depends upon your earned income. For example, if you're married and your spouse doesn't work, they rely on your income to live. If you die, your income stops. Therefore, you should get enough life insurance to cover your spouse's living expenses until they can generate their own income.

As you can imagine, there are many scenarios where life insurance is needed. A non-working spouse is only one example. You should factor in children, other dependents who are unable to work, and anyone else who relies on your income. This can include life partners, live-in lovers, fiancés, and more. You *do* love them, don't you? Determine who relies on your income (if anyone) and how much money they would need if you died. Remember, insurance should replace your income for a certain length of time. If you earn $75K a year, your beneficiary doesn't need $5M in life insurance. I suggest about 15 times the amount of your salary. For example, a $50K income would warrant a $750K term policy. That estimate should provide a reasonable income to your beneficiary and a little cushion (clearing debt, funeral, legal expenses, etc). You must adjust based upon your entire financial picture. Do I have term life insurance? Yes, I do…

When I retired from active duty, I took out a 20-year term policy. That would provide my wife and kids with financial security if I had died. Luckily, I'm still alive and our kids are now adults. However, as that policy nears its expiration, I started an additional 15-year term policy. The two policies overlap a bit, but as the first one expires, this new policy will extend my insurance coverage until I'm almost 70 years old. That policy will provide financial security for my wife if I die first. It would essentially replace my military/VA monthly benefits. (For those who are unfamiliar, my military pension dies with me because I declined what's called the Survivor Benefit Plan (SBP). In a nutshell, our term life insurance was cheaper than the SBP monthly premiums.) We're also debt free, have an emergency fund, savings, and some investments. I love my wife too much to have it any other way.

Online insurance calculators can help you determine your needs but ultimately, you'll have to decide what's necessary. If you're healthy and don't smoke, term life insurance is quite affordable. However, you can become uninsurable due to certain health conditions so keep that in mind. The premium is largely determined by the term (policy duration), the benefit payout amount, any high-risk lifestyle, and your health. It's very sad to hear about a parent dying and their family left in a financial bind simply because they didn't have life insurance. **Please love your family enough to have the proper life insurance.** Also, keep your beneficiaries current as life changes occur (marriage, divorce, kids, etc). News flash – life insurance beneficiaries usually take precedence over beneficiaries in your will.

Do your research, learn more about coverage and limitations, and get life insurance if your situation warrants it (before you become uninsurable).

General Liability and Workers' Compensation Insurance.

If you're self-employed, this protects you and/or your company from any damage caused during the course of business. It also protects your workers from work-related injury or illness. It may even be required by law in some states, so do your research and contact a certified insurance professional for advice. If you're self-employed, run a small business, or hire workers to earn an income, look into this insurance.

Proper and timely insurance is vital to protecting wealth. I've covered the basics of insurance. This is by no means an all-inclusive list. There's insurance for identity theft, gun owners, vision care, phones, electronics, and much more. Everyone's insurance needs are different. Be intentional, do your research, run the numbers, assess the risk, and think critically to determine the appropriate insurance for your situation. Consult an expert who specializes in the area of insurance you're considering. Have them educate you and answer any questions you may have. As you get your insurance in order, there's another element to generational wealth.

Estate Plan

Your estate plan is a key component to generational wealth; it's the financial and legal link between generations.

As you may recall, the opening line of this book told us, "News flash – we're all gonna die!" It's still true. What we rarely know is precisely *when* we're going to die (or become incapacitated). That's just one reason to create an estate plan *sooner* rather than later. More reasons will soon become obvious. But you might say, "I don't have an estate. I don't need a will. I don't even have any money." Nice try, as my daughter likes to say.

An estate plan is a packet of legal documents that helps to carry out your wishes when you're dead *and* when you're alive. Plans are unique to every individual's circumstances – even if you have *no* money. There are various online resources that help you create these documents in DIY fashion. However, I highly suggest you consult with an estate planning attorney. These documents are state specific and a good attorney can also help you devise an efficient tax strategy as part of your plan. Plus, I assume law school exists for a reason. Therefore, I don't play DIY attorney. In general terms, below are some documents that may be part of your estate plan. You may only need a select few. The laws are very complex and it's best to talk directly with an attorney to discuss your specific situation. These documents may not invoke thrill and excitement, but they're certainly critical to have if when stuff hits the fan!

- Last Will and Testament.
- Power of Attorney (POA).
- Health Care Surrogate.
- Advance Medical Directive (i.e. Living Will).
- Do Not Resuscitate (DNR).
- Pre-Need Guardianship.
- Trust.

As you can see, these documents do more than simply "pass your belongings to your heirs." Some ensure a smooth transfer of guardianship for your children if you die while they're still minors. Some may provide asset protection or minimize tax liabilities. Others convey your healthcare wishes should you become incapacitated in some fashion or suffer cognitive decline and are unable to communicate. They all have their purpose.

In addition to these important documents, there's something else vital to estate planning. That is, designating a **beneficiary** for your financial accounts. The designation of a beneficiary can often be called pay-on-death (POD) or perhaps transfer-on-death (TOD), depending on the institution and type of account. There are differences between POD, TOD, and trusts, so be sure to discuss the details with an attorney or your financial institution.

In basic terms, you should designate a beneficiary (or beneficiaries) for your financial accounts. This is typically done through the financial institution where your account is held (bank, credit union, brokerage, etc). Contact each and learn their process. Usually, you complete a simple form or assign beneficiaries through your online account portal. (Hint: the bank doesn't always ask when you open an account – when's the last time you checked?) Designate a beneficiary for all checking, savings, money markets, investment, and retirement accounts. The same is true for insurance policies, annuities, pensions, and more. By doing so, you designate who gets that money when you die.

This is super important. Why? Because in many instances, these beneficiaries *supersede* beneficiaries in your will. Whoa, what?! Yes, here's a hypothetical example. Your spouse is listed as a beneficiary on your 401(k) retirement account worth $500K. You remarry and wisely update your will to include your new spouse. You die soon thereafter. Your *ex-spouse* gets your $500K retirement account because you forgot to change the beneficiary on your 401(k) to your *current* spouse. Oops. There you go, *The Torch of Life* may have just saved your beneficiary $500K! (You're welcome.) Now, this is just one simple example and the laws are very complex. Remember, this is also true of life insurance policies. They, too, generally *supersede* beneficiaries in your will. The lesson here is to keep your beneficiaries updated in a timely fashion…all of them! Resolve any questions with an attorney.

Depending on your state of residence, some of these documents may require signatures, witnesses, and/or notarization. Also, be sure to keep your documents updated! Major life events may warrant changes to your plan. For example, we just discussed getting married or remarried. Presumably, you'll want your current spouse listed as beneficiary. You may also have kids one day. Who will be their guardian if you and your spouse die? Are they still minors? Is a trust required? Who do you want as your healthcare guardian if *you* should become incapacitated? Yes, an estate plan requires upkeep. Another true story…

When our youngest kid turned 18 years old, my wife and I made a major revision to our estate plan. We dissolved the pre-need guardianship and our living revocable trust. Everything got simplified since our minor children were now adults and able to function independently. Yay! Then, we had them each meet with an estate planning attorney and complete *their own* estate plan documents. Their paperwork allows us to make decisions on their behalf if ever required (accident, major health issue, life support, etc). The takeaway here is to think about your own personal situation (and any time it changes).

Even though you've completed all of the documents for your estate plan, you're not done quite yet. Once your documents are complete, protect them! There are many ways to do this. We store ours in a small waterproof and fireproof safe. This prevents water or fire damage in the event of fire, flood, or natural disaster.

Then, *tell someone* where they're stored. Your carefully prepared documents will be *useless* if nobody knows they exist! If you died today, would anyone know where your documents are stored? My wife and I have briefed multiple close family members on the location of our estate plan.

They should also know exactly how to access them. If your storage requires a key, where is it kept? If it requires a combination, where is it written? For example, our safe combination is… (oh, wait). Kidding aside, ensure *more than one person* knows where to find the key or combination.

It's also wise to store other important papers with your estate plan: beneficiary designations, marriage certificates, insurance policies, etc. You should also include emergency contact names, phone numbers, and other key information that you feel is relevant to your estate. Mind you, nothing of monetary value is stored here, only things that will make life easier for your heirs *when* you pass away. Sort of a one-stop shop. Ok, now you're done, right? Well, just one more thing.

So, your documents are completed and safely stored away. Everyone knows where they are and how to access them. What now? The last thing is to *discuss* your estate plan with interested parties...

- Talk to the personal representative (executor) of your will. Do they have questions?
- Talk to your beneficiaries (heirs) and *tell them* what to expect (or not) when you die.
- Explain the contents of your will, who gets what, and why.
- Discuss your health care wishes with any surrogate(s) and/or powers-of-attorney. If you have a DNR, keep that document readily accessible.
- Convey your burial, cremation, or funeral wishes and how it's all documented. Do you prefer a certain burial site?
- Discuss preferences for potential long-term care. Do you prefer a nursing home or in-home care?
- Discuss any other relevant issues.

Don't leave people guessing. The time to discuss all of this is when you're *alive* and *able* to. It's difficult, if not impossible, to convey your wishes once you're incapacitated. Therefore, talk to the appropriate people *today*. Answer any questions. This will allow you to sleep well at night. Once your estate plan is complete, there's one final reminder to wealth building.

Remember to file your federal taxes (and state taxes, if required) on time, every time! This is typically every year. If you're self-employed, you may have to file quarterly taxes. Check with a tax professional. Some people prepare their own taxes but do so at your own risk. I don't play DIY tax professional because the laws are complex and constantly changing. I have bigger fish to fry, so I pay a certified professional to file our taxes – it's money well spent. I recommend the same to anyone who asks.

All of these principles should lead to a very prosperous life. Your wealth building journey should continue right into and through what most people call 'retirement' and beyond. It's lifelong. Here are some thoughts on retirement.

Retirement

Are you approaching retirement? Are you currently retired? Retirement can be defined in many ways. I'd guess most people view retirement as when they can stop working – usually at a certain age such as 65, plus or minus. Some people think of it as a financial finish line. This is 'yes and no' and everything in between. As with other things, you should have a clear vision of retirement and what it means to you.

For example, am I personally retired? Yes and no. I retired from the military at age 39. That simply means I served more than 20 years and now collect a military retirement check, among other benefits. It certainly was not and is not the last of my "career" or working years. I then went on to work as a civilian employee. Since then, I've also been working at other things, writing being one of them.

Others may work a government position that eventually leads to a retirement check. That can be another form of retirement. If you hit the lotto for $25M, are you retired? I don't know. These are questions you alone need to answer. Perhaps your idea of retirement is changing careers, starting a business, working part-time, volunteering, writing, speaking, teaching, or any number of things. All reasonable and valid. Just don't sit on the couch eating potato chips!

The core requirement to all of this is affordability. Achieve the financial freedom to do what you *want*, instead of what you *must*. If you follow the principles that have been laid out so far, you'll be on track to possibly retire sooner than you think. It depends on when you start and how hard you work. Your age doesn't dictate your ability to retire; your *finances* do. Remember, your age (59 1/2) affects withdrawals from a retirement account without penalty, but not when you retire. Here are some factors to consider…

Monthly Expenses.

Look to your budget for answers. How much will it cost to live in retirement? This is yet another reason to live debt free and own your home; it minimizes expenses (and risk).

Monthly Income.

Again, look to your budget. Add up all income from all sources. Do you have a pension? When will you take Social Security? Do you have rental income? Do you receive any other sources of income (royalties, business, dividends, interest, alimony, etc)?

Hopefully, you've amassed a retirement nest egg by the time you plan to retire. Remember, you typically can't withdraw it until age 59 1/2 or later without penalty. Even then, you must account for any applicable taxes. Suppose you withdraw 5% per year; that gives you $5K for every $100K in your retirement account. So, at that same withdrawal rate, $500K provides $25K per year. A $1M account provides $50K per year income, and so on. A 5% withdrawal rate should leave enough so as not to deplete your retirement account. I'm not suggesting you withdraw 5% – it's merely an example. There's endless debate about the proper withdrawal rate, but the actual answer is, *it depends*. You must adjust accordingly because, as you'll see, there are no exact answers.

[Your retirement account and other investments should act as the goose, not the eggs. That means your goose provides you with endless golden eggs (income) for the rest of your life. Never kill the goose.]

Your Age and Life Expectancy.

These two factors greatly affect your investment withdrawal rate and overall finances. How old are you and how long do you reasonably expect to live? This is somewhat of an educated guess based upon family history, current health, and lifestyle (smoking, drugs, diet, exercise, alcohol, etc). If you retire healthy at 60 and live to 90, you'll need sustainable income for 30 years! If you retire at 72 with cancer and die at 74, that's a huge difference. Get the point? I lean toward a more conservative approach that's likely to make my money last longer.

The goal is to tailor things to your situation, factoring in your investments, expenses, income, age, life expectancy, inflation rate, tax rates, and expected returns. As pointed out earlier, it's reasonable to expect the S&P 500 to average about 10-11% per year over time. However, you must account for any extreme market downturns. Your retirement account should only be *part* of your overall retirement plan, so adjust accordingly.

P.S. One retirement challenge for many people is calculating their Social Security benefits. The retirement calculator on the Social Security Administration's website can provide a benefit estimate. Run some 'what if' scenarios based upon your earnings history, projected earnings, and when you plan to claim benefits.

I certainly would not advise relying on Social Security as your *sole* source of income. However, it pays to be aware of what you may receive and factor it into your overall retirement plan. It won't make you wealthy on its own, but take everything you're entitled to; after all, you paid in for many years! The longer you wait to claim it, the higher your monthly benefits will be. That said, you don't want to die before you collect anything either. It's a tough decision, which is why you should think it through carefully. Consider talking with a social security claims specialist.

Where does this leave us on our path to wealth? Here's a condensed summary of the overall blueprint.

Summary

(Wealth Blueprint)

Follow these 6 Principles (in this order):

1. Follow a Written Budget.
2. Always Grow Your Income.
3. Live Debt Free.
4. Keep a 6-Month Emergency Fund.
5. Invest 15% into Retirement.
6. Own Your Home.

As you follow these principles, remember…

- ✓ Buy the right **insurance** at the right time. Not doing so can lead to financial ruin.

- ✓ Complete your **estate plan**, store it safely, and brief your loved ones on its contents and accessibility. Your estate plan is the key financial and legal link to generational wealth.
- ✓ **Adjust** your investing, insurance, and estate plan as your life situation changes. This includes beneficiaries (POD, TOD, and trusts). Consult a certified professional in those areas.
- ✓ Pay your **taxes** on time, every time.
- ✓ Reflect on **retirement** and what it means to you. Adjust your overall financial plan to get you not only *into*, but also *through* retirement.

As you can see, this blueprint to wealth is simple. It's certainly not easy, but it is simple. This brings us now to three key behaviors to follow and the rationale behind each. Remember, money should be more than simply transactional.

Wealth Behaviors

You don't follow certain behaviors because you're wealthy; you're wealthy because you follow certain behaviors.

Have a Plan for Your Money

This behavior displays intentionality. It leads to financial success, a core component to prosperity. Why able-bodied people *choose* to struggle is a mystery. And make no mistake, it is a choice. By not following these principles, you're *choosing* not to grow wealth. Have a balanced and prioritized plan for your money (all of it). Your budget can help with this. The six principles to wealth leave you debt free with an emergency fund. You'll also be steadily investing into retirement and on your way to becoming a multi-millionaire! That's all a given. You may also be in the process of paying off your home. Or maybe you've done that already. But what then? What to do with money above that?

Here, I'm talking about what to do with the *extra* money? That's the fun part! And the more money you have, the more fun you can have. Extra money is breathing room. It's also called freedom, security, and options. By including money in your budget, *you* decide where it goes.

A good rule of thumb is to have a balanced plan. The principle of *balance* is key to many things (chapter 7).

Consider a plan that uses a ratio (or percentage) to allocate your money. Remember, money extremes are rarely a good idea. Die with nothing or hoard every penny? Umm, no. Spending every penny and dying broke is not a wise plan. Likewise, hoarding every penny and living like a hermit defeats the purpose of building wealth. It's your money, so do as you please. However, I suggest balanced and healthy stewardship of your money. A more mature approach. Why? Because it works. Remember, your money management is largely a visible reflection of your underlying values. For me personally, stinginess (hoard it all) or financial gluttony (spend it all) are not part of my values. If you choose to follow this playbook, you'll take a healthy and balanced approach to budgeting.

Keep in mind, you're trying to achieve a steady-state rhythm for your money. Think of a diet and exercise plan; extreme, yo-yo, trendy, and fad diets don't work. The same is true for your money. Your plan should be flexible and adjust as your life evolves. Here are some suggestions to balance your extra money…

- Allocate a percentage to *always*: save, give, spend, and invest.
- *Always* save for vehicle replacement and/or upkeep (they don't last forever).
- *Always* save some fun money; enjoy life.
- *Always* save for giving & hand-*ups;* be generous.
- *Always* save for surprises (newsflash – most are not surprising).

The more consistent you are, the less you have to think about it. Your plan should also apply to money outside of just your *earned income*. For example, how will you spend your retirement nest egg? What about an inheritance? Or life insurance money. How about the sale of a business? You may profit from the sale of property one day. What will you do with that money? Whatever you decide, give it thought. In addition to balance, you should also *prioritize* your money plan.

This is where I stress the importance of personal values (chapter 8). Most people prioritize their money based upon what they value. Do you know anyone who has money for alcohol and eating out, yet they "can't afford" life insurance to protect their family? Do you know anyone who has money for multiple streaming and TV subscriptions, yet they "can't afford" to complete their estate plan? Hey, everyone has their priorities. However, if you wish to prosper financially, I suggest you give some serious thought to yours.

This brings me to my marriage and my amazing wife. It's no surprise that money fights are a common reason for divorce. As I'll share in chapter 10, a strong marriage is built upon a common value system. Among other key values, my wife and I strongly agree on money. Our money plan is *prioritized* on things we value. For example, our retirement investing comes before fancy shoes or purses. We prioritize living debt free (and stress free) over car payments and credit cards. We prioritize our family's financial security over eating out every week. We also have combined finances and bank accounts; it's not her money or my money, it's *our* money. Suffice it to say, this system has afforded us the ability to do *all* of the above…and much more!

The prosperous advice is to prioritize necessities over niceties. After all, if you follow the principles in this book, you'll cover your necessities and have *ample* money for niceties! Whatever your money plan is, be intentional about it. The desired behavior is to have a balanced and prioritized plan and adjust as necessary. If you discover you need more income, you can (and should) *always*…earn more!

Give (Hand-Ups)

This behavior reinforces generosity and contributes to a prosperous life. Offer helpful hand-ups, give to others, and be generous. There are many ways to do this, but here I refer mainly to what financial security can provide. All things equal, wealthy people can be more generous than poor people – and they *should*. Give generously when people hit a rough patch. Give for holidays, birthdays, graduations, and other life milestones. Pick up the bar tab. Pick up the dinner tab. Never show up empty handed. There are countless ways to be generous. However, you certainly don't need to be wealthy to give. Although I can't give as much as a billionaire, I still give proportionate to what I can afford. It's not the amount that counts. Anyone can be generous – and they *should*. Either way, be sure to have a mindset of helping others.

Financial security also allows you to be more generous with your time and knowledge so that others may achieve independence and prosperity of their own. Mentor, teach, parent, guide, instruct, and inspire others to reach their full potential. That's the core reason I wrote this book. Be especially kind when others are at their worst. Everyone hits bumps and potholes in life…sometimes a huge crater! Rather than ignoring someone's misfortune, walk alongside them, guide them with sincerity, and help them get back on track. I talk more about helpful hand-*ups* in chapter 7 and generosity in chapters 8 and 12.

Leave an Inheritance

This important behavior is the financial link between generations and, in turn, generational wealth (a core component to *generational prosperity*). What does it mean to leave an inheritance? It can mean many things, right? After all, people can inherit nearly anything. However, here in this instance (financial wealth), I refer to money and other financial assets. It also circles back to the mindset of values and behaviors that accompany that financial inheritance. It's a package deal. What do I mean by that?

If I suddenly throw 300 pounds on someone's shoulders, they'll likely collapse under the weight. However, if I first help them carry 100 pounds, and then 200 pounds, they'll eventually be able to carry 300 pounds. They will have built the necessary muscle to hold the weight.

Likewise, if I suddenly hand a pile of money to anyone who's unprepared, it has the potential to ruin their life (drugs, entitlement, ego, laziness, hedonism, etc). A person who cannot lift 100 pounds is ill-prepared to lift 300 pounds. Likewise, a person who has little money is ill-prepared to manage a lot. At least not without first building the necessary money muscle to do so. So, don't hand a large sum of money to anyone who's unprepared for it. And people without money have not proven their ability to manage it. Thus, they never have any money. Even some people *with* money are unprepared for it, which is why their money doesn't last very long. Therefore, it's wise to leave an inheritance only to those who are prepared for it. So, who to leave an inheritance to? Whether you have kids or not, please read on. Either way, leaving an inheritance requires the proper behavior…

Broke behavior is *selfish* behavior. Some people blow it all while they're alive; to heck with the kids or anyone else! Good luck, but that's not for me. That strikes me as broke behavior. The immature and greedy behavior is to devour all that you have. It's thinking only of yourself. Broke behavior leaves you destitute and struggling in your final years (or decades) of life. Broke behavior leaves your kids (or others) to pay for your funeral and final expenses. Broke behavior *certainly* does not achieve generational prosperity. There is a better way.

Wealthy behavior is *selfless* behavior. It provides a very fruitful life with plenty of leftovers. It allows you to be generous. Wealthy behavior reminds you that life is about far more than racing to spend every penny. If spending equaled happiness, 99% of the world would be depressed compared to the top 1%. True happiness is not so shallow. Wealthy behavior affords you a comfortable and dignified retirement. Wealthy behavior pays for your final expenses and leaves an inheritance to your loved ones.

So, if you have kids, it's time to change your family's financial tree. After all, money isn't everything but it sure does help. **How can you promote generational prosperity by dying broke?** If you hope to die broke, you're reading the wrong book.

My wife and I have two kids. We practice wealthy behavior and we share the same values. Whoever dies first wants the survivor to be financially secure. For example, if I had 6 months to live, I *guarantee* you that I wouldn't rush to spend it all and leave my wife penniless. No, that would speak very poorly of me. Plus, my wife would choke me (and rightfully so). Thinking about how quickly I can spend money would not even cross my mind. My character and values are much better than that. Rather, my *behavior* would be to spend my remaining time with family, friends, and loved ones – you know, what truly matters. She feels the same, vice versa.

That said, we've lived a very fruitful life. However, there's always *plenty leftover*. We're financially balanced and content, not greedy or gluttonous. We're not compelled to devour everything we have. Neither do we *deprive* ourselves in order to leave it all to the kids. No. We live life to the fullest – any leftovers will go to our kids (if they're good). There will be plenty for all of us.

My wife and I foster generational prosperity and we hope our kids follow suit. Our kids inherit everything upon our death – any leftovers. They should not *count on* receiving anything, but we hope they *honor* whatever they do receive. It should not *cause* their financial prosperity, but should *contribute* to it. They can honor their inheritance through wise stewardship. If they properly care for the goose, they'll have endless golden eggs.

Like many parents, we want our kids to do better than we have in life. They're off to a great start – let's hope they keep it up. Their behavior, in turn, will dictate what inheritance they leave to *their* kids. If they don't have kids, I hope they choose someone close to their heart to leave their inheritance to. That will be their choice.

Either way, my wife and I can proudly and lovingly say we've done our part. It's official…we have broken the back of generational struggle! That doesn't mean just a pile of money, but rather we've taught our kids a holistic path to financial prosperity. We've taught them the principles in this book and how to not only earn money, but also how to manage it wisely. They have ample money muscle and are prepared for a financial inheritance. Mission accomplished. Obviously, not everyone has kids. So, what to do then?

If you don't have kids, leave an inheritance to your spouse, nieces, nephews, cousins, significant other, charity, or a special loved one. Anyone come to mind? Anyone…? Hmm. If there's not even *one* person in your life that you love, well…I'd think about that!

The point is to lend a hand-up in some way to those who follow you. Regardless who you leave an inheritance to, it should contribute to their financial wealth in some manner. What a shame to be the 2nd, 3rd, or 4th generation and *still* living paycheck to paycheck. *Sigh.* Yes, it's true – you can live a great life and *also* leave an inheritance. My wife and I are living proof. Each generation should be better off than the one prior. (I showed you in principle 5 how just *one* generation can be worth $53M by following these principles.) Let's each do our part. If you haven't done so already, think about who you'll leave an inheritance to when you die.

Please notice I refer to financial inheritance and not legacy. Many people speak of leaving a legacy by way of money or other assets. I do not. Money is not legacy. Wait, what?! That's right, while a financial inheritance certainly is *part* of generational prosperity, legacy is much bigger. I save that thought for chapter 8, where I share my views on living and leaving a legacy.

[A final note on inheritance: if you're eager to *receive* an inheritance, be just as eager to *earn* it! Be there to care for aging or ill parents with *your* time, money, love, and support.]

There you have three wealth behaviors to follow: have a plan for your money, give hand-ups, and leave an inheritance. I'm sure you can think of even more. Use these behaviors in conjunction with the six principles to building wealth.

In conclusion, financial wealth is achievable by every able-bodied individual and every generation. So, after reading this book there's one thing you *cannot* say. You cannot say you don't know *how* to build wealth. Now it's a choice; you either follow a path and do the work...or you don't. If you have better ideas, go for it! There are *many* ways to get wealthy. Just ask yourself how it's working out so far. It's my sincerest hope that *you* and all readers of this book take these principles to heart. I hope you achieve far more financial success than I have.

Perspective
(Parting Thoughts on Wealth)

As you can see, every able-bodied person can achieve wealth. It requires the proper mindset, blueprint, and behaviors. As I alluded to in the opening of this chapter, my mindset on wealth is more of a *feeling* than it is a dollar amount. It's the journey, not the destination. While wealth can provide comfort, peace, and security, it certainly does not make you better than anyone. Most importantly, your mindset should be one of *helping others*. That's why chapter 8 is devoted entirely to personal *values*...because they matter.

Remember, *The Torch of Life*, includes a path to wealth as just one component in a broader playbook for achieving generational prosperity in life. So, whatever you do, don't confuse millionaire status and financial wealth with true *prosperity*. There's much more to it than that. Wealth must be combined with many other principles in life. Read on. Let's continue to widen our perspective even further.

Secret Sauce:

Don't focus on building financial wealth. Rather, focus on the mindset, blueprint, and *underlying actions* that lead to wealth; follow principles 1-6 and the 3 basic money behaviors. Step by step, wealth will follow.

CHAPTER 5

HEALTH WEALTH

"Knowing what I know today, I'd rank health wealth as the #1 ingredient to generational prosperity." — An older, wiser me.

How much would you pay to live one more year? How about one more day? Money's great, but it's worthless if you're dead! How much would a blind person pay for sight? What would a paralyzed person pay to stand, walk, and run? While it's true that money can buy healthcare, by and large, it cannot buy health. It certainly can't buy more life. Even billionaires will succumb to disease, disability, and death.

Health is precious. You have only one body. You must prioritize health wealth along with financial wealth. Fortunately, there's plenty of time to do both but ultimately, health trumps money. Like most things in life, health is relative. Sadly, too many people focus on their careers and neglect their health. They spend more time binge watching TV or scrolling online than exercising. How about you? What are you doing to build your health wealth? Make no mistake, poor health wealth can *destroy* your prosperity!

How many people…

- Live in an abusive situation?
- Murder themselves (suicide) each year?
- Suffer from depression, anxiety, stress, and other mental illness?
- Are in prison for assault, rape, killing, or other violent offenses?
- Perpetrate violent and hateful acts of extremism?
- Suffer from obesity?
- Neglect and abuse their body?
- Struggle with some ailment, illness, injury, or condition?
- Die from preventable disease?

The above questions are a mere fraction of endless possibilities. What do they all have in common? You got it…our *health*. And guess what? Most, if not all, can be avoided or managed with qualified care! (You're welcome.) That's right, read on to live the healthiest life possible.

Yes, mental health professionals can help you manage abusive, stressful, violent, and suicidal issues with proper therapy and/or medication. Medical providers can also control or completely cure preventable disease – but you must first *seek the care*. In other words, *you* play a key role in your own health and quality of life. Many elements of our physical, mental, emotional, intellectual, spiritual, and relational health all have a direct impact on not only *our* lives, but the lives of those around us: our family, friends, co-workers, classmates, and community.

You should focus on your *health wealth* more than anything else. It's tough to be prosperous (or do much of anything) if you're not healthy. You don't have to be a certified financial planner to build financial wealth. Likewise, you don't have to be a professional healthcare provider to build health wealth. (Even many of them are unhealthy.) When it comes to maintaining health wealth, my focus is heavily on the *controllables* (chapter 7). The underpinning of health wealth is controlling what you can. For what it's worth, and with my own two adult children in mind, here's what I think about health wealth and how it contributes to generational prosperity.

Two Caveats

First, we must acknowledge that life is complex and many factors affect our health. I realize that people can (and do) experience health issues because that's simply part of life. Yes, there are many *uncontrollables* in life. It's possible to properly diet and exercise and still succumb to illness or disease. Doctors, scientists, and medical professionals are very educated but they don't have all the answers and cannot cure every ailment in existence. There's no magic wand. Not yet, anyway. That's the sad part. So, if you're suffering from an untreatable condition, I sympathize with you. My heart goes out to you and others who are in pain and/or debilitated in some way. I have my own issues to deal with but I'm keenly aware that many others have it much worse (*relativity*, chapter 7).

Second, is regarding some of the questions that opened this chapter. I'm well aware that people commit crimes, acts of violence, and other things for many reasons, not only because of their mental, emotional, relational, or intellectual health. Behavior is affected by parenting (or lack thereof), culture, environment, peer pressure, and many other things. Here, I simply refer to the *controllables* of our health, particularly our *mental, emotional, intellectual, and relational* health. That's it, simple. It takes a qualified healthcare professional to diagnose clinical mental health and/or other issues. They can determine what degree of illness is uncontrollable and what is *controllable* through medicine, counseling, therapy, and other procedures. It should be clear as you read on that the controllable factors of our health have a huge impact on generational prosperity.

Perspective

Everyone has their own perspective on their health. On one extreme, some believe we should go full-speed ahead, no brakes, twenty-four hours a day and throw caution to the wind! We should eat, drink, and smoke anything we want and run our bodies to the ground. On the other side, some think it's safer to stay indoors, wrapped in bubble wrap, eating salads, and sleeping precisely 8 hours per night. I guess neither approach is right or wrong – to each their own. I happen to fall somewhere in between. As with many things, I subscribe to a *balanced* approach. I believe life is meant to be lived to the fullest, but with a degree of responsibility. What follows is strictly my opinion. It's what I believe will lead to a healthy and prosperous life. However, you be the judge and live your own life, accepting the consequences of your actions (and inactions).

Like many people, I wish I could go back in time and do some things a little differently. Just as I wish I had invested more money, I also wish I had taken better care of my health when I was younger. Live and learn. I've discovered much about my own health in the past half century. Yes, I have my own health issues (mostly out of my control), but given my age, I think I'm doing okay. Let's just say I keep on keeping on and am grateful for every day I'm given.

I view health wealth as far more than just diet and exercise. Focus on your *total* health: physical, mental, emotional, intellectual, spiritual, and even relational. Do whatever you can to be the best and healthiest you. Why? Because all things equal, you'll live longer and have a much better quality of life during those years. Proper health can give you energy, stamina, strength, and even a more positive attitude. You'll also get to spend more time with family and loved ones. Let's see how our health wealth unfolds in our daily lives.

Controllable vs Uncontrollable

It's best to focus on the things we can control and find a way to accept the things we cannot. Caution: be careful how you define uncontrollable. Why? Because we don't know what we don't know. I don't play DIY doctor. Be sure to involve healthcare professionals and let *them* determine what's controllable or not. For example, it may be easy to throw up your hands and say, "I have issue X, so that's why I'm so angry or depressed." Or, "I have issue Y, so that's why I can't lose weight." By doing so, you're playing doctor and *ass*uming that nothing can be done about your condition. However, doctors may determine otherwise. In this instance, the *controllable* part includes seeking professional help to diagnose, treat, or manage issue X or Y. Allow me to get on my 'dad soapbox' for a moment...

If I could tell my kids (or anyone) just one thing about their health, it would be this...

"Don't ever play doctor. If something's bothering you, see a doctor; they can't help if they don't know. Don't assume. Don't guess. See a doctor! When in doubt, check it out."

So, if you don't see a doctor for a condition you're facing, then you're not controlling what you can. In other words, you're not doing your part. Doctors certainly don't know everything. However, I'm amazed at what's possible today. Plus, new medical breakthroughs occur seemingly every day. Between my own health issues and that of my wife and family, I've seen and learned a lot. I've discovered that although many conditions may not be curable, they certainly are manageable (controllable). Even though we didn't think so at first! Here's a little true story...

My wife suffers from severe migraines. The doctors have diagnosed the issue, but have also explained that other factors can contribute to migraines and some things are still unknown. As such, I've driven her to *countless* appointments for her care for well over a decade. To their credit, doctors have offered *countless* treatments for my wife's migraines. The treatments have included injections of many types, biofeedback, electrical nerve stimulation, intravenous (IV) fluids, various therapies, *eight* lumbar punctures (aka spinal taps), and dozens of pharmaceutical combinations. Yes, we've encountered many good doctors who have tried their best. However, not all doctors are created alike.

One doctor told my wife that it's best to learn to live with the migraines and essentially, "We've done all we can." With all due respect, doc…try again. Since choking him was not going to help, we carried on to see the next doctor. Long story short, after more than *10 years* of this, we stumbled upon an IV treatment that had never been offered before. Although it's not a cure-all, this particular IV (every 3 months) helps manage my wife's pain to a somewhat tolerable level. Sadly, nobody told us about it, we had to actively seek it out.

So, the lesson in my story is **not** how to diagnose or treat migraines. It's **not** about bashing doctors; they don't have all the answers. To the contrary, I **thank** them with tears in my eyes for all they've done for my wife. The lesson is that *you* can't determine what's controllable or not. Heck, in our case even a *doctor* thought it was uncontrollable and thankfully…he was wrong. If we had listened to that doctor, my wife would still be in unnecessary debilitating pain. And by the way, you have never truly "tried everything." Remain proactive and don't *ever* give up!

So, what parts of our total health can we control and how can that affect our prosperity? As part of *total* health, I focus on a few general areas: physical, mental, emotional, intellectual, spiritual, and relational health. Each plays its own role in our overall health. Let's first look at each general area and then some things we can do overall for total health.

Physical Health

It's critical to care for our physical health. If our body shuts down, we shut down – nothing else matters. We can do certain things to help maintain our physical health. And remember, we're all different, so adjust according to your body and your doctor's advice. To keep things simple, we control at least three main daily things: diet, exercise, and hygiene.

Diet.

How many obese people do you see walking around? Good grief. Before you send me hate mail, please realize obesity is not a vanity issue, it's a *health* issue. It's not a criticism, it's a *concern*. Trust me, I'm not exactly twiggy but come on now. Obesity is practically everywhere you look. After all, we have fast food restaurants seemingly on every street corner and processed sugary foods out the wazoo. I believe people should eat healthier for their own benefit.

There's no perfect diet, but it's wise to eat a balanced and healthy diet. To me, this means generally following the food pyramid suggested by the U.S. Department of Agriculture. The food pyramid may now be called MyPlate, but regardless of what it's called over the years, the concept is to eat a balanced and healthy diet. Some may call it 'clean eating' or something similar. Basically, consuming more natural foods and less processed ones. Whatever the label, don't follow stupid hacks, tricks, and gimmicks on unsocial media; follow professional advice! Most of us learned the basics of this in grade school. When you're young, it feels like you can eat anything you want. Not so much as you age. Stay in tune with your body, how it reacts to different foods, and adjust your diet as necessary.

Admittedly, my diet was horrible during my younger adult years. Chalk that up as another lesson learned the hard way. I ate stupidly. If I could rewind the clock (or had better guidance), I would have eaten much healthier. Nowadays, I eat much better and cleaner, as they say. (Although I must confess to drinking too much caffeine while writing this book...I hope it was worth it.) I challenge you to reflect on your own diet. A poor diet can make you feel sluggish and tired. Body weight aside, it can also lead to many physical problems such as high blood pressure, high cholesterol, heart disease, liver conditions, and countless other bad things. Do yourself a favor and eat healthier.

Some people like to watch their caloric intake for a more stable diet. My wife is an expert at that and it pays off for her. She'll use an app to track how many calories she eats. Just like magic, she achieves her weight and caloric goals...simply by *tracking* things. *Where you focus, you prosper.* My wife has this principle down to a science!

Action plan – review your diet. Try journaling what you eat for 30 days…it may be quite shocking! Use the food pyramid (MyPlate) as a baseline. Make changes as needed, but eat as healthy as possible. Become familiar with nutrition labels but *don't obsess*. Cut back on junk food with little nutritional value…maybe cut it out completely. Eat fewer processed foods. Limit your intake of salt, sugar, and unhealthy fats. Also balance how much you eat (portion control). Avoid nicotine products, drugs, and alcohol or at least limit them as much as possible. I've never been much of the "food police" and don't judge people by what they eat. It's more important for *you* to establish *your* diet. After all, *you're* the one that has to live with yourself. And remember, some people will need more or fewer calories, nutrients, vitamins, and minerals than others. Be mindful of food allergies. If you struggle, consult a nutritionist or other qualified health provider.

Exercise.

Exercise is the yin to diet's yang. Enjoy your youth because it only lasts for so long and time flies. Physically, getting old stinks. Savor your vitality, energy, flexibility, youthful appearance, and everything else that comes along with being young. If and while you're able to…skip, jump, play, climb, and run like the wind! Don't go out of your way to endanger yourself, but don't baby yourself either.

My younger years consisted of weight lifting, running, and various recreational sports. Unlike my poor diet, my exercise was consistent and on point. I'm currently in my mid 50's. I exercise regularly, usually 4-5 days per week. My routine consists of walking, light workouts, and physical therapy exercises prescribed by my physical therapist. No running due to back pain. I adjust as needed for any dad-bod issues: aches, pains, cramps, strains, or muscle pulls. If you don't exercise regularly, you don't know what you're missing. It's far more than striving for 6-pack abs. There's something therapeutic and rewarding about being sore from a good workout. You can get lost in the moment working up a good sweat and getting your blood pumping. In fact, if a genie blessed me with permanent 6-pack abs, I would *still* exercise on a regular basis! Exercise can improve your mood and reduce stress. It can also increase your energy, strength, and stamina. More stamina enhances your performance at work, at play, and in many other areas <wink>.

The important thing is to remain active, even as you age. Our bodies are meant to *move*, not to hold the cushions down on our sofa. As you start to age, do things within your limits but *do* things.

Don't confuse your body weight with your fitness. What do I mean? Sadly, too many people think fit and healthy equals *skinny*. Wrong! You can be skinny from anorexia or bulimia and be *very* unhealthy. I see people desperately grasping at pills, potions, lotions, and injections…all to lose weight. They're easy to spot because they have zero muscle tone and look gaunt. Who knows what's happening to them long-term. Yikes. Quit looking for an easy button; it doesn't exist. No matter your body weight, exercise is required!

Action plan – if not already doing so, start your own exercise routine. Start slowly, but *start*. Strike a balance between cardiovascular, strength, flexibility, and stamina exercises. Maintain a healthy body weight, not so much for vanity, but rather for your *health* (heart, back, joints, cardio-vascular, etc). If necessary, consult a qualified health provider before starting an exercise plan. If you're able to, exercise outdoors for even more fun. If it's been a while, give it a shot…you'll thank me later!

Hygiene.

Everyone knows that one *nasty* person…don't be that person! Good hygiene is part of health wealth. Say what you want, but it's utterly shocking how many grown adults are simply nasty! Come on now, most of us learned this stuff as kids. Most of us anyway. It's sad that proper hygiene is not common sense for some people but it certainly affects our daily lives. When it comes to physical health, there are at least three main hygiene areas to focus on. Here's a 3-part action plan for healthy hygiene (body, dental, and sleep)…

First, keep your *body* clean. Basic hygiene is more than just aesthetic, it can keep you from getting sick, developing nasty skin problems, infections, and/or other medical conditions. Not to mention, you'll simply look better, smell better, and feel better! Shower at least once daily, but ideally, morning and night. Use hot water and soap. If you're a 'shower minimalist' or have a skin condition, at least consult a doctor about your routine. Trim your nails; fingers and toes. Keep your hair clean and groomed. Wash your laundry and bedding regularly.

Second, and more specifically, be sure to maintain proper *dental* hygiene. Follow your dentist's advice; brush, floss, rinse, and apply fluoride as recommended. Also, remember to protect your teeth with an appropriate mouthguard when participating in contact sports or other dangerous activities. Specialty care may be required for things such as overbites, underbites, misaligned or damaged teeth, and so on. Your dentist can refer you as needed.

Third and finally, maintain healthy *sleep* hygiene. Good sleep is important. Healthy sleep is typically consistent sleep. Try to get the same amount of sleep each night; not too little, not too much. Some people sleep during the day because they work at night (been there, done that). Either way, be consistent. How much sleep you need will vary depending on your age, health, activity level, medical conditions, medications, and other factors. If you have trouble sleeping and/or feel unusually tired, consult a doctor.

Also, as part of your physical health, be sure to discuss any health concerns with your doctor in a timely manner. Other physical health concerns are discussed under the 'Total Health' section.

Mental/Emotional Health

I've received (and taught) plenty of training on suicide awareness, resiliency, mental wellness, and the toll of trauma, PTSD, and human trafficking on mental health. The training I received was provided during my military service and was very basic. The focus was primarily on identifying and recognizing signs and symptoms so that professional help could be obtained. I believe *everyone* should seek out that same basic knowledge. Think of it as "first-aid for mental health"; a lay person's training that could potentially save lives! Once again, I'm **not** a healthcare professional. If you struggle with *any* health issue (including mental health), consult a qualified provider.

Some people act as if physical health and mental health occur in isolation. The reality is they're intertwined and they do affect each other. Not only that, but many mental and emotional health disorders are not visible and don't show up on an x-ray. Nevertheless, this issue is important. It's tough to prosper if you're not mentally and emotionally healthy.

As I opened this chapter with a few sample questions, it's evident that mental illness can have severe consequences. One question I asked was how many people live in an abusive situation. You may think, "What the heck does that have to do with health?" Well, if you're the abuser it may have to do with your mental health. At a minimum, it shows that you're relationally unhealthy. If you happen to be the one being abused, it may indicate an unhealthy relational or mental health issue. It's possible that you may feel 'less than' or somehow 'deserve' to be abused. Make no mistake, a diagnosis requires a mental health professional. However, my point is simply to illustrate the power of health wealth on your life – including mental health. Simply put, abusive relationships are *not* healthy. The other questions are also just as pertinent.

It doesn't take a psychologist to know that serial killers, rapists, and other such people are not mentally and emotionally healthy. However, it does take a trained professional to diagnose and unravel that level of illness. I'd argue that many criminal behaviors are at least partly due to some level of mental unwellness. Hey, we all have bad days on occasion. However, some things can seriously cross the line. In my opinion, a mentally or emotionally healthy person does *not*…

- Abuse others; either physically, verbally, financially, or in any other fashion.
- Allow others to abuse them in any manner.
- Plot or commit murder, torture, and violence.

These sad things (and many others) are reason for concern. They affect us all in some way and it's important to seek professional help. Maybe not all, but *much* of it can be controlled with professional help. That help may come from medical professionals and/or it may involve legal help from the courts or law enforcement. Each situation is different, but please prioritize yourself because you're worth it! Did you hear that? **You're worth it!** In order to be as mentally and emotionally healthy as possible, you must work at it, just like your physical health. Talk with your healthcare provider, read books, practice, and learn about ways to build mental strength and resilience.

Being human, I have my own emotional moments. I consider that healthy. After all, we're human beings, not robots. People *should* have varying emotions. For example, it's normal to be *sad* when a loved one dies. It's normal to be *excited* about an upcoming vacation. It's normal to get *irritated* when people act stupidly or disrespectful. However, I strive for a healthy balance and avoid unhealthy extremes. I continue to learn and practice new ways of improving my own mental and emotional health. Here are some things that have worked for me personally regarding mental and emotional health…

- While it's true that I have an eye toward the future, I strive to live in the present – the here and now. No dwelling on the past. Unless it serves to learn a lesson of some kind, no "woulda, coulda, shouldas" allowed!
- Maintain positive habits and healthy routines. Remember, diet, exercise, and sleep affect mental wellness.
- Avoid (or severely limit) negative habits that do not contribute to overall well-being: alcohol, gambling, overeating, overspending, oversleeping, etc.
- Control the controllables and accept the rest.
- Focus largely on *others*, especially family. It seems counterintuitive, but I've found a more selfless focus is far more emotionally rewarding, comforting, and fulfilling than a more selfish (self-centered) one. How best to love and support my spouse. How best to raise, mentor, guide, and love my kids. How best to help others in the world around me.
- Not to sound mean, but I simply don't care about what other people think about me or how I live. There will be critics no matter what, so be yourself and do what you do.
- I live in ~~virtual~~ actual reality! (chapter 6)

These things work for me, but you must explore your own approach. Folks, your mental and emotional health are critical. Although today's world appears more 'connected' than ever due to the Internet, too many people are disconnected, empty, and lonelier than ever. The content in today's online media not only feeds into our mental health (if we allow it), but it also reflects our mental health as a society. Be aware of your own mental wellness and seek help if needed.

Luckily, many people do seek help when they need it. In fact, my daughter has personally volunteered well over 200 hours with an online organization providing mental health support to those in need. She served as first-line contact for people reaching out for help with anxiety, loneliness, sadness, and other mental health issues. Her training also taught her when to escalate the issue to a more qualified health supervisor as needed. I like to think she's made a positive impact in many people's lives. Good for her and good for those people who are reaching out for help.

However, there are too many people who are mentally unstable and do **not** receive professional help. Sadly, in extreme cases, their issues can lead to acts of physical harm and violence towards themselves and/or others. Think about political or religious hatred, domestic violence, gang violence, human trafficking, riots, and similar atrocities. Sadder still, some people act as if this is new – it is not. Just like war and armed conflict, societal violence has been occurring since the beginning of time. Remember when politicians dueled? How many U.S. Presidents have been shot? How long have mafia and gangs existed? Even today, some people seem incapable of civil debate and discourse without resorting to violent rhetoric, hate, threats, and/or physical violence. They may suffer from mental problems and are unable to control their own behavior. I'll leave that up to the psychologists and human behavior experts to figure out. All I'm doing here is emphasizing the importance of mental/emotional health on your prosperity. It's just as important as physical health…in some cases, even *more* important. What's the takeaway?

Just as there are countless physical health conditions, so too, there are countless mental ones. They're both *health* concerns and you should treat them with equal importance. Regardless of your struggles, work to manage or resolve the issue. If you started urinating blood, I hope you'd see a doctor. Likewise, if you suffer from anxiety, depression, suicidal ideations, addictions, emotional outbursts, hate, anger, or any other mental/emotional health concern…see a professional immediately! Don't let problems fester and get worse. Don't be ashamed. Don't be a hero and try to tough it out. Rather, be courageous and wise…get help. Here's a visual…

Scenario 1: you're having a heart attack. Do you call 911 or say, "No worries, I can handle it"?

Scenario 2: you're feeling suicidal. Do you call 911 or say, "No worries, I can handle it"?

In this visual, I see two life-threatening scenarios. One is physical and the other is mental. Both can be deadly. A heart attack is not normal or healthy. Suicide is not normal or healthy. Both can be treated. I've witnessed the sad consequences of suicide up close and personal. I've also seen how professional help can save lives! Mental or emotional health issues don't have to be potentially fatal to warrant help. If you suffer from trauma, behavioral disorders, or self-image issues, seek help. Why? Because again…**you're worth it!** I want you to live the most prosperous life possible. I hope *you* do too, and that's why you're reading this book. Right? So, for your loved ones and most importantly for yourself, if you suffer from a mental/emotional health issue, please…*get help today*!

Intellectual Health

I'm certainly no rocket scientist, but I've taken pride in working hard to build my intellect over the course of my life and continue to do so. Yes, learning should be lifelong. I believe a key component to intellectual health is mental stimulation. Some people suffer from learning disorders which can make educational, creative, and intellectual tasks quite challenging. In those cases, it's important to seek professional help. However, under normal and healthy circumstances, be sure to exercise your mind like you exercise your body. Some ways to exercise your intellect include reading, puzzles, brain teasers, learning creative and artistic new skills, and solving riddles. There's plenty more but you get the idea. Also, as you know, chapter 2 is packed with suggestions for keeping your intellect healthy in the interest of lifelong learning. Remember to plant seeds, not weeds!

Exercising your mind can help keep you mentally sharp as you age. In his later years of life, my late father struggled with cognitive issues. His doctors advised him that working on small puzzles, crosswords, and word jumbles can help slow cognitive decline. It may not be a cure-all, but every little bit helps. Do what you can to keep your intellect healthy and strong. There's another benefit to intellectual health as well.

I hope I've stressed the importance of lifelong learning so far and the importance of building intellectual biceps. But let's not stop there. A strong intellect is absolutely, positively, and unequivocally *vital* to fighting and dispelling ignorance. What do I mean? Well, again, some of the opening questions in this chapter referenced hate, extremism, abuse, killing, and other nasty deeds. Yes, some of that is related to mental and emotional health issues. For example, if you support crime, I believe there must be something wrong with you. Yet, there are plenty of people that do exactly that. It's simply unreal.

However, we could also argue that much of this comes from *ignorance* (lack of knowledge, facts, understanding, and comprehension). Oh, if only. If only people would build their intellectual health. A strong intellect can help eradicate *many* of our societal woes. Intelligence can help people grow a career, raise a family, become wealthy, build a marriage, vote properly, support law and order, and many other things that lead to prosperity. In addition, just wait until you see how a strong intellect can come in handy when we get to *individualism* in chapter 9. Folks, this stuff all ties together!

Spiritual Health

Spiritual health relates to your beliefs and/or religion; a sense of your connection to, and place within, something larger. I dive deeper into spirituality in chapter 14, but emphasize here that it's an important component of overall health. In fact, it has been (and is still) so important in my life, that I devote the *bulk of that entire chapter* to the benefits of spirituality and beliefs. Therefore, I don't duplicate that information here. Religion can certainly be part of your spiritual health. So, too can assorted types of meditation, yoga, prayer, and other worship.

Maintaining spiritual health may involve reflecting on your values, the relationship between your body and spirit, or even your spiritual beliefs about death and the after-life. There's no right or wrong answer, provided you're not harming yourself or others. Again, the benefits of spirituality, beliefs, and religion will become even clearer in chapter 14.

Relational Health

Ok, relational health is absolutely critical for successful relationships. Imagine how successful you'd be as an athlete if you had poor physical health. Likewise, imagine how successful your relationships would be if you had poor relational health. Yikes, talk about a hot mess! Strong and healthy relationships don't happen by accident. Yes, relational health basically spans any human-human interaction. This includes family, friends, classmates, co-workers, neighbors, and anywhere there's a relationship between people. In fact, I touched upon the service-oriented mindset and relational behaviors you should exemplify in your *career* in chapter 3. I also covered selfless, helpful, and generous behavior towards others in chapter 4. However, for the purposes of generational prosperity, I want to really hammer home the importance of relational health in your *marriage* and *parenthood*!

Arguably, the strongest human-human relational bonds most people will build in their lifetime occur in marriage and parenthood. Agreed? Agreed! It seems to me that some people get married and say 'there, now I have a spouse' or they reproduce and say 'there, now I have a kid'. While technically true, if you wish to truly prosper in either area (marriage or parenthood), you should maximize your relational health. Like most anything else in life, this takes work, practice, and patience. Darn it, why is everything so much *work*?! Hang in there. After all, you're essentially doing an interactive relational dance with another human being; it takes nuanced synchronization and patience. The playbook for this involves selecting various avenues for building your relational skills. Some resources that may be helpful include…

- Pre-marital counseling.
- Parenting classes.
- Books on marriage and/or parenthood.
- Advice from older/wiser folks who have been there, done that.
- Marriage and parenting seminars.
- Mentorship from seasoned and experienced church elders.
- Relevant training (personality assessments, situational leadership, transactional analysis, etc).

Those are just a few options for leveling up your relational health, especially in marriage and parenthood. Having taught some of that relevant training myself, I know first-hand how valuable it can be! Now, relational health is certainly not the *only* thing essential to marriage and parenthood. There are also many skills to acquire and other things to learn if you wish to excel at either (or both). As luck would have it, there's an entire chapter on each in *Part II* (chapters 10 and 11). However, if you wish to be the best spouse and/or parent possible, improving your relational health is at the top of the list!

Although relational health is important in marriage and parenthood, not everyone is a spouse or a parent. However, *everyone* interacts in some way with other people: social gatherings, school, work, travel, sports, etc. Knowing this, it's in your best interest to build your relational health. You can read about this and/or you can *practice* it. Here are a few tips…

➢ Be situationally aware; observe your surroundings and others in your space.

➢ Live by strong personal values (chapter 8); they strengthen interpersonal bonds.

➢ Maintain healthy personal space; don't crowd others or remain distant and detached.

➢ Make eye contact when speaking with others; don't stare or dart your eyes in every direction.

➢ Be an active listener; ask open-ended questions and do not dominate the conversation.

➢ Display positive body language; smile, stand/sit up straight, and face others.

➢ Respect other people's beliefs, cultures, and lifestyles (it's not all about *you*).

➢ Please…put the phone down.

P.S. – if you're having a relationship with chat-bots or 'artificial intelligence', umm…get professional help **immediately!** *Sigh.*

All in all, great relational health leads to great relationships. This stuff doesn't happen by accident, so if you wish to have the most prosperous relationships possible…work at it!

Total Health

Aside from tending to the above specific areas of your health, it's also important to focus on your total health. Here, I include things not already mentioned earlier. Think of these as collective pointers for your overall health.

Annual/Routine Checkups

Visit your healthcare provider at least annually and your dentist every six months. Think of routine visits as a "tune-up" for your body; preventive maintenance can go a long way. Your doctor and dentist can also refer you to other specialists if/as required.

Your primary care provider is the 'head coach' of your overall health, so rely on their advice to stay as healthy as possible. They should track your vitals such as body weight, heart rate, oxygen levels, blood pressure, lab results, hearing and eye exams, and much more. They can schedule you for preventive tests as appropriate (colonoscopies, breast exams, skin cancer screenings, etc). Also, discuss recommended vaccinations with your doctor.

Your dentist and oral hygienist will perform cleanings, exams, imaging, and other things to keep your dental health in top shape. They can detect and treat cavities before they become major issues. They can also spot other issues or abnormalities that may require the care of a specialist. Ensure they address any questions or concerns you may have. You only have one set of adult teeth, so take care of them!

Specialty Care

Your primary doctor or dentist may refer you to a specialist for certain care. If you have any health conditions or ailments, be sure to manage them proactively. Your job is to follow your specialist's advice and ask clarifying questions as needed.

A Team Approach

When it comes to overall health, doctors and dentists are great. However, it's also helpful to surround yourself with a team. Depending on the care you may need, it's great to have family, friends, counselors, and other professionals on your side. You may require emotional support, accountability partners, in-home care, transportation, bandaging assistance, and a host of other things. Lean on your team as needed and be sure to repay the favor.

Advice and Follow-up

Follow your *doctor's* advice; not the advice of unqualified friends, co-workers, classmates, or online videos. A few controllables include following doctors' orders as prescribed…

- Taking medications or supplements.
- Performing any required therapies.
- Wear and use of any medical or dental devices.
- Bed rest, exercise, and/or dietary restrictions.

If you have concerns or disagreements with your doctor's advice, get a second (or third) opinion…from a *doctor*. A key component in your health wealth is *you*. Be proactive. Schedule appointments and follow-up as needed. Don't let problems fester. Seek help in a timely manner.

General Health Awareness

Most of us are not trained healthcare professionals. Even doctors don't have all the answers. However, we should all strive to learn the basics about our own health and the health of our loved ones. Be in tune with any changes in your five senses: sight, smell, hearing, touch, and taste. Be aware of changes or disruptions in bodily functions, mood, or behavior. In short, pay attention to any abnormal changes to your body of any kind. Don't obsess or be a worry wart, but if anything feels off in some unusual way, check with your doctor. It could be nothing, but you never know. An ounce of prevention is worth a pound of cure. Sometimes, recognizing signs and symptoms is the important first step in getting the help you (or loved ones) need. When in doubt, check it out!

Some areas of life are easier to blueprint success than others. For example, being a lifelong learner is pretty straightforward and will always be beneficial. Another example is managing money; it's hard to go wrong with the six financial principles and three wealth behaviors outlined earlier. I've also provided common elements to achieving success in nearly any career.

However, personal health is complex, unique in many ways, and highly individualized. There's an entire science to diet, exercise, medical conditions, and total health. Doctors attend many years of medical school, residency, and specialized training for a reason. I've intentionally kept this chapter short and stayed within my lane of knowledge and suggestions. But just because there's no simple or easy path, that doesn't mean health is any less important. It's also not an excuse to shrug your shoulders and do nothing. To the contrary, your health wealth is arguably the *most important* area of your life. I've covered some principles and general behaviors that can stack the odds in your favor. There are entire books written on health. You can find books on physical, mental, emotional, intellectual, spiritual, relational health, and more. Put the phone down and read a few. There are books on almost any disease or medical condition imaginable; learn about what affects *you* (and your family) and how to manage it. You can obtain basic-levels of training on things such as CPR, mental wellness, diet, exercise, and more. And remember to **consult qualified healthcare providers** on a regular (and as-needed) basis. Don't get your information from random online searches and/or video clips. Control the controllables…your health (and prosperity) depends upon it!

One final but important note on health…

Realize that everyone on Earth has some condition they're dealing with, whether it's known or unknown, minor or major…seen or unseen. Absolutely no one is in literally *perfect* health. (And if you *think* you are…just wait.) We're all in the same boat. For everyone that you think has it 'better off', there are many, many others who have it 'worse off' (whatever *it* is): deformities, disabilities, height/weight issues, skin conditions, sight or hearing issues, mental health issues, or anything else you can imagine. The principle of *relativity* will remind us of this (chapter 7). Life catches up with us all…no exceptions. Don't compare yourself to others, just do the best you can. No pity parties. Love and support each other. Measure your health only against yourself and that of your doctor's advice. We are (thankfully) all unique. Regardless how 'perfectly' we diet and exercise, we will all die. Know that your body has an expiration date. Enjoy the life you've been given and live each day to the fullest.

CHAPTER 6

UNPLUG

(~~VIRTUAL~~ ACTUAL REALITY)

Oh, where to begin? Let me start by saying technology offers many great things in life and it will continue to get even better. Having worked in IT for 25 years, I'm a big fan of what it can do for us. Technology has automated many things and improved the speed at which we work, live, and play. Corporations use enterprise software, high-tech hardware, cloud computing, and many other technologies to make our lives better in some way. All great. However, that's not what I'm talking about here when I say you should unplug. Here, I'm referring to common digital devices and how they're used every day by ordinary people: laptops, tablets, phones, Internet content, applications (apps), navigation, gaming, and the like. This technology will exist in some form for the rest of our lives and well into the future. However, it is but a mere baby in the scope of humanity. This stuff didn't even exist when I was a kid just two eye blinks ago. If it did, it was only in its infancy and certainly not mainstream. Yes, I'm a relic. When I was a child, we played with sticks, rode our bikes, built forts, and spent much of our time in what mom called *outside*! We used rotary dial phones to call each other, fold-out paper maps to navigate roadways, and read books in the library to do our research. It was quite the thing. Somehow, I'm still alive.

The point is, society is still finding its way in this relatively new digital age. Many are bumbling and fumbling through life as if blindly feeling their way in a dark room. With each passing year, fewer and fewer people will know of a life without technology. Heck, my own two kids have never lived a day without its existence. Therefore, for society at large it becomes more and more difficult to comprehend a life not connected to virtual reality. If you don't pay attention, it becomes the new norm. If you're not careful, you become numb to it. Or even fall *prey* to it. Perhaps society is the proverbial frog in slow boiling water. I'm not suggesting we go back to the stone age. I don't believe we should resist change and never evolve. To the contrary, I believe change is good – if managed properly. Embrace change.

However, if you wish to live a prosperous life with meaning and purpose, I strongly suggest that you learn to *balance* the use of technology. Human beings are emotional and social creatures, not robotic androids. We operate on feelings and emotions, not ones and zeros. You must step back and widen your lens. Look at the bigger picture and view life more objectively. More maturely. Without the proper values, experience, mindset, and knowledge, it's easy to get sucked into the vortex of the digital world – allow me to call it *virtual* reality. You know, like when people have a virtual meeting or a virtual medical appointment. This, as opposed to physical, face-to-face, *actual* reality. Yes, an online meeting is actually real. Yes, a video call is actually real – just as your friends on 'social' media are actually real. However, the meeting, video call, or friendship taking place on a digital device is hardly the same as an in-person, face-to-face encounter. It is virtual. I make a clear distinction here between *virtual* (online) and *actual* (physical) so we're on the same page.

It's my hope that as you read on, my message will become crystal clear and you'll become highly adept at balancing the two realities. If you're reading this, it's possible that you've never lived in my world. That is, a world before *and* after the aforementioned technology. It's possible that virtual reality is all that you've ever known. If so, I understand some of my advice may sound foreign or even weird. That's okay. Hear me out and keep an open mind – it could change your life for the better. When I boil down my advice in this area to one central idea for a prosperous life, it is this...

Unplug. You should *use* virtual reality and *live* in actual reality.

So, exactly how can we use virtual reality and live in actual reality? Like many things, it's simple but not easy. This is where intentionality comes in again. I'm telling you, intentionality is like a super power. But remember that's not all; we must also do the work. I'm sure you know that by now. We must walk the walk. I'd like to start by stressing the importance of owning your situation. This is where I remind you that I'm not a certified therapist, psychologist, or mental health professional. I say this because I believe many people are, at some level, addicted to their devices. A digital addiction, if you will. Their devices and some of its contents are like digital opioids. Now, I use the term addiction in a facetious, tongue-in-cheek fashion, but the matter is hardly funny…it's quite serious. If not an addiction, perhaps an overly out-of-balance and unhealthy obsession. I could be wrong but I sincerely believe many people are unable to recognize they're stuck in the vortex and unable to escape on their own.

Therefore, by owning your situation, I'm reminded of the first step in common 12-step programs used to combat substance addictions. The first step is to *admit that you have a problem*. Admit that you're unable to control your usage of technology. If you're unable to do this, it's an uphill battle to living your best life. If this is you, I seriously recommend you seek professional help. For real. I'm not joking. It's no cause for shame. To the contrary, seeking help shows a strong self-awareness and a great strength. A specialized healthcare professional can help you figure things out. There are many reasons I believe some people are addicted to virtual reality. The good news? You can (and should) first learn to recognize some unhealthy habits and behaviors and then adjust accordingly in order to prosper.

Driving while addicted

Must I even say anything? I'm utterly astonished (and saddened) at how many people are glued to their phones while behind the wheel. Even when it's against the law in that area. It's unreal. The things I've seen are unbelievable. Cars swerve from side to side, sit at green lights, brake at the last second, and all kinds of crazy stuff. One time, I saw someone with their phone clipped to their dashboard *watching a video* while they were driving! Sadly, deadly accidents also occur due to texting and driving. It doesn't take a genius to know that many people are simply out of control. You *might* be addicted to your phone if you can't drive to the store and back without using it.

Adjust. Take a deep breath. Unplug your brain from your phone (or your phone from your brain). Look around and drive. We *must* ensure we're smarter than our "smart" phones. You may choose to use your phone for navigation. If so, practice following the *voice* directions so you won't have to look at the map. Diverting your eyes from the road only increases the chance of an accident. If your vehicle is equipped, make use of your head-up display (HUD). A HUD will help to keep your eyes up and forward instead of looking down or around to see your phone. Minimize phone calls (if any) while driving. If you feel it's critically necessary, at least use hands-free technology. Think of this – how would you feel if you *killed* someone while texting and driving? Put the phone down and drive!

Dining while addicted

My wife and I enjoy dining out fairly often (maybe too often). Once again, I'm saddened by the number of people sitting at their table glued to their phones. Here, I'm referring to a table of two or more, all of them swiping and scrolling throughout the entire meal. No eye contact. Little conversation. Digital zombies. It's extremely rare for me to even *have* a phone in a restaurant, never mind use it. It reminds me of a time my wife and I went to a restaurant and they didn't have a single physical menu to view. The waitress instructed us to scan some code with our phone for a copy of the menu. Umm, no. I didn't even *have* my phone – it was in the car, as usual. Needless to say, we left and found another restaurant next door. Problem solved.

Adjust. Here's a challenge – leave your phone in the car when you're dining out. Does that make you anxious just thinking about it? Try it. Enjoy the moment. Look your company in the eye. Have a conversation. Savor your meal. Strike up small talk with the waiter or waitress. Laugh. Smile. Live. Likewise at home…no phones at the kitchen table. This may sound like heresy to some, but try it, you may grow to like it.

Text-a-thon addiction

I see it all the time. I've coached my kids through this one. They'll be texting or emailing someone about an issue they're trying to resolve; perhaps it's a payment issue, a scheduling conflict, or similar admin-istrative issue. It's a game of ping pong – back and forth, back and forth. They tell me, "Dad, they're saying this. Dad, they're saying that." Ok kids, bring me the phone, please. I hit the 'dial' button and the person answers. After a one-minute conversation, the issue is resolved. Another problem solved. Cut through the BS and *communicate*, person to person. Yes, there's a time and place for texting. However, you must discern when to use it. Remember, *people* get things done, not apps or devices.

Adjust. Here's another challenge – before texting someone, stop for a moment and ask yourself if a phone call is more appropriate. Try a short phone call, then put the phone down and move on with life. You've got things to do and places to go. Minimize texting, maximize living.

Sleeping while addicted

Sadly, some people can't even go to bed without their phone. Look, it's great to have on your nightstand for emergencies or as an alarm clock but that's not what I'm referring to here. Some people even bring it into bed with them! If you must constantly check your phone for every bleep, buzz, and blip, you *might* be too attached to it. I'm just saying.

Adjust. Treat your bedroom as a no phone zone. By that, I mean keep it for emergencies or use as an alarm clock. However, put it on silent mode and keep it out of your hand. Set it across the room and out of reach. Throw it out the window, if you must – I don't care. Unwind. Rest. Relax. Sleep. Sshhhhhh….ZZzzzz.

Out & About while addicted

Have you been shopping lately? The digital zombies are everywhere! People are so obsessed with their phones, they stand there blocking the aisles, earbuds implanted in their ears, blabbing away on their phones. Productive? Hardly. Holding up checkout lines. So distracted that their kid's about to fall from the seat of the shopping cart or topple over a shelf of glass jars. Then you have the people walking in front of traffic with their eyes glued to the screen. They risk getting run over…and for what? Are they talking someone through open-heart surgery? Geez. You wouldn't believe how many zombies I see on my morning walks. People are walking their dogs glued to their phones. Jogging on their phones. Skate boarding on their phones. And yes, they're sitting on exercise equipment at the gym…on their phone. Wake up people.

Adjust. Here's a thought – go for an early morning walk and leave your phone at home. Breathe in the air, observe the wildlife, admire the sunrise, and just enjoy the moment. When you go shopping, leave your phone in the car. Dare I say it, you might even want to go biking, swimming, surfing, or play a game of tennis – all <gasp> without your phone.

Phone tree addiction

Even businesses are addicted! Sadly, many of us know this one. There used to be a time when companies had actual *people* answer the phone to provide *actual* customer service. Imagine that. Today, way too many of them have implemented these ~~worthless~~ automated phone trees and/or virtual ~~idiots~~ assistants <cough, cough>. Press 1 for this, press 2 for that, press # for something else. "I don't understand you." "Repeat what you'd like to do." "Please tell me what you want." Ok, here's what I want – someone with a brain to answer the phone! Good grief. I can't tell you how much business I've taken elsewhere when a company wastes my time like that. If you'd answer the phone, you'd *know* what I want. How much money do they spend on phone tree technology, hardware, software, and ongoing maintenance? It's not cute, trendy, or efficient; it's *stupid*. If a company would *lead* and not follow, they might even 'go viral' by actually answering their phone and providing world-class service. I'd be first in line as their customer. I know many, many others who would follow suit.

Adjust. Since I don't run these companies, all I can do is take my business elsewhere. And I do. Whenever possible, I seek out companies that provide top-tier customer service. That *may* include an *option* to use an app or phone tree, but it will certainly include the option to interact with a real-life *human*. If you don't answer the phone, you don't get my business.

I could go on with these addictions (obsessions?), but you get the idea. I'm sure these scenarios, and many others, look familiar…perhaps a little *too* familiar? Yes, having a phone can be great for emergencies (accident, medical issues, tracking or monitoring, etc). Very true. Just know how and when to engage. I'm weird but hear me out. Folks, it's a digital epidemic. I challenge you in *whatever* you're doing, even if just for a day. Put. The. Phone. Down. Call it digital detox day. Unplug from virtual reality and engage in actual reality. Live in the moment. Make things happen. Look around you. See the sights. Hear the sounds. Dance. Sing. Love. You may be surprised at what you've been missing – almost like (re)discovering a whole new world.

Whether you feel you struggle with device addiction/obsession or not, I encourage you to monitor your daily usage. One good thing about most devices is the ability to track your time online. Either in the program settings or perhaps a separate application, the device will display your cumulative screen time. This provides you a concrete number (i.e. 4 hours, 22 minutes) instead of a vague notion of "Well, I don't spend *too much* time on my device." I talk more about the principle of *balance* in chapter 7, but too much of anything is usually not a good thing. This is especially true of screen time. Again, if you're unwilling or unable to unplug, you may have a problem and should seek professional help.

In addition to unplugging from our devices, it's also critical to be smart when we do use them. What's the nature of the content that we're consuming? I love many things about computers and smartphones – they can be quite useful at times. However, I cringe at the stuff some people are rotting their brains with. This is certainly where we should apply our critical thinking. It saddens me to witness the dumbing down of society and humanity through the garbage we consume on our devices. This occurs in many ways, but I'll focus on what I believe are some of the worst offenders. First off, let's focus on <ahem> news.

Tabloids (news?)

I must say, the definition of 'news' has changed over time. Maybe it's just me but I remember decades ago when news was almost actually …news. A reporter would track down a lead, ask probing questions, dig deep, and usually present the reader or viewer with a relevant, balanced, and useful story. Today, stuff is shot-gunned out as fast as possible to the point of information overload and I use the word "information" loosely. In my opinion, many so-called news agencies should be called tabloids. Remember those in the grocery store checkout aisle? The headlines screamed that aliens took the baby or a celebrity was back from the dead. Good grief, reading today's "news" is like wading through a cesspool of sewage. First, you must click through a barrage of annoying pop-ups, ads, pay walls, and sponsored click-bait junk. Then, you get to sift through all of the grossly biased political junk and hateful biased opinions. When you're done navigating through *that* stuff, what's left is one or two nuggets of actual news. Sadly, many people consume this junk on a daily basis. Remember what happens when you plant weeds in your mind.

Adjust. I get smarter each day not because of the so-called news agencies, but in spite of them. It's unreal how hateful, divisive, biased, and irrelevant the content has become. The good news? Well, since *The Torch of Life* contains advice on living a more inspired and fruitful life, I'll share a secret regarding said news. My wife and I ignore it. All of it. You can, too. Simple. Yep, another problem solved. We gave up reading that junk long ago. Oh sure, we'll occasionally tune-in to actual local news for severe weather updates or other significant issues now and then. After all, I don't live under a rock. I also check in on a particular site or two for economic and market information (factual data). That's it. The rest has gone bye-bye. The result? We're still alive. And we're actually smarter and much happier! We're smarter because we read unbiased and factual information from legitimate sources. We're happier because we're no longer bombarded with sensationalized headlines, half-baked reporting, click-bait, or irrelevant sound bites. It's great. So, that's one tip for a better and more prosperous life. But sadly, so-called news is not the only thing rotting people's brains.

Unsocial Media

Ah, good old unsocial media. Just like news, what started out with good intentions has turned into another cesspool. Admittedly, I used some 'social' media apps many years ago. At first, my friends and I would use it to share funny stories, pictures of family, celebrate holidays, and just stay in touch. You know, fun *social* stuff you do with family and friends. However, at some point my circle of connections grew and somehow paid or sponsored "news" feeds started showing up. Before I knew it, this unsocial media was now infested with hateful and half-baked political trash, paid advertisements, links to scams and viruses, and all things negativity. Not to mention, anything and everything was now somehow racist or sexist. Good grief. I'm not sure where these people lived, but the picture of that *virtual* world was certainly **nothing** at all like the *actual* world where I lived. Not even close. The sad part? Some of my 'friends' were never like that in real life (you know, *actual*, face-to-face life). But somehow, they became spineless and weak enough to fall in with the sheeple and keyboard warriors. Or perhaps it was their true colors coming out. I don't know.

Either way, I don't partake in drama, so I deleted my accounts. That's right, at the time of this writing, I don't have a single unsocial media account and haven't for many years now. Neither does my wife. She uses a certain app as a messaging feature with out-of-country family but that's it. Guess what? Once again, we're both smarter and happier as a result…living life full-speed ahead! We both keep in close contact with family and friends through a quick text or email, phone calls, or face-to-face visits. Anyone who wallows in negativity, lies, drama, and racist/sexist innuendos is outside our circle – problem solved. Other than that, we're too busy having fun and enjoying prosperity. I believe other people are not so lucky. I've read some horror stories.

My daughter is studying psychology and planning to attend medical school to become a psychiatrist. (She'll have plenty of patients!) Occasionally, I bravely search out stories that are related to her future profession and forward them to her as learning opportunities. As a result, I've read about many so-called social media apps and their devastating effects on people's mental health. It's especially rampant in the younger demographic, teenagers in particular. There's a myriad of idiotic 'dares and challenges' for people to take on. Some are not only idiotic but down-right dangerous, if not deadly. Culling the herd, I guess. I've got a challenge for you – delete those stupid apps! If you're a parent, please pay particular attention to what your kids are viewing on unsocial media. That is, if you even allow them to have access at all.

As most of us know, unlike actual reality, when people get on unsocial media, the sheeple, trolls, and keyboard warriors are all around. People say and do things online that they would never consider doing face-to-face in real life. (*virtual* reality vs. *actual* reality.) I've read about people suffering from bullying, body dysmorphic disorder, fat shaming, anxiety, depression, and a whole lot more while being bombarded by their so-called social network. Sadly, some even contemplate or commit suicide because they were unable to cope with the pressures. Folks, we must spread the word. We must parent our children. We must involve mental health professionals and behavioral specialists when necessary.

These unsocial media apps can be a nightmare. Just to clarify, it's not only teenagers who are suffering from these apps.

I know people of all ages who get sucked into the unsocial media vortex. Even full-grown adults. Instead of using these apps for thoughtful and *intentional* purposes, they mindlessly scroll long enough to start believing that virtual reality is actual reality. They fall prey to the junk that's inserted into their news feed or what someone says is trending. Sadly, it's usually neither news, nor trending. It's simply something promoted by an algorithm, paid advertisement, or someone with an agenda. My advice is to be a pace setter, not a trend follower. I've seen very little value in anything trending online. Have you ever opened a search browser and glanced at the 'trending searches'? I just shake my head. If that's what's trending, it's no surprise that people are unhappy, unsuccessful, anxious, depressed, and living paycheck to paycheck. Wow. It's certainly not trending in *my* world. Chances are, if something is trending, hash-tagging, or going viral, it's usually irrelevant (yawn) and probably idiotic. Likewise, if you judge success by clicks and views, you *might* be missing the mark in life. Do you equate popularity with success? Remember, even some serial killers have been popular, but most would question their success. It's no wonder I don't use unsocial media! (And no wonder I'm so happy.)

Adjust. Try closing your unsocial media accounts and deleting all of the apps. If you're unable to do that, then at least monitor how much time you spend on these apps. Perhaps limit yourself to only one app. Also, give yourself a limit to how much you use it – say, one hour per day *maximum*. Keep in touch with actual friends via phone calls, face-to-face, or an occasional text. Ask yourself what you're actually trying to accomplish via the apps and are there better ways of doing so. How could your time be better spent? Whatever you do, find a way to remain engaged in actual reality.

Online Pornography, Gambling, and Gaming

It doesn't take much research to know that online pornography, gambling, and gaming are costly addictions in many ways. While the Internet is not the cause of these addictions, it has certainly amplified the situation through easy access. These addictions can cost people valuable time and money, including bankruptcy. Additionally, they can take a toll on relationships and quality family life, including neglectful parenting and spousal infidelity. As if that's not bad enough, people addicted to these vices can start to neglect their diet, exercise, sleep, and overall health. Some even neglect their personal hygiene in order to spend more time online. If you suffer from addiction to online pornography, gambling, or gaming, please…seek professional help. Immediately.

More Virtual Reality Dark Sides?

So, tabloids, unsocial media, pornography, gambling, and gaming play their part in the dumbing down of our lives. However, there are still more things to be aware of in virtual reality. There will always be bad people up to no good, but they especially thrive in the virtual world. There, they can be anonymous or easily masquerade as someone else. Plus, they can reach a much wider audience than would be possible in actual reality.

Children are at particular risk in virtual reality. For instance, it's much easier for some creep to approach your young child on unsocial media than it is face-to-face. These creeps can reach right into your home and right into your bedrooms via online messaging platforms. They use social engineering to lure children from their homes, obtain lewd photos, make false promises, spread lies, and a host of other nasty things. Their tactics include phishing, ransomware, malicious logic, viruses, and a host of other dirty deeds to take advantage of unsuspecting victims. Do these people have a life? Good grief. And it's not only kids that are vulnerable.

Adults are victimized as well. Virtual reality can lead to many actual health problems, including death. Death?! That's right. The improper or over-use of virtual reality can lead to eye strain and sight issues, sleep disorders, carpal tunnel syndrome, mental wellness problems, and even death. People can suffer seclusion, loneliness, and isolation from real human beings in virtual reality. Sadly, for some, it's more than they can bear. Even adults are at risk of being lured into dangerous and deadly situations by online perverts. Please, folks…use your digital devices but do so responsibly and safely.

Don't have a heart attack, but our two kids didn't even *have* a phone until they were 13 years old. Unbelievably, they're still alive. Caveat, our daughter got hers a few months prior to age 13 only because of circumstance. Our son (who's 3 years older than her) got in trouble for something. As a consequence, we took his phone away and gave it to our daughter. Maybe that's one reason why they each earned 4.0+ GPAs in high school, but who knows.

Here's something (not) funny. I've read reports suggesting people can improve their health by taking breaks from online activity. They claim it helps reduce bullying and increases self-esteem in children. By eliminating comparisons with "the Joneses" on social media, people have less anxiety and self-image issues. Again, what a shocking surprise! By cutting down on wasted time and rotting brain cells, people actually perform better in school, earn more money, and have better relationships. Really? Who'd a thunk it? Is this some new *viral* trend to unplug for a more successful life? Yawn. No…it's not new *or* viral. It's been that way forever and will continue to be that way. Unplug from virtual reality and back into actual reality.

Potential Consequences?

This book is not one of statistics, empirical studies, or behavioral research. It's mostly just common sense. As with any of the aforementioned risks of virtual reality, education is key. Please take some time to learn about these topics on your own. If warranted, you might even consider consulting a behavioral specialist for advice. I highlight these issues as potential life landmines and encourage you to be on guard, not only for yourself but for your family as well – especially your kids. It would be a shameful disservice to pass along a Torch of Life on generational prosperity without including the risks and negative consequences that virtual reality can carry. The potential exists to destroy your life. I suggest a way of life that minimizes use, obsession, or addiction to virtual reality and simultaneously implore you to seek professional help if required. It's very tough, if not impossible to achieve generational prosperity if your digital life rules your actual life and/or you suffer from debilitating addiction of any kind. Here are just a few examples of potential negative consequences…

➢ Adult children who live in their parents' basement and play video games or mindlessly scroll unsocial media all day. No hopes. No dreams. No job. No career aspirations. No ongoing education. They rarely get outside, exercise, or have healthy interactions with other people.

> Employees jeopardize their job/career because they're unable to work without a phone in their hand (or at their desk). They don't work while at work and constantly have one eye on their phone for the latest blip, buzz, or bleep.

> Spouses and/or couples are detached from one another due to a digital divide. They spend more screen time with their device than quality time with each other. Too many are committing virtual infidelity and having online relationships with someone else.

> Kids are not fully developing because they're glued to their devices all day and night. They get little exercise, struggle academically, struggle emotionally, and/or are socially awkward.

> People struggle financially. They have hours to scroll on their phone but don't have time to complete a degree or certification to increase their salary. They're up-to-date on the latest celebrity happenings but don't have a budget or retirement account. Wow. Simply wow.

Additionally, consider how virtual reality is revealing some people's true character in times of crisis. Have you seen videos of people filming a horrific accident, violent fight, medical emergency, or other tragedy? These people record someone's plight rather than offer aid or even call 911 for help. It reveals their disgusting character and complete lack of values. How many of these videos are out there? I don't know because I don't go searching for them. I also don't revel in watching these events either – that would show a lack of tact, decorum, and respect for the victim on my part. I don't let virtual reality rule my life or dumb down my values. Others may not be so thoughtful.

Is it possible...?

> ➢ Are some people losing basic navigation skills because they can't get from Point A to Point B unless navigation software instructs them turn by turn?

> ➢ Are some people afraid to actually *talk* to others instead of hiding behind a text message?

> ➢ Are some people losing their attention span, imagination, and creativity such that they're 'bored' without a device in their hand?

> ➢ Have some people's memory and *critical thinking* skills been reduced to performing an online search for every answer in life?

> ➢ Are some people losing the skills to simply write with pen and paper?

Perhaps the verdict is still out; more data, studies, and research are required. Time will tell, but you get the idea. All in all, there are far too many potential negative consequences to list here. I'm sure you can think of (or have experienced) many more.

In summary, be mindful of how you use virtual reality and the content you consume. Remember, this technology is relatively new and society is still learning to adapt and adjust as we continue to integrate virtual reality with actual reality. We've had centuries to study and learn the behavioral and addictive effects of things such as nicotine, alcohol, opioids, and other substances. However, we've only had a few decades to do the same with digital technology. As we look across the digital landscape of the future, things such as virtual reality, quantum computing, artificial intelligence, digital currency, and technology of all sorts will be an integral part of our life. It's critical to balance those technologies in a healthy manner. Join me...be ahead of your time and lead the way for the generations that follow. Be a role model and walk the walk in actual reality. And if you're a parent, be sure to teach your kids to own their technology instead of it owning them. Give them guidance and rules for using their devices responsibly and enforce those rules. Parent.

In case you think I'm anti-technology, I'm not. As I said in the opening of this chapter, I believe we *should* use technology. I'm not a dinosaur and I'm not anti-technology. If you can believe it, I love technology. It *can* be used for good. In fact, it can be used for *much* good. I just hope everyone uses it wisely and safely. One reason I wrote this book was to shine a light into the dark side of virtual reality. This dark side of technology affects all of us in some fashion. Don't rely on artificial intelligence, but rather *actual* intelligence. Monitor your screen-time and use devices productively. Use devices as tools, not as replacements for real-life social interaction with other human beings. Use them for increased productivity and with kind intentions. Don't allow them to numb down and dumb down your life.

In closing, I encourage you to assess your own relationship with virtual reality. Your prosperity depends upon it. Remember to *use* virtual reality but *live* in actual reality. Don't be a digital zombie. Put your device down. Look people in the eye. Shake their hand. Smile. Hug your loved ones. Communicate with words, touch, and emotion, not ones and zeros. Grow socially, intellectually, spiritually, psychologically, and emotionally. Keep your head up and engage in *life*! This has worked extremely well for me and my family...I hope it does for you and yours, too.

CHAPTER 7

LIFE PRINCIPLES
(RULES OF THE ROAD)

As you've noticed, this book contains useful concepts, repeatable processes, and strategic approaches to success in many areas of life. However, it doesn't stop there. This playbook also offers some *rules of the road* to guide you along your journey. While driving to your destination, it's wise to follow the rules of the road: speed limits, traffic signals, stop/yield signs, rights of way, and others. Likewise, *universal life principles* are the *external* rules of the road that contribute to a prosperous life. The rules are timeless and universal. I've found them to be very useful. Follow the principles on your journey to prosperity.

The Merriam-Webster online dictionary tells us that a principle is "a comprehensive and fundamental law, doctrine, or assumption; a rule or code of conduct." As I reference the following life principles, I'm not very legalistic or scientific about the whole thing. However, just as two plus two always equals four, I've found these principles to be universally true for everyone, everywhere, all the time, whether they believe them or not. I've learned that adhering to these principles results in success and ignoring them leads to struggles in life. To each their own. Just know that if you touch a hot stove, you will get burned. Follow them for your own success; disregard them to your own detriment. I'm sure you've already discovered (or soon will) other life principles that are equally relevant and useful in life. Feel free to add these to your repertoire.

Hand-ups Help; Hand-outs Hurt!

Admittedly, this principle is not as intuitive as some others. If we were to climb the tallest Himalayan mountains, peer through the shrouded mist, and seek out a wise Zen Master wearing his hooded robe, he might say this principle is akin to, "Give a man a fish and he'll eat for a day; teach a man to fish and he'll eat for a lifetime." But you may ask, "How can I *hurt* someone by giving them a handout?" Let's find out.

Lending a hand *up* is fairly clear, which we'll get to shortly. However, allow me to clarify a hand *out*. First of all, *giving* is not a handout. Giving is part of generosity. I *give* often. This includes gifts for holidays, birthdays, graduations, weddings, charities, and many times 'just because'. However, I don't believe in giving hand-*outs*. As the term describes, you can envision someone with their hand out, in dependent expectation or entitlement. I find handouts disrespectful, demeaning, and even hurtful to both the giver *and* the recipient. What do I mean?

Cue the old movie scene with a disheveled beggar on a dreary cobblestone street. Along comes the rich guy in suit and top-hat who drops a few gold coins in the beggar's open hand. How condescending. A momentary feel-good, look-at-me handout from the rich guy only perpetuates the beggar's condition. The beggar may eat for a day or two, but then what? He's back to begging and dependence on the metaphorical aristocracy; a nearly slave-like relationship, holding the beggar subservient, reliant, and beholden to the almighty giver of coins. Thus, the poor beggar is robbed of his dignity and independence. Sadly, this principle is not only on display in movies.

There are people and entire organizations who, bless their hearts, attempt to feed the hungry. I applaud their intent, but their heart is bigger than their head. They even boast about growing bigger to "help even more people"; they go from feeding 10K people from a corner store to building a food warehouse to feed 100K people. *Pssst…*they're going the wrong way! To truly solve hunger, you must feed *fewer* people each year. The goal is to make people independent so they can sufficiently feed themselves. Bailing out the leaky boat is good, but fixing the hole is best! Fix the *root* issue; teach people job skills, money management, and life skills that lead to independence. Does that mean we shouldn't feed hungry people who are temporarily down on their luck? Of course not. But we should do so in a respectful and caring way that sets them up for long-term independence. Yes, this takes a bit more time and effort but it's worth it. The lesson is crystal clear — handouts are demeaning, ineffective, and perpetuate dependency. So, if that describes hurtful hand-*outs*, let's look at the gold star winner…that is, helpful hand *ups*.

One of the most compassionate and respectful things you can do for another human being is to lend them a hand *up* when they've stumbled in life. We've all been there before, and will probably be there again at some point. It's simple – when someone falls, lend a hand to lift them up. But don't carry them around like a sack of potatoes for the rest of their life. Don't make them dependent on you (or anyone else for that matter).

A hand up, by definition, should be temporary in nature. Giving someone hot meals after their home was destroyed by a tornado makes you generous. However, providing them hot meals for years makes you their almighty provider and makes them your dependent.

A hand up should also improve the person's position in some way. Paying someone's rent after they're laid off will leave them in the same position next month. However, teaching them to budget and build an emergency fund will cover future layoffs for the rest of their life.

A word of caution here – unfortunately, some people don't want a hand up because that requires them to take ownership of their own situation. It requires responsibility and work on their part. No, some people would rather take as many handouts as possible and then complain when they stop. In their mind, it's easier to blame someone or something else for their circumstances: politicians, society, racism, sexism, the rich, the neighbors, the cat, the dog, or who knows what else. Let's look at a few hypothetical examples of hand-ups versus hand-outs. See if you recognize any…

It Starts at Home

Hand-out. A parent allows their adult child to sit at home, not pay any bills, and play video games all day long. The child remains undeveloped, lazy, immature, and dependent on mom/dad's charity.

Hand-up. A parent teaches their child how to land a job, become financially stable, and transition to a home of their own. The child matures into a hard-working, responsible, and independent young adult – confident and dignified.

Student Loan Debt

Hand-out. Politicians want to take money from tax payers who did *not* borrow money and give it to tax payers who *did*. This encourages others to borrow even *more*, hoping their loans will be paid off too. It unfairly shifts the debt burden from borrower to taxpayer and rewards irresponsibility. It also raises expectations for *more* handouts and *additional* debt to be paid off (why not pay off mortgages, vehicle loans, medical debt, credit cards, etc). It's a self-perpetuating cycle of stupidity.

Hand-up. Politicians and education officials incorporate classes on basic financial literacy in high school; there's an entire chapter on money management in this book. The politicians shift the loan risk from taxpayers to lending institutions and borrowers, thus placing debt ownership where it belongs. Better yet, politicians and education officials educate parents and students on how to attend college debt-free; there are at least 8 ways to do so listed in chapter 2. That puts student loan debt to rest, once and for all.

Inheritance Waiters

Hand-out. My wife and I don't want our kids to become waiters; that is, sitting around *waiting* for an inheritance with their hands out in expectation. It's kind of like vultures waiting for a creature to die so they can eat it. Sadly, some people wait around, *expecting* an inheritance, as if they're somehow entitled. Relying on an inheritance to live is a total disgrace. These waiters don't work hard or manage their own finances. They don't visit or spend time with their parents while they're alive. They don't lift a finger to help them in old age or when they require long-term care. If they do receive an inheritance, it's usually gone in no time and they're right back where they started from.

Hand-up. Some kids don't expect any inheritance, but appreciate and honor it if there is one. Either way, they spend time with their parents while they're alive. They help provide long-term care for their parents and look out for *their parents'* best interest. This includes their parents' money being spent on their parents' care while they're alive and ensuring a proper burial when they pass. If there happens to be any money left over, any heirs are grateful and honor the inheritance by stewarding it wisely. Since they're already educated, hard-working, and financially secure, any inheritance would simply be icing on the cake.

Yes, even some of our fearless "leaders" (ahem, politicians) don't understand the principle of helpful hand-ups over hurtful hand-outs. If you reflect on some of the government proposals and policies over the decades, it should be pretty obvious this principle is foreign to many officials.

As mentioned earlier, maybe it's handing out tax payer money for student loan debt instead of borrowers working to pay it back. Promise and pander; pander and promise.

Maybe it's some condescending suggestion for handing out 'universal basic income' (more taxpayer money). Yes, keep the peasants beholden to the almighty giver of paltry handouts; rob them of the dignity and independence they're capable of achieving on their own. If the peasants grow dependent enough, they'll worship the almighty politicians with their vote.

Perhaps it's a disrespectful funding program aimed at certain racial or ethnic groups. That's right, they're too stupid or lazy to succeed on their own. How patronizing and belittling.

I guess I think too highly of people to do such a thing. I respect people too much. But hey, you're paying for it with your hard-earned tax dollars. Something to keep in mind the next time you vote. Anyway, I'm confident that you can apply this principle to many areas of your own personal life.

As you can see, offering a hand-up takes a bit more time and effort than simply throwing money at the problem. Hand-ups are more heart-felt, longer lasting, and often come in the form of mentoring, teaching, guiding, coaching, and instructing. Oh, and the recipient is held accountable for his/her participation. However, the trade-off is worth it because the recipient is left more self-sufficient and earns the dignity of independence. Handouts are short-lived, disrespectful, merely transactional, and mostly impersonal.

So, remember, people will stumble at times. Let's not disrespect them or cause further harm with a condescending and hurtful hand-*out*. Go ahead, reach down and lend a truly caring and helpful hand-*up*. I can honestly say this principle has never failed me once…ever.

Order > Chaos

Order over chaos. A place for everything and everything in its place. Let's face it, order saves time, saves money, reduces mistakes, and cuts unnecessary duplication. Living in chaos does just the opposite. *Order* is you happening to your environment. *Chaos* is your environment happening to you. With order, you decide where things go, when things happen, and how things happen. When you succumb to chaos, you're more reactive than proactive. Think about how this applies to your life…

Diet

If your diet is **chaotic**, it's likely that you eat meal-to-meal, throwing together whatever happens to be convenient at the time. When you're hungry and pressed for time, what happens? You get *hangry* (hungry-angry)! When you're hangry, you reach for the quickest thing to eat, which is usually not the healthiest (or cheapest). That's when you gorge on fast food or dive into the workplace vending machines because you're starving. Your diet is heavy in junk food. You go grocery shopping without a list – you shop willy-nilly, waste time, and buy mostly unhealthy processed foods. Much of your food spoils, expires, and/or goes to waste due to poor planning. Over time, you become unhealthy, overweight, and waste lots of money.

An **orderly** diet consists of planned meals. You may even meal prep for the week – chicken or fish, fruits and vegetables, a healthy starch, and portioned meals. On average, home-cooked meals are healthier and cheaper than fast food, vending machines, and other highly processed junk food. Also, when you drive around town, fight through traffic, and wait in fast food lines, eating out takes more time. It's far simpler to reheat your healthy pre-made meals at home. You use a list for grocery shopping – you stick to the list and buy mostly healthy foods. You save time and waste very little food. You also don't go shopping when you're hangry because you'll buy much more than you should. Over time, you grow fit, lean, and healthy – and save money! Order or chaos.

Money

Money and **chaos** are a bad mix. Think about the money you work so hard to earn each day. I mean seriously, most people work *hard* for their money. Then what happens? They chaotically throw their hard-earned money out the window. It sifts through their fingers like sand. No budget. No plan. No order. The money comes in, the money goes out. Where did it go? Who knows. All of that hard work and little or nothing to show for it. You live paycheck to paycheck and broke. A rat in the wheel. Sadly, you don't even know where your money goes every month.

Contrast money chaos with **orderly** budgeting. As covered in chapter 4, having a written budget is one of the most important wealth building principles. A budget is order for your money. Simple and organized. Powerful. Order eliminates debt and builds an emergency fund. Order prioritizes life insurance over drinks at happy hour. It prioritizes financial independence over new purses or more fishing gear. You live debt free and stress free! You eventually become a millionaire. Order builds generational wealth. Order or chaos.

Career

A **chaotic** career involves job-hopping and going sideways. You run, run, run and get nowhere fast; you're the rat in the wheel. You settle for whatever job conveniently falls in your lap. Your resume has no recent upgrades (certifications, education, etc). Your pay is usually minimal and you're afraid to ask for a raise. Companies are hesitant to hire you.

An **orderly** career involves a clear and intentional path. It entails relevant and ongoing education, training, and experience. You climb the corporate ladder. Entrepreneurs build a profitable business model and scale at a sustainable pace. An orderly career takes your income higher and higher each year. Companies are petrified to lose you and/or begging to hire you! Order or chaos.

Life

A **chaotic** life is unproductive, reactive, and unrewarding. You don't happen to things; things happen to you. You're late to almost everything. You chase your own tail. A life of chaos is a game of whack-a-mole. You struggle. You spend your time doing what you *have* to do, instead of what you *want* to do. Your kids have no structure in their life and often end up going astray. A chaotic life is a messy one.

An **orderly** life is productive, proactive, and rewarding. You make things happen and have plenty of time to do what you *want* to do. You dictate your schedule, not vice versa. You get to travel, dine out, have fun, and enjoy life. You parent your kids proactively and guide them on a path to prosperity. An orderly life is a wonderful one! Order or chaos.

Those are just a few small examples of how order is greater than chaos (order>chaos). I'm sure you can think of many other ways in which chaos has cost you time, energy, money, or even your health! Here are a few tips to live an orderly life…

- ✓ Use a list for shopping and running errands; it saves time and money.
- ✓ Put things back where you found them; you'll find them when you need them.
- ✓ Maintain a calendar of your schedule; you'll be punctual and avoid scheduling conflicts.
- ✓ Perform regular home & auto maintenance; it saves time and money on large repairs.
- ✓ Where possible, put your bills on auto-pay; avoid late fees and ruining your credit score.
- ✓ Get regular health/dental check-ups; you'll be healthier and minimize costly medical bills.
- ✓ Have an orderly file plan; keep key documents safe, organized, and accessible.
- ✓ You can think of many others; save time and money; do less work and have more fun.

Remember, the principle of order over chaos applies to all of us. You'll also note that it works, whether you believe it or not. It's a choice, so be *intentional*; choose a life of order, not one of chaos.

Different Input = Different Output

Huh? Is this some complex engineering formula? Nope. If we were to consult our wise Zen Master again, he may re-state this principle as…

"If you want different results, you must do things differently." Or perhaps…

"If you keep doing what you're doing, you'll keep getting what you're getting."

Quite right. I guess that's why he's the Zen Master. Of course, this principle applies to all areas of your life. And again, whether you believe it or not.

Is there one single area of your life that you'd like to improve? A stronger relationship? More money? Better health? How about a career that you love? Whatever it is, ask yourself what you can do *differently* to effect a positive change. If you're sick and tired of being broke…change! If you're unhappy with your weight…change! The person best suited to help you make a change can be found in your mirror.

When I stopped spending like a fool in my youth and started to invest wisely, I actually started building wealth. When I started working out and exercising at a young age, I saw positive results in my strength, stamina, and overall fitness. These are just two simple examples of a positive change by doing something different. It's amazing how that works.

I believe this is possibly the simplest of all principles and perhaps the most difficult to follow. Why? Because it takes *self-discipline*. After all, if you can get the person in the mirror to change, there are no limits to what you can achieve. That's what it takes – *change*. Do. Something. Different. How many people do you know complain about their finances and do nothing about it? How many people *wish* they could lose a few pounds but don't lift a finger to exercise? The list is endless.

In fact, we could also apply this principle to the aforementioned organization trying to solve hunger. By doing something *different* (solving the *root* cause), the organization stands a much greater chance of eradicating hunger. Instead of just handing out food, they can also teach job skills and money management. The hungry people will gradually become independent and able to feed themselves (and others). They'll stand tall and proud, charting their own course in life. Reframe your thinking to change the status quo…solve hunger permanently!

Following this principle first requires you to be self-aware and intentional. It's very easy to keep doing what you're doing and remain in a rut. That's how the rat in the wheel goes through life. Instead of jumping off the wheel, he just keeps doing what he's doing and thus, he keeps going where he's going…nowhere! Imagine that. So, wake up and break free from your rut. Then, set about doing something different. That's not always easy, so here are a few tips…

> ➤ Start small. By taking small steps, change may not feel so overwhelming. Instead of trying to lose 30 pounds, first lose 10 pounds. Instead of trying to become a multi-millionaire, first follow a budget and apply the principles in chapter 4.

> ➤ Have a clear vision of your desired results. Start with the end in mind. Picture that loving spouse and strong marriage. Envision

a rewarding career doing XYZ instead of hopping from one dead-end job to another.

➢ Write down your plan. The power of the pen cannot be overstated. Be specific about what behavior or actions you will change. For example, you may wake up one hour early three days a week and do a workout or ~~run~~ walk 2 miles (start small). You may work to become 100% debt free within one year. It doesn't matter what you do, but be intentional about it. Have a written plan. Don't need one…? *How's that working out?*

So, if you want to change a part of your life for the better, do something *different*. Make a change for the better. Different input = different output. And by the way, if something is working, leave it alone. If it ain't broke, don't fix it!

Control the Controllables

"God, grant me the serenity to accept the things I cannot change, the courage to change the things I can, and the wisdom to know the difference." – The Serenity Prayer

Amen. To me, this principle is one of efficiency. Spending time and energy on things you can't control is wasteful, frustrating, and inefficient! (Not a good combination.) Every minute wasted on an uncontrollable takes away a valuable minute from one that's controllable. Let this wisdom guide you towards a better life.

Health Issues

It's no secret that my wife was hit with severe health issues in our peak earning years. That's only part of the story. What matters significantly is what we *did* and *didn't* do along the way. In short, we controlled the things we could control and let go of the things we couldn't. What do I mean? Well, here are some things we could (and did) control…

➢ We ensured my wife was getting the best health care possible. This remained priority #1 at all times and still does to this day. We proactively worked with every doctor and followed their advice to the letter. We still do.

➤ We moved from Maryland to Florida in order to be closer to family and within driving distance of a military veteran's hospital.

➤ We started saving every spare penny we could, anticipating loss of income. We rented a house not based upon how fancy it was but rather how affordable it was. This was survival mode, not play time.

➤ We kept our kids informed and their lives on track (schoolwork, diet, exercise, hobbies, etc).

➤ We kept our heads up and eyes forward. We scratched, clawed, hustled, and got it done.

Likewise, there were things we could *not* control; therefore, we didn't waste precious time, money, or energy trying to do so. Here are some things we could **not** control…

➤ The "what if" scenarios of my wife's health. We took one day at a time. Wringing our hands and losing sleep over possible outcomes served no purpose and would only cause unnecessary worry.

➤ Whether or not my wife would get her job back and resume her career. That would be determined at some future time and based on her health. First things, first.

➤ She was unable to apply for life insurance due to her health issues. Lesson learned – have it in place *before* you become uninsurable. We factored her limited life insurance and disability benefits into our overall financial picture and planned accordingly.

➤ Answering the "why us" question. Everyone goes through their own tough times. Sitting around fretting and whining never helped anyone. We didn't control why she had health issues but we could control how we responded.

For us, controlling what we could from day to day helped us move forward and still does today. It helped us remain focused on our priorities and kept our family on track. It kept us financially sound and allowed us to provide the best care possible for my wife. We could've let things spiral out of control and sit around the house while things collapsed down around us. Not happening. Take control of what you can and let the other stuff go!

Pandemics

I'm sure most of us remember the COVID-19 pandemic. This principle could not have been any more pertinent during those times. Sadly, millions of people lost their lives. At the time, there were many unknowns and therefore uncontrollable factors that led to sickness and even death. As the healthcare professionals evolved practices such as social distancing, face masks, and vaccines, things slowly began to get better. Herd immunity began to progress.

However, as you may have noticed, there were many people losing their minds over "what if" scenarios and misleading or fake information. Losing their minds over uncontrollable events. Meanwhile, the government gave out trillions of dollars in stimulus money. How much of that money was spent on frivolous things instead of paying down debt or saving for uncertain times? Completely controllable. Many people used the money for necessities such as rent and food while others went on a spending spree as if they'd won the lottery. Some used the pandemic as an excuse to sit on the couch and play video games.

Conversely, there were many others who stepped on the gas! They took on jobs that nobody else wanted and/or worked tons of overtime, raking in more money than they ever have in their life. Many accepted remote, work from home jobs.

While student loan payments were on hold, some seized the moment and paid down as much debt as possible, using "found" stimulus money to pay off their debts in full – boom!

Some businesses shuttered up and collapsed. Others pivoted to home delivery, drive-up service, outdoor dining, ghost kitchens, social distancing, and many other practices to accelerate their business – boom!

The pandemic taught us many lessons about what we control and what we don't. In hindsight, I remember those who got sick or lost their lives and those who were devastated by truly uncontrollable circumstances. But I've also learned many lessons about the difference between shrinking back in fear and allowing *life to happen to me* or leaning in, taking the reins, seizing opportunities, and controlling whatever I can so that *I happen to life.*

Parenting

In addition to certain elements of a pandemic, there are other things we control in life. As a parent, I was in tune with school policies and rules when my kids were still in school. I can't tell you how much drama there was over cell phone usage in class. Parent-teacher meetings. Local news stories. School robo-calls and voicemails. Messages from principals to parents. Unreal. My wife and I, in our usual fashion, kept it simple. We ignored it all. Why? Because our kids simply did not bring phones to school, period. We didn't wait for the school to enact a policy; we simply took *control* and parented our kids by setting our own policy. Our kids did not bring phones to school, problem solved. Again, control the controllables.

Government

Are you one of those people waiting on Washington D.C. to solve your problems? Just like you shouldn't wait for school administrators to solve your problems, nor should you wait on politicians. Don't beg for student loan "forgiveness"; take *control* and pay off your loans. Don't scrape by waiting for a minimum wage increase; follow the career advice in chapter 3 and *triple* your income! Don't hope and pray you'll retire on social insecurity; follow wealth building principles in chapter 4 and retire a multi-millionaire! Do you complain about the national debt and deficit? How does *your* budget and *your* net worth look? Grab the bull by the horns and control the controllables – for *your* benefit and *your* prosperity.

In short, there are countless other situations that are within your control. By taking ownership of your life and controlling what you can, you can live life on your terms. One thing to remember about this principle is that it doesn't guarantee success; it only stacks the odds in your favor. You can follow a doctor's advice, but cancer can still kill. You can wear a seatbelt, but still die in a car wreck. But I'd argue every single time that you can and *should* control what you can and shrug off the rest. Remember, the principle is that you control the controllables; it's not that controlling guarantees success. By the way...*you* control whether you follow the principles in this book or not.

Relativity

"It's all relative", as they say. So true in so many ways. The better we understand this principle, the better our lives will be. Think about how many people are unhappy with a *relative* aspect of their life. I mean some people are down-right depressed or obsessed over some things. Their obsession can rule their life. Think I'm kidding? Exaggerating? How about an example.

Allow me to focus on body weight as one example of many. There are people who are overweight and others who are underweight. If they're not careful and intentional, some of those people may grow to view their weight out of proportion with reality. In extreme cases, this can lead to body dysmorphia that causes shame, anxiety, and an unhealthy fixation that may require professional help. This can be true even when their weight is actually within normal limits and *healthy*! There are people who are nearly skin and bones that view themselves as fat. Only a qualified medical professional can determine if your body weight is normal and healthy. However, let's stick to the concept of relativity. I'm sure it's understandable for most people to want to add or lose a few pounds from time to time. The key is to keep things in perspective. For example, health professionals provide us with body weight guidelines and advice. If you're within those guidelines, then don't obsess. News flash – there will always be someone lighter (skinnier) than you and someone heavier (bigger) than you. Compare yourself only to the advice of your doctor, not to who you see on TV or unsocial media. The important thing about your weight is *health* (heart, back, joints, cardio, blood pressure, etc) and not so much *vanity*. So, weight is just one small example that highlights the power of relativity. Let's broaden this principle up a bit. Here are a few questions to ponder. Are you…

- Tall or short?
- Black or white?
- Rich or poor?
- Smart or dumb?
- Fast or slow?
- Strong or weak?
- Pretty or ugly?

So, what about it, how did you answer? The real answer is neither (and both) – more than one thing can be true at the same time. It's all *relative*! Let's estimate the world population at *8 billion*, give or take. Line everyone up and ask the same questions – you'll discover the same thing. The answer is relative. Someone is tall (or short) when compared to another. Someone is black or white when compared to another. Oh, by the way, I've never seen a literally 'black' or 'white' person in my life. Some people are darker or lighter than others, and everything in between, but not pure black or white. Someone is rich (or poor) when compared to another. So on and so on. You get the point and I'm sure you can formulate many other similar comparisons. As you can see, this principle is universally true, period. These aspects, and many others, of your life are all relative. So, how do we leverage this principle? How does this help us live a more prosperous life?

The point is to keep things in perspective and don't dwell on the uncontrollables (remember those?). Unfortunately for them, too many people put themselves (and others) incorrectly in a *box* instead of correctly on a sliding (relative) *scale*. I believe they do this mostly subconsciously, out of habit, ignorance, or even because of peer pressure. You'll be much happier and can focus your energy more productively in life by viewing things as relative. Since comparison is the thief of joy, I've learned to compare myself only to myself. I couldn't care less what 'the Joneses' or anyone else is doing.

Some people put absolute labels on themselves and it becomes, at least partially, their identity. The labels I speak of are absolute as opposed to relative. It could be race, health, net worth, or many other things. They're black or white. They're healthy or unhealthy. They're rich or poor. In recent years, I even hear people whining about "privilege". They whine about the concept of privilege (whatever that means) as if it's something you either have or you don't. News flash – welcome to life! Depending on your perspective, *everyone* in the world is privileged in some way and to some degree – it's all **relative**. Here's an example…

A baby born on a dirt floor in a shack in the back woods of a country town in the USA is more *privileged* than a baby born in some communist country prison camp after its mother was raped by a guard.

Heck, now that I think about it, I guess I'm also affected. I'm less privileged than thousands of other men who are taller, faster, and stronger than me; which is why I never succeeded in the Olympics or professional sports. I'm also not privileged to be born a debonair movie actor or male model. I wasn't privileged to have raw intelligence with an IQ off the charts. I wasn't privileged to be born into a billionaire family (or even a millionaire family). I wasn't privileged to have healthy eyesight, which prohibited me from becoming a military pilot. Hmm. I guess life's unfair and someone else is to blame. Not!

Get the point? Don't place yourself (or others) in a self-imposed box. Another example relates to money…

Do you know people who are jealous of millionaires? They say things like, "Nobody needs that much money." But *relative* to billionaires, the millionaire actually has very little. (1 billion = 1,000 million!) And if we took away their millions, those same jealous people would whine because others have *half* a million. And if we took that away…and so on. The jealousy exists because they don't understand the concept of relativity. The terms rich and poor are relative. Who cares how much money other people have? How is that affecting you? Why does it seem certain politicians, socialists, and other hypocrites only criticize and attack people who are doing *better* than themselves? Hmm. Jealousy? Hate? Hypocrisy? How about low relational or intellectual health (chapter 5)? As for me, I congratulate success! Oh, wait, my wife can also tell you about privilege…

She immigrated to the U.S. as a teenager with nothing and unable to speak English. Today, she's an awesome mother of two successful adult kids, a college graduate, a proud military veteran, a published poet, financially successful, and my wonderful wife. She wasn't privileged to have been born in the U.S. She wasn't privileged to have been a native English speaker. She wasn't privileged to…get the point? (Just don't tell her that.) My wife simply gets it done! Guess what? So can *you*…just don't place yourself in a box.

As you can see, the principle of relativity is important. It plays hand-in-hand with the value of *contentment* (chapter 8). It's funny how some people can be content *until* they discover that someone else has more. Remember, you have much, much more than many people in this world.

174

Yes, you.

It's also critical to the power of *individualism* (chapter 9). No matter your race, gender, age, ethnicity, or other demographic, there's always someone else with more or less. Remember, out of about 8 billion people on the planet, we're all (thankfully) different!

Always strive to be better, but love who you are. Respect others. Remember, you're rich *and* poor, tall *and* short, fast *and* slow. And neither. When compared to others, it's all relative. Start from where you are and walk your own walk. Don't worry about your neighbors, co-workers, classmates, the Joneses, athletes, celebrities, so-called influencers or anyone else – they're all irrelevant. Be careful who you idolize and be wary of a public facade. Many of the Joneses are secretly unhappy, going broke, and uneducated. The news will often reveal their legal troubles, broken families, and poor value systems. There's not a single person in this world that I'd rather be…not for a second. I hope you believe the same for yourself!

And besides…it's all relative, right?

Balance

This is one of my favorite life principles. In some ways, balance pairs well with relativity; together, they're like yin and yang. As such, I've taught and continue to remind my children that *balance* is important in life. As I mentioned earlier, when I asked my daughter if she could ask only *one* single question about life, what did she ask? She wanted to know how to find a work-life balance with education and career. Very thoughtful. However, the principle of balance applies not only to work-life, but many other key areas of life. Therefore, I was darn sure to incorporate extra advice on balance here in *The Torch of Life*…it's *that* important! I believe the principle of balance is best described through example. Since I already discussed work-life balance in chapter 3 (career tip 1), let's look at two others…

Appearance

One Extreme: Obsessing over every blemish, wrinkle, or imperfection. Spending *hours* in the mirror. Bordering on body dysmorphia. Not conducive to relationships. Ironically, a vain or narcissistic person is rarely considered attractive by others.

The Other Extreme: Lack of hygiene. Dirty, nasty, and smelly. Disheveled clothing and unkempt hair. Unshaven. Bordering on a caveman /cavewoman. Not conducive to relationships or a good impression at work.

Balance: Healthy hygiene. Wearing clothes that are clean and well pressed. Showered and clean shaven. Dressing and grooming appropriate to the occasion. Taking pride in your appearance, but not defining yourself by it.

Diet

One Extreme: Eating donuts for breakfast, lunch, and dinner. Drinking bottles of sugary soda daily. Consuming 2-3 times (or more) the calories of a healthy diet. Eating mostly processed foods that are high in salt, sugar, unhealthy fats. Gluttony.

The Other Extreme: Eating lettuce for breakfast, lunch, and dinner. Missing out on healthy fats and essential nutrients, vitamins, minerals, etc. Neglecting one or more food groups entirely. Consuming fewer total calories than recommended in a healthy diet. Suffering from anorexia or bulimia.

Balance: Eating a healthy and balanced diet. Eating a diet relatively proportionate among the five food groups. Limiting salt, sugar, unhealthy fats, and processed foods to a reasonable and moderate amount. Following a professional's advice to suit your individual dietary and medical needs.

So, those are yet two more examples of how balance can improve your life. Recall, I *also* emphasized the value of balance with money in chapter 4. So, whether it's work-life, education, career, appearance, diet, money, or any other area of life, *balance* is usually key. Pause. Take a moment to reflect on *other* areas of your life where balance is important. Taking anything to the extreme is normally a bad idea. For many people, balance does not come easily; you must work to build bigger balance biceps.

A word of wisdom here. Balance rarely happens in perfect equilibrium every hour of every day. There will be times when you're *temporarily* out of balance in life. You won't work precisely 8 hours every day. You won't always eat perfectly balanced meals. There may be moments when your appearance is slightly out of balance. Your spending, saving, and investing tempo will ebb and flow over the years. However…strive to maintain balance over the long run. On average, over time. Remember to practice balance in life; it contributes greatly to prosperity!

The Cost of Procrastination

This principle is perhaps the shortest & sweetest of them all, but very powerful. If left unchecked, procrastination will eat your life away! This doesn't mean you should never rest (remember balance). However, if something *should* be done, then do it sooner rather than later.

Think back to the ant and the grasshopper in chapter 4. The grasshopper procrastinated preparing for winter while the ant got it done! When winter struck, the ant was able to enjoy the fruits of his labor while the lazy grasshopper was hungry and cold. What if the ant and grasshopper were investing for retirement? For illustration purposes, let's assume they each invest $300/month and achieve a 10% average annual return. Here, the ant starts early whereas the grasshopper *procrastinates…*

Ant:

- Starts investing at **age 21** & stops at age 31 (**10 years**)
- **Total invested $36,000**
- Has about **$2.2M at age 67**

Grasshopper:

- Procrastinates investing until **age 31** & continues until age 67 (**36 years**)
- **Total invested $129,600**
- Has about **$1.3M at age 67**

So, the industrious ant started investing at age 21, whereas the lazy grasshopper procrastinated until age 31 to start. The result of the grasshopper's late start? He invested $93,600 *more* than the ant, yet he ended up with about $900K *less* than the ant! That's the power of compound interest over time. The grasshopper's *procrastination* cost him nearly $1M! Be the ant, not the grasshopper. By the way, the same math works at any age; the longer you procrastinate, the more it will cost you. (Imagine if you invest *nothing*!)

Procrastination also costs you dearly in other areas of life. Chapter 2 taught us the value of formal education. The salary difference between a doctoral degree and a high school diploma can be over **$2M** in lifetime earnings! What are you waiting for?!

Hard work now = less work later (not procrastinating). By investing *now*, as the ant did, you work less later in life. Also, think about things like preventive maintenance. By performing routine maintenance *now* on your home and auto, you'll save lots of work, time, and money on major repairs down the road. My mother used to say, "An ounce of prevention is worth a pound of cure." That means a small amount of work now saves much more work and money later.

Less work now = more work later (procrastinating). Procrastinating on home and auto maintenance now will cost you more later. Try not changing the oil in your car for a few years. Try never changing your brake pads. No, seriously, don't…but I think you get the picture. Likewise, prolonging leaky roof repairs on your home can cost *triple* to repair water-damaged walls and floors later on. This holds true in many other areas as well.

Consider preventive healthcare. Have you ever had a small cavity? What if you let it fester for a few years? I'm sure a filling is cheaper than a root canal, not to mention less painful! By dragging your butt and doing less work now, you only cause yourself *more* work (and money) later. To put it succinctly…

Hard work now = less work later
Less work now = more work later

The next time you find yourself procrastinating, stop and calculate the cost. Remember, the early bird gets the worm!

Where You Focus, You Prosper

By now, this should be the most *obvious* principle. However obvious, this one often goes right over many people's heads! I don't know why.

So far, you've read how this principle has worked very successfully in my own life....

- ❖ I've prospered in life thanks to a *focus* on my 3-part personal mission statement (chapter 1).
- ❖ My kids succeeded in school by *focusing* on learning how to learn (chapter 2).
- ❖ My wife and I have grown our careers by *focusing* on productivity, higher education, progressive certifications, and ongoing OJT (chapter 3).
- ❖ We build generational wealth by *focusing* on the mindset, principles, and behaviors (chapter 4).
- ❖ My wife achieves her weight goals by *focusing* on her caloric intake (chapter 5).

Is this all happenstance, coincidence, or luck? Perhaps, but I don't think so. I believe it's the result of a laser focus. In fact, what *else* do you remember reading about the above examples? Answer…they were *written* down in some fashion…

- ❖ My mission statement was *written*; in fact, I've even etched it onto an acrylic plaque.
- ❖ My kids *wrote* down their grades in a notebook while in high school.
- ❖ My wife and I *wrote* job credentials on our respective resumes (degrees, certifications, etc).
- ❖ My wife and I follow a *written* monthly budget by using a spreadsheet.
- ❖ My wife *writes* her caloric intake into an app.

The power of the pen. (A pen can mean any equivalent method of writing things down.) Is it *necessary* to write things down? No, not at all. However, I've found it very helpful. Whether you write things down or not, the point of this principle is the power of focus. The act of writing simply puts an exclamation point on your focus – it shows you mean business! After all, if you can't even spend a few minutes writing a monthly budget, how can you expect to become a millionaire?! Good grief.

Remember, this principle can be applied to any aspect of life. This includes marriage, family, career, education, finances, health, and a whole lot more. In fact, as I age and my life winds down, I slowly shift my focus to include death, spirituality, and beyond. The options are limitless and the choice is yours.

Go ahead, assess yourself. Would you like to prosper at something specific? If so, how seriously are you focused on that area? If you can't take the time to write down your goal(s), I'd question your level of commitment.

Some people focus on who's dating who. Some focus on how much beer they'll drink this weekend. Others focus on the latest celebrity trends or gossip. I'd encourage you to set your sights a little higher. In fact, a lot higher. Your focus should be part of who you are and what you value. It shouldn't be a passing fad or a one-and-done, but rather a lifelong endeavor. *Where you focus, you prosper.* The only question left is…where's *your* focus?

In conclusion, these eight universal life principles are external rules of the road. I've found they apply to everyone, everywhere, all the time. Use them to your advantage. Use them in your pursuit of generational prosperity.

CHAPTER 8

PERSONAL VALUES (WHO ARE YOU?)

In addition to following life principles (external rules of the road), you should also adopt a system of personal values that help define who you are. Your *personal values* are the *internal* beliefs that shape your character and guide your actions. As such, I've found that certain values lead to prosperity more so than others. Values matter. A lot. These values are by no means all encompassing, but rather a 'starter set', if you will. As you move through life, you'll discover others and continue to build upon your own personal value system. Whereas you *follow* life's principles, you should *live* your values.

If I could pass along only *one* single thing to my kids when I die, it would not be money, jewels, autos, or real estate – it would be values!

Know what you stand for. Values help shape your character, morals, and ultimately, who you are as a person. The beauty is that we all get to choose our own personal values. Our choice in values, by the way, also includes the resulting consequences – it's a package deal. In other words, be very careful and intentional about what you stand for and the behaviors you exhibit. Do you display envy, dishonesty, gluttony, arrogance, selfishness, laziness, hatred, or lack of self-discipline? If so, you're on the wrong path. Negativity such as this rarely leads to anything good…yet the world is full of it. I find that ironically puzzling.

As you read, use this as an opportunity for self-reflection. Create a list of your own values. Be sure to list your *actual* values (that you exhibit) and not values that you *wish* you lived by. Are you happy with your list? I hope so, because your list is a reflection of you. If you're not happy with yourself, then change. Realize that you can change your value system at *any time* in order to become a better person.

Below, I share some of my own personal values – not only general definitions but also what they mean to me. I include similar values below each heading (in parenthesis) that I feel are closely related in some way. Remember, this is not an exercise in splitting hairs over word definitions, but rather a much bigger goal of building (and living by) a strong and virtuous value system. Feel free to associate with whatever word(s) you desire; after all, you get to define and live by your own personal values. I just share what works for me. I strive to be extremely open and accepting of people and their value systems. Live and let live. I hope you're just as accepting as I am and do not judge my values too harshly. After all, this is part of who I am and what I stand for. These values form the bedrock of my success. I would be remiss to write a playbook for generational prosperity and not include such a value system.

Also, nothing in my value system results in any negative effects on anyone else. To the contrary, I continually help others, but only if they want to be helped. Some people enjoy being stuck and don't want to change. Fair enough. You can lead the horse to water, but you can't make it drink. But if you choose to adopt any part of this system, I hope it works even better for you! Either way, take it or leave it – you won't hurt my feelings. Just know that it works.

The last thing I'll mention is that nobody is perfect. Don't be fooled into thinking you (or anyone) will adhere to some flawless set of values or be perfect in any way. Not happening. We can spend our lives debating the nuanced meanings of every value and squabble over the definition of every word. I call that stepping over dollars to pick up pennies – quite silly, actually. My values are neither legalistic nor absolute; yours aren't either, whether you admit it or not. Never say never, there are always exceptions. I wasn't born with my values and neither were you born with yours. People hone their values over time and continue to do so as they learn, mature, and grow. That said, just as you should be a lifelong learner and you should always grow your wealth, so too should you *always* strive to adhere to (and refine) your value system. If you should falter, dust yourself off and get back in the saddle. Without further ado…

Thoughtfulness

(I also include intentional, analytical, logical, reflective, intellectual, objective, and reasoned.)

Thoughtfulness is versatile and it informs *intentionality*, which I devoted an entire chapter to earlier (chapter 1). In fact, there I shared the one question my son asked me about life and my response to him. It was mostly centered around finding fulfillment, purpose, and meaning in life. I put much *thought* into my personal mission in life. I view thoughtfulness as broader and more reflective, whereas intentionality is focused and more action-oriented. My thoughts drive my intentions. When intentionality is broadened up to thoughtfulness, you reflect on the very essence of who you are and how you treat others; your personal character and values. After all, if you're going to stand for something, at least understand *why*; I call that critical thinking (remember that?).

Thoughtfulness should cause you to choose your values (and live life) based upon facts, data, evidence, accuracy, context, logic, reasoning, and reality. In other words, why would you value laziness, theft, unfairness, greed, or any such other negative trait? Oddly, some people do. I don't believe most people *intentionally* do so. I think they do so *unintentionally* because they're not being very *thoughtful*. I'm convinced that thoughtfulness is very rare today. Many people simply don't think; at least not as often as they should. Perhaps they're too concerned with how someone *else* is living. Or maybe they're simply too preoccupied with their phones.

This value should serve as the foundation for your views on important topics such as religion, politics, spirituality, parenthood, marriage, career, wealth, and the like. In fact, I apply thoughtfulness all throughout *Part II*, especially chapters 10-14. Don't follow fleeting and irrelevant trends. Don't be a Bumbling Dumbledorf. Don't follow the band wagon. And certainly, don't follow the sheeple. Be thoughtful; it will serve you well.

Dependability

(I also include reliability, trustworthy, and punctuality.)

Have you ever played the trust-fall game? It's when someone stands up straight, folds their arms across their chest, closes their eyes, and then falls backwards, *trusting* that you will catch their fall. It's often used in team-building exercises. Can you trust someone to catch your fall? Better yet, can someone trust *you* to catch their fall? I guess it depends. (After all, you might *accidentally* get distracted while trying to catch that 'special' boss, right? Oops!) Ok, kidding aside. Just ask yourself…

- Are you on time, every time?
- Do you *do* what you say you'll do?
- Do you pay your bills and debts – on time, in full, every time?
- Do you get the job *done*?
- Do you make excuses or get *results*?

During military life, dependability was ingrained in me. If I wasn't early, I was late, period. I can't speak for other branches, but the enlisted promotion system within the Air Force was very structured and formal. Promotion up to paygrade E-4 was mainly based upon performance, time in service, and time served in your current grade. However, promotion to paygrades E-5 and above *also* involved written testing. When you became eligible, that testing occurred *once a year*. When your test date arrived, you better be on time! If the test started at 8:00am, doors were locked at 7:59am. If you were late for any reason, better luck next year! (Requesting a second chance required commander approval and was very rare.) The point was to be *dependable* if you want to be trusted at the next higher rank. I strived to be dependable and I never missed a single test.

If you're not dependable with small things, how can you be dependable (or trusted) with big things? Ironically, some people want big money but they can't dependably manage the little money they have by following a simple budget. Some people want a pay raise but can't be depended on to earn additional skills, education, or certifications. Being dependable makes you valuable at work. It also makes you a great friend and someone that people want to be around. Your spouse depends on you to love and support them. If your spouse gets sick, care for him/her and stand by them; don't discard them and move onto someone new. Your children depend on you to protect and guide them. If you love your kids, have the necessary life insurance and estate planning documents in place. You can bet your *life* that my wife and kids can depend on me. If you tell someone, "I've got your back", well…*have* their back! Do this not only when it's easy or convenient. People admire others who are dependable – why not be dependable?

Respect

(I also include courtesy, humility, and politeness.)

I can't tell people who or what to respect. Nor would I, even if I could. Neither should you. No, respect is something personal and as such, it must come from within; that's what gives it value and meaning. Respect cannot be forced; it must be earned. Yes, we're sometimes forced to be respectful to others because of their position. For example, a sergeant who is disrespectful to their commander can be reprimanded. A defendant or lawyer who is disrespectful to the judge can be held in contempt. A student who is disrespectful to the teacher can be suspended. And so on. That type of respect is generally codified in some manner for the benefit of society at large. As we've learned, without order, there is chaos. Everyone loses. If you're even the slightest bit aware of lawless societies that are rife with organized crime, corrupt governments, gang violence, militant in-fighting, and the like, then you understand (or should) exactly what I'm talking about. If not, I strongly suggest you learn about such places. It's tough to have a civilized society without some level of formalized respect, law, and order. In my opinion, that's a given. Therefore, allow me to set the concept of formal (forced) respect to the side for now.

Here, I mainly speak of individual (personal) respect – the kind that you and I choose of our own free will. It's not forced. If you want to truly prosper, your value system should include respect; for other people, for other things, and for *yourself!* I believe if you internalize and live this value, then the aforementioned formal (forced) respect becomes a non-issue…a no-brainer. Why is that? Because I set my standards for individual respect *higher* than formal (forced) respect. Shortly, I'll share some small examples of how I do this.

My personal take on respect? Well, you know by now that I like to keep things simple. Perhaps I'm old-fashioned. Maybe I'm not cool, viral, and trendy or whatever, that's fine. By default, I respect *everyone* and *everything*, period. What?! That's right, you already have my respect; it's yours to lose. Crazy, right? What does this look like in daily life? Why is this value so important to prosperity? How does that play out in action? Here are just a few examples of how I display respect, but this is just me...

I respect the law; therefore, I obey it. In America, laws are placed upon society through elected officials. Respecting a law doesn't necessarily mean *agreeing* with a law. If I disagree with a law, I work to change it. Otherwise, I respect you and my fellow citizens enough to obey the rules. Pretty simple, I know. If I break the law, I own the consequences (yes, I've been ticketed for speeding). I don't break into my neighbor's house or steal packages from their door step. I don't distribute illegal drugs, weapons, or traffic other human beings. I don't burn down buildings of random, innocent store owners. I don't disrespect police officers by acting combative, argumentative, evasive, or threatening simply because they're doing their job. I'm not special, privileged, entitled, or above the law. I respect my neighbors, the society I live in, and the laws they've established, even if I disagree with said laws. Pretty simple.

I respect nature and other living creatures. I remember humility; the world does not revolve around me, me, and me. I've visited countless national parks and am in awe of such places; I admire and respect their beauty and grandeur. I don't pollute, litter, and throw my trash all over the place as if the world is my personal dumpster. If I have a pet, I care for it instead of neglecting and abusing it. If I hunt or fish, I do so legally, humanely, and with proper permits. If I don't hunt or fish, I respect others' rights to do so; I don't throw a temper tantrum over it. Yes, I may be weird.

I respect the U.S. Constitution, which in part, includes the right to bear arms. If I choose to own firearms, I do so legally, safely, and responsibly. If I choose not to own firearms, I respect others who do; I don't force my beliefs on others. Odd, I know.

I respect other people's beliefs and religions. People are free to worship as they see fit, provided they're not harming others. I don't feel the need to criticize, belittle, or rant against their beliefs. After all, I have

186

a life and I have better things to do anyway. Don't you? Live and let live. If we all thought alike, we'd be boring robots. Just don't force your beliefs on me. Heresy, right?

I respect people's freedoms and equality. *All* people's freedom and equality, not just a select few.

I've stood inside the Statue of Liberty and reflected on her welcoming symbol of freedom and liberty.

I've visited Ellis Island where millions of immigrants became U.S. citizens (legally).

I've looked down at the city streets from inside the World Trade Centers (Twin Towers) in New York many years before they were attacked by sick cowards on Sep 11, 2001.

I've been to the top of the Gateway Arch, a symbol of America's pioneering spirit and westward expansion.

I've been to Mount Rushmore, a tribute to four of our past presidents and their contributions to the founding of our nation.

I've toured the U.S. Naval Academy (Annapolis, MD), the U.S. Army Academy (Westpoint, NY), and my favorite...the U.S. Air Force Academy (Colorado Springs, CO). Each of these institutions is a reminder that freedom isn't free.

I understand the meaning and significance of those historical landmarks, institutions, and many others. Make no mistake, our nation's history has included many ugly and tragic events. We have scars just as every other nation and every other people who have ever existed. However, for better or for worse, the evolving course of history has led to the freest and most prosperous country on earth – and still improving every day. I respect who we are today as a nation.

I served on active duty to protect our freedoms, including yours. I respect the millions who have served (or died) before me to protect *my* freedoms. I respect the millions who fought and/or died in the Civil War, in part, to eradicate slavery. I respect the millions (of every race, creed, ethnicity, and gender) who fought and legislated to advance rights for *everyone* – including women and all people of all colors. I respect a country that is the freest in the world and is a beacon of hope and opportunity to all. I respect the millions of people who legally immigrate (or die trying) to call the United States home, which includes my wife who immigrated here as a teenager. People of every race, ethnicity, and gender risk their lives not to leave the U.S. but to *enter*; what a wonderful country it must be. There are countless other countries still being run in socialist, communist, and/or dictatorship fashion; people are imprisoned, tortured, or killed on a whim. People leave there to come *here*. Yes, I simply respect the freedoms and rights of everyone and America is the gold standard for freedom when compared to the rest of the world.

That is why I don't kneel for freedom – I *stand* for it. I stand for justice and equality and have served over two decades to protect it for everyone. I encourage you to do the same. Serve to protect law and order. Serve to fight fires. Serve to govern in the public's interest. Serve to uphold our judicial system and democracy. Serve to defend our nation. Do something to help and heal instead of whine, criticize, hate, and hurt. I advocate servant leadership. But that's just me.

So, those are just a few examples of how I display respect for others. A core aspect of respect is humility – realizing that it's not all about you. Humility involves thinking less about yourself and more about others. (Notice I said thinking less *about* yourself, not less *of* yourself.) Thinking of others and the world around you demonstrates respect. Keep in mind, showing respect doesn't always have to be a big ordeal or take much effort. You don't have to serve in the military or become a first responder. There are countless smaller ways to be respectful as well. Many occur on a daily basis and all they require is to be *courteous* and *polite*; it won't cost you a dime. Here are some ways I go about it…

> ➢ Silence my phone when out in public.

> ➢ Lower my voice in restaurants, movie theaters, shops, and the like.

> ➢ Hold the door for someone.

> ➢ Honor the rules of others' homes (wipe feet, remove shoes, refrain from alcohol/smoking/etc).

> ➢ Allow others ahead in line – especially if they only have a few items or appear in a hurry.

> ➢ Raise my hand to speak in classes, conferences, or seminars instead of shouting out.

> ➤ Respond timely to missed calls, voicemails, emails, and text messages (yes, I'm weird).

> ➤ Allow a fellow motorist into my lane instead of inching up and blocking them out.

> ➤ Display good sportsmanship in all things – win or lose.

I've found those small but meaningful gestures go a long way towards respecting others. I'm sure you can think of many other ways to be respectful, humble, courteous, and polite. However, you should also respect yourself. How so? Well, I have some thoughts on that. After all, a key part of raising my two kids was teaching them how to respect themselves. It's hard to respect others if you don't respect yourself.

First and foremost, I've taught my kids that *who* they are matters far more than *what* they are. Don't judge yourself by the *what* (hair, height, skin color, nails, gender, etc). Rather, judge yourself by the *who* (character, values, personality, etc). Make no mistake, we should strive to maintain our bodies (the what) in order to be healthy. It's okay to want to be pretty and handsome – that's fine and normal. However, we should not *define* our identity by such a fleeting and material thing. People can experience loss of *what* they are physically. They can suffer loss of limbs, eyesight, hearing, uncontrollable health issues, disease, disfigurement, and crippling disabilities. However, let nothing or no one take away *who* you are; things such as your hopes, beliefs, thoughts, values, character, and personality. As you continue defining and shaping who you are, there are many actionable ways to demonstrate respect for yourself. With everyone in mind, but especially my own kids, below are two key ways that I like to think of as defense and offense.

Defense – protect yourself and your space.

Respect yourself enough to defend yourself. Provided you're not harming others or breaking laws, you have the right to a safe and peaceful existence. Do not allow others to walk all over you. Do not allow others to put their hands on you in an unwanted manner. Do not allow others to assault you physically or verbally. Do not allow others to invade your home, vehicle, or other personal space. Do not allow others to steal your belongings. How do you protect yourself? You use a progressive approach; apply a mild tactic at first and increase as needed. If someone is violating your space, tell them to stop. You may need to involve school staff or faculty, workplace management, senior leadership, or even the law (i.e. police, restraining orders, etc). In the rare event that you're unable to remove yourself from the situation, you may have to be more forceful with your tone of voice and/or body posture. In extreme situations, you may have to *lawfully* defend yourself by fighting or use of a weapon. Having situational awareness is key to defending yourself; be aware of your surroundings.

When it comes to belongings, I've taught my wife and kids to 'let them take it' and contact the law afterwards. If a carjacker is that pitiful and desperate, simply hand them the keys and report it to the police as soon as you're safe. I've also taught them *never* to allow someone to kidnap or take them away to a remote location. Even at gunpoint. You'd rather get shot in public than be taken away, never to be seen again. Don't try to play the movie hero. Nonetheless, my focus here is not on self-defense techniques but rather standing up for yourself in the interest of self-respect. There's no cookie-cutter answer, but ultimately you must respect yourself enough to defend yourself.

Offense – demand more of yourself.

A big part of self-respect is to see yourself as worthy. Set the bar high for yourself. Know that you can do anything and be anyone you want...and then do it. Don't settle for mediocrity. You should respect yourself enough to excel in all spheres of life, but three common ones come to mind: education, relationships, and career.

Having self-respect is extra important in your formative years, especially as you start your education. I'm sure you've heard kids say things like, "I'm not smart enough to do math. This homework is too hard. Only the smart kids did well on the test. I'm just not good at taking tests." All baloney! While it's true that some things are harder than others, my wife and I taught our kids a system for 'learning how to learn' discussed in chapter 2. However, that system sits on top of an underlying foundation of self-worth, self-confidence, and self-*respect*. Kids must believe they can do it – whatever *it* is. I'm not sure where the old mantra came from, but, "what you believe, you can achieve" is something we should all subscribe to, especially kids.

Then, as you grow up and start to seek a relationship, remember not to settle for just anyone. Although you'll never find the 'perfect' person, you hope to find someone who's perfect for you (and vice versa). They must not abuse you in any way. They must not hold you back from achieving your dreams. They must add value and contribute to the relationship in a positive manner. A mate who truly loves you and cares about you should also be your accountability partner. That means you both should look out for each other if one of you should start to 'go off the rails' in some manner. I share more on relationships (marriage) in chapter 10 but be sure to respect yourself enough to build a strong, long-lasting, and loving relationship.

Lastly, we've all heard kids tell us what they want to be when they grow up. Their eyes light up and they're excited to share their hopes and dreams! We've been there ourselves. They want to become astronauts, firefighters, doctors, professional athletes, and all sorts of things – good on them! But then…somewhere along the line, many kids start to lose some of that confidence and swagger. The hope that anything is possible slowly begins to fade. They start to settle. Maybe it's too much work. Perhaps it will take too long or cost too much. Who knows why, but self-doubt starts to creep in. Stop it. Don't settle. Remind yourself (and your kids) that you can be *anyone* and do *anything* you want in life. And with rare exception, it's never too late. You know what it takes; I devoted an entire chapter to growing a rewarding and prosperous career. I'm your biggest fan. I know you can do it and I hope *you* do, too. Go for it!

I share more thoughts on respecting yourself and others in chapter 9. I told you, *The Torch of Life* ties all of this stuff together.

Diligence

(I also include stoicism, grit, determination, fortitude, perseverance, grind, resilience, and self-discipline.)

In chapter 4, the ant, the tortoise, and the third little pig taught us what it takes to achieve financial wealth. What value was common to all three…? Answer: *diligence*!

Are you diligent (disciplined) enough to save $80 a month? Just $80. If so, you're in luck...

- Invest $80/month from age 25 to 65 at 10% growth = about **$500K** in retirement!

That's $80 measly dollars. Yes, the lack of diligence may be costing you dearly! Up that to $800 per month and you'd have $5M! Diligence is the ability to stick to something. It's having (and building) an attention span that involves work. The ability to apply yourself over a long period of time. So, we learned that building financial wealth occurs slowly and steadily over time. That is, through *diligent* effort, saving, and investing. Likewise, many other things can be accomplished in life through diligence. Allow me to share a personal story to demonstrate just one example of what I mean. This one involves my daughter...

As part of her USF college pre-med classes, my daughter took organic chemistry (student nicknamed 'orgo'). According to the student grapevine and college lore, orgo is an extremely tough class. In fact, my son, who I mentioned also attended USF (3 years ahead of my daughter) once said, "Oh, dad, that class is hard! One time, I saw kids coming out of class *crying*, it was so hard." Some students refer to orgo as a 'weed-out' class, meaning it's intended to weed out the kids who are not smart enough, good enough, or *diligent* enough to get through the degree plan. Lazy, perhaps? Suffice it to say, my wonderful daughter enrolled in orgo (the weed-out class) and diligently followed her learning model from chapter 2. It must be true that organic chemistry is tough because she did work hard...*very* hard. She put in many hours of self-study, studied with a fellow classmate, attended office hours (teacher tutoring), and took copious notes. The result of her diligence? She earned an "A" in the class (tears not included)!

However, that's only part of the story. As if that wasn't enough, she *voluntarily* enrolled in organic chemistry **2**. What?! If orgo was a weed-out class, what pain and torture would await my daughter in orgo **2**?! Why inflict such misery on herself with an *optional* class? Actually, for good reason – although not a mandatory class, it would help her on the MCAT (medical college admission test) and she'd be more competitive when applying to medical school. In other words, it would be hard but worth it. So, after another semester of diligent studies, orgo **2** was in the books. How did she do? You guessed it, another "A"!

And to put the final nail in the weed-out coffin, she applied to be a *tutor* for organic chemistry. Boom, cry about that! I love my daughter. She's humble, gracious, hard-working, and yes…diligent. She won't toot her own horn, so I'll do it for her, not in a braggadocious way, but in a proud and loving dad way. I'm most proud of the way she volunteers to help her classmates along the way.

So, if it's not fully clear yet, being diligent is hard but worth it. If you truly want something in life, buckle up buttercup and do the work…get it! In my view, diligence is closely related to self-discipline; the propensity to *self*-motivate and *self*-correct. When you stumble, get back up. When you're tired, don't give up. Scratch, claw, hustle, and persist. Keep grinding. Where else can diligence take you?

- If you'd like to lose weight, *diligence* will take you there. Not overnight. Not this weekend. Properly losing weight (and keeping it off) happens over months, years, and across a lifetime. Diet. Exercise. Sweat. Work. (pills, injections, potions, and lotions not included.)
- Would you like to raise kids into successful adults? It takes **over 18 years** of parenting *diligence*. Diapers. Bedtimes. Chores. Homework. Questions. Answers. Love. Praise. Guidance. Discipline. And yes…you better believe it's worth it!
- How about earning an education? Whether it's a college degree, a certification, trade school, or a so-called weed-out class, you know what it takes. Yep, *diligence*.
- Care for a black belt in martial arts? Start as a white belt (beginner) and never quit. Do the work. Train. Practice. Study. Spar. Be *diligent*.
- Building a loving marriage, a rewarding career, and a prosperous life all call for the magic ingredient of *diligence*.

I believe it's difficult (impossible?) to prosper in anything of significance without being diligent. This usually means a *long-term* mindset, not a short-term one. By definition, if you spend *every* penny today, you'll *never* have any tomorrow. A one-day diet never works. In fact, neither does a one-month diet; a healthy diet is life-long. You don't grow lean and fit over the weekend; you do so over the course of years and decades. Giving up when the going gets tough makes you a quitter. Don't be a quitter. Hard work lays ahead of you – embrace it. Although diligence is the long road, it pays off in the end.

Integrity

(I also include truth, honesty, consistency, and accountability.)

While serving in the Air Force, we subscribed to a set of core values. At the time I served, there was a small book that outlined these core values and their related virtues. That book was called *The Little Blue Book*, presumably because its cover was Air Force blue. We were expected to study it, know it, and live it. Of course, the values mapped to expectations within our military profession. After retiring from the Air Force, I continued subscribing to many of these values, adjusting them to suit civilian life. One of the core values was *Integrity First*. Like any other value, integrity can mean different things to different people.

First, my definition of integrity is being honest and truthful. It's doing the right thing, even when no one is looking. Don't cheat at anything: academics, career, relationships, games, sports, etc. **Hold yourself accountable.** Follow the laws, rules, ethical and moral standards, and values set in place by society and yourself. Don't be a hypocrite; if you talk the talk, then walk the walk. Be principled and deep-rooted in your beliefs, not fleeting, shallow or spineless. Have strong convictions that bend but don't break; you want to be principled, not stubborn or egotistical. Don't easily bend in the wind or cater to the latest fleeting 'trend' or whatever happens to be popular at the time. Do what's right, not what's convenient or easy. Popular does not equal right. That said, how does integrity affect our prosperity?

Do you like people who lie, cheat, and steal? Who does?! Hmm. Then why do so many do it? Hmm again. Without integrity, it's hard to get very far in life. Hard to find a job. Hard to make good friends. Hard to be trusted. Hard to find a quality spouse. Hard to respect yourself. In fact, it's hard to do much of anything because nobody wants to be around a person without integrity.

Think about this…

- If you win a marathon by jumping out of the bushes near the finish line, did you really win?
- If you print a fake training certificate, do you really have the skills?
- If you cheat on an exam, do you really know the material?
- If you embellish your resume, do you really have the credentials?
- If you forge a college degree, do you really have the education?
- If you could magically steal *anything* you wanted and never get caught – would you?
- If you could lie about *anything* and people would believe you – would you?

Questions to ponder, although the answers should be obvious. By applying thoughtfulness, you can formulate your own hypothetical questions (and answers). That's what integrity is about. I've taught my kids that even if they didn't get *caught*, they'd still be liars, cheaters, thieves, or (fill-in the blank). Getting caught is irrelevant as far as integrity is concerned. It may be relevant to your parents, spouse, teachers, supervisors, and law enforcement, but it's not relevant to integrity. Those people may hold you accountable if you're caught. Then again, they may look the other way; it depends on *their* integrity. It's a vicious cycle that ends with *you.*

Ultimately, you alone hold yourself accountable. Stay true to yourself. Live by your personal values. Stand by your principles. Even when it's not easy or popular. Even when no one's looking. Live with integrity.

Excellence

(I also include extraordinary and world-class.)

At the time I served, *Excellence* was another Air Force core value in the pages of the *The Little Blue Book*. If you're content with mediocrity or average, then skip excellence. Otherwise, strive for excellence in all you do. Aren't you worth it? Excellence is a key ingredient to elevating yourself in many ways! How does this look in daily life? Let's see…

Lifelong Learning

ordinary.

Sit on your couch. Scroll and click on your phone or other devices. Subscribe to all the channels and streaming services. Consume all of the unsocial media, reality shows, and/or brain-draining videos. Repeat.

EXCELLENCE!

Learn something valuable that can improve your life. Earn a college education. Obtain a new certification. Gain a new skill. Learn a new language. Read a non-fiction book. Read many books. Apply your knowledge. Follow chapter 2.

Career

ordinary.

Slip on a wrinkled t-shirt. Trudge to work, punch the clock, and work the proverbial 9-to-5. Do the bare minimum and waste the remaining time on your phone. Over a 5-year span, do the same work and receive the same pay (or very close). Don't level-up your skills or add anything of value to your resume. Stagnate.

EXCELLENCE!

Dress for success. Gallop to work like a stallion; arrive early and eager to add value. Hustle, smile, and do the best job possible. Network with others and work in the team's best interest. Over a 5-year span, learn new skills, complete on-going education, earn a degree and/or certifications, and apply new found knowledge to your job. Follow chapter 3.

Financial Wealth

ordinary.

Live paycheck to paycheck. Don't budget. Keep a car payment. Keep a house payment. Wallow in debt. Invest little or nothing into retirement.

EXCELLENCE!

Follow a written budget. Grow your income. Live debt free. Have an emergency fund. Invest for your future. Own your home. Become a millionaire. Don't just exist; thrive! Follow chapter 4.

Health Wealth

ordinary.

Live on fast food, junk food, nicotine, and alcohol. Sit on the couch. Allow your mind to be overrun with weeds. Neglect your hygiene. Neglect your relationships, intellect, and mental wellness.

EXCELLENCE!

Eat a balanced and healthy diet. If you choose to consume junk food, nicotine, or alcohol, do so in moderation. Exercise regularly (scrolling on your phone doesn't count). Plant intellectual *seeds* in your mind. Regularly visit your doctor and dentist. Continually hone your relationships, intellect, and mental wellness. Follow chapter 5.

Marriage

ordinary.

Sit on your couch. Scroll and click on your phone or other devices. Have a few drinks. Watch TV. Have a few more drinks. Repeat.

EXCELLENCE!

Put your phone down. Have deep and meaningful conversations with your spouse. Travel to exciting places with each other. Enjoy fine dining. Build strong bonds and values together. Surprise each other with gifts, flirty notes, loving poems, or something new. Laugh with each other. And (keeping it clean)…love each other. More in chapter 10.

Parenthood

ordinary.

Have a kid. Be a parent (the noun). Repeat.

EXCELLENCE!

Be an active parent (the verb). Protect your kids. Provide structure and guidance to your kids. Spend quality time with them. Read to them. Play games with them. Mentor them through progressive stages of life. Praise and discipline them. Love them. Contribute to *their* prosperity. Teach them a strong value system. More in chapter 11.

Play/Live

ordinary.

Sit on your couch. Scroll and click on your phone or other devices. Subscribe to all the channels and streaming services. Consume all of the unsocial media, reality shows, and/or brain-draining videos. Repeat.

EXCELLENCE!

Put your phone down. Put on your walking shoes. Take a road trip. Take *many* road trips. Travel the country. Travel the world. Check out museums, zoos, aquariums, amusement parks, plays, concerts, musicals, comedy shows, and magic shows. Get a fun hobby: sports, painting, drawing, woodworking, hunting, fishing, scuba diving, or even sky diving! Read fascinating books. Play challenging and fun games. Seek out adventure. Grow, develop, mature, and evolve. More in chapter 12.

By now, you probably think I have something against phones and devices. I don't. I use phones and devices. However, I'm convinced they're rotting people's brains and ruining their lives. If you value *excellence*, there's no room for digital zombies. Break free from virtual reality. Put some thought into your *actual* life. Where can you make some changes? How can you shake things up? Strive for excellence in everything you do!

Generosity

(I also include selflessness and kindness.)

Be generous. Don't overthink generosity, just do it. Some people think you must create a big, fancy nonprofit or donate millions of dollars in order to be generous. Nope, nothing fancy is required. It doesn't require lots of money either. In fact, it doesn't require any money at all. Giving money is fun, but you can also give your time. I've given, and continue to give, both. Ironically, I've found that generosity often does more for the giver than the receiver. So, what are some simple ways to give your money and time?

Giving money can be fun and satisfying. Again, it doesn't take much. The simple act of buying a $5 or $10 toy for a needy child during the holidays can warm that child's heart (and yours). Occasionally, I get a random desire to do something spontaneous...

One day, I was having dinner at a restaurant in Salt Lake City. In walked an elderly gentleman with a woman who clearly appeared to be his wife. I guessed they were in their late 70's. He walked very slowly, careful to keep his balance as the wait staff helped him and his wife to their seat. The gentleman was proudly wearing attire that, to my eye, told me he was a military veteran; a service patch on his jacket was the giveaway. His hair was neatly trimmed and his clothing looked sharp and freshly-ironed. He and his wife were clearly dressed 'fancy' as they say and holding each other's hands as they sat. My heart told me to do something nice for this lovely couple and thank the gentleman for his military service. So, after I paid for my own meal, I handed the waiter an extra $100 in cash. I asked him to apply it to the couple's bill and be sure to tell the gentleman, "Thank you for your service." Then I quietly left the restaurant. I can't tell you what happened thereafter, but I know how good that one simple act made me feel.

That, and many more examples of both spontaneous and planned generosity can be amazing. Keep in mind, if you don't currently have much money to give, you can donate time.

Giving time can often be more effective and more heart-warming than giving money. It's usually more personal. Consider being a volunteer. Search online for 'volunteer opportunities near me' or something similar (see, phones are good for something). You'll find ample organizations in dire need of volunteers. Ask your local schools and churches if they need volunteers; trust me, they do. I've volunteered hundreds, if not thousands of hours all over the world and it's been very rewarding. Just a few things include…

➤ Donating my labor to nonprofit home-building programs for those less fortunate.

➤ Serving on teams to conduct both preparation and post-recovery cleanup efforts during natural disasters such as flooding and catastrophic hurricanes.

➤ Organizing, cleaning, and repainting schools in underfunded communities.

➤ Raising money for cancer awareness, poverty, hunger, and other similar causes.

So, you can be generous in many ways. Yes, life is busy, but make the time to lend a hand-*up* to others. Keep in mind that generosity should come from the heart. Be sincere. Be careful not to come off as patronizing or condescending. Also, giving on a personal level is often more satisfying than from arms-length. In other words, spending the day helping a disabled person recover from storm damage may be far more rewarding than donating $100 to a random online charity.

Lastly, don't confuse generosity with hand-*outs* (covered earlier). Give for the sake of giving and don't overthink it. There are countless ways to be generous. Whatever you do, wherever you are, and whenever you can…live generously!

Contentment

(I also include satisfaction and **happiness**.)

My contentment is an *internal* appreciation for what I *have*. This value is a golden nugget for everyone, but especially for my daughter since it's been on her mind. I mentioned earlier how she asked me two questions about life. The first regarded work-life balance; I addressed that in chapter 3 (career) and also in chapter 7 (under the principle of *balance*).

My daughter's second question was essentially, "Do we ever find true happiness in life or do we eventually just settle?" Although they're not exactly the same, I use 'happiness' and 'contentment' interchangeably at times. So, will we ever be truly happy, or do we just have to settle? The answer is yes and yes; we find true happiness (contentment) *and* we settle at times. It's not a cop-out, it's true. This is where the principle of relativity also comes into play. For example, I'll share in chapter 10 how I was *happy* when I was single…I might even say *content*. But now I'm *wow happy* in my marriage (way more than content). In other words, contentment is relative – the intensity level varies like adjusting a dial knob, not flipping an on/off switch. The same for happiness. Let's explore contentment a little further.

I describe contentment as an *inside* appreciation or satisfaction. Coincidentally, you could argue that contentment is not only a value, but also a feeling or emotion. Contentment makes me feel calm and appreciative inside. It's that *full* feeling after enjoying a big, delicious meal. So, if I only eat 16 ounces of my 22-ounce ribeye steak, I'm quite content, but I also settle to some degree by not finishing the entire steak. Likewise, it's hard to describe precisely why, but I feel very content *and* happy in my overall life. Although I eagerly look forward to tomorrow, I feel *full* today. Content *and* happy. Perhaps it's also what I *don't* feel that makes me content.

I don't feel empty, lacking, or greedy. Also, importantly, I have zero care about what the Joneses or anyone else is doing. Not in a mean way. I just don't feel the need to *compare* myself with others. The old saying is true; comparison is the thief of joy. Remember, there's always someone else with more (and less). Does that mean you settled if you have less than others? Absolutely not. Plus, having more doesn't make you better than anyone. Therefore, eliminating comparison will dial up your level of contentment. By the way, that's difficult if you spend half your life in *other* people's newsfeeds, profiles, and unsocial media posts. Hmm, maybe *that's* why I'm so content <wink>. There's also another consideration at play.

Be careful not to overthink or over analyze contentment. Sometimes, I can use intellect or thoughtfulness to be content. For example, I'm not a billionaire, but I'm perfectly content financially. However, other times contentment just happens – intellect or thinking not required. For example, when my kids were babies and one of them fell asleep in my arms, contentment (and happiness) instantly filled my heart. I'm sure you've felt similar contentment or happiness many times in your own life. Perhaps you got married, had a baby, earned a promotion, or simply held a loved one in your arms. That said, there's a constant balance between 'settling' and finding contentment (or happiness) in life.

It's healthy to strive for excellence, but you should also practice contentment. After all, I'm content with my finances, but I still work for more. I'm content with my education, but I still continue learning. And so on. *They're both true at the same time.* There is no perfect. So, by definition, we all settle to some degree. Contentment allows us to let go of non-existent perfection and be happy with what we have. Just do. Just be. Contentment (and happiness) is found in the journey; not an impossible state of perfection.

So, if contentment is an *inside* appreciation, I view its soul-mate 'gratitude' as an *external* appreciation.

Gratitude

(I also include thankfulness.)

My gratitude is an *external* appreciation for what I *have* or what I've *received.* Allow me to cut to the chase on gratitude. Back when I was working in the office, many of my cube-mates filled their cubicles and desks with plants, pictures, knick-knacks, and all kinds of other *stuff.* I'm sure people still do that today; I guess it makes them feel more at home. Me? I had one single thing tacked to my wall. (I told you I'm simple.) It was a one-page 'poem' for lack of a better word. I don't even remember where I found it, but wherever it came from, I made a few minor tweaks (I can't remember which ones) and held on to it. Whenever I moved offices, I took it with me and hung it up in my new space. For about a decade, wherever my desk was, this poem hung on the wall. Here it is…

I AM THANKFUL…

FOR THE WIFE
WHO SAYS IT'S HOT DOGS TONIGHT,
BECAUSE SHE IS HOME WITH ME,
AND NOT OUT WITH SOMEONE ELSE.

FOR THE CHILDREN
WHO ARE SCREAMING AND MAKING A MESS,
BECAUSE IT MEANS I AM A PROUD FATHER
OF HAPPY AND HEALTHY KIDS.

FOR THE TAXES I PAY
BECAUSE IT MEANS
I AM EMPLOYED.

FOR THE MESS TO CLEAN AFTER A PARTY
BECAUSE IT MEANS I HAVE
BEEN SURROUNDED BY FRIENDS.

FOR THE CLOTHES THAT FIT A LITTLE TOO SNUG
BECAUSE IT MEANS
I HAVE ENOUGH TO EAT.

FOR A LAWN THAT NEEDS MOWING,
WINDOWS THAT NEED CLEANING,
AND GUTTERS THAT NEED FIXING
BECAUSE IT MEANS I HAVE A HOME.

FOR ALL THE COMPLAINING
I HEAR ABOUT THE GOVERNMENT
BECAUSE IT MEANS
WE HAVE FREEDOM OF SPEECH.

FOR THE PARKING SPOT
I FIND AT THE FAR END OF THE PARKING LOT
BECAUSE IT MEANS I AM CAPABLE OF WALKING
AND I HAVE BEEN BLESSED WITH TRANSPORTATION.

FOR MY HUGE HEATING BILL
BECAUSE IT MEANS I AM WARM.

FOR THE PILE OF LAUNDRY AND DRY CLEANING
BECAUSE IT MEANS
I HAVE CLOTHES TO WEAR.

FOR WEARINESS AND ACHING MUSCLES
AT THE END OF THE DAY
BECAUSE IT MEANS I HAVE BEEN
CAPABLE OF WORKING HARD.

FOR THE ALARM THAT GOES OFF
IN THE EARLY MORNING HOURS
BECAUSE IT MEANS I AM ALIVE.

I AM THANKFUL AND WILL GIVE 100% EVERY DAY.

Kudos to whoever wrote that! Now, please don't take the words literally; the message is what counts. The sentiment is what captures my heart and expresses the *gratitude* that I have in my life. I'm probably the most grateful person on Earth. I am truly humbled by all that I have and will remain ever thankful. That, in a nutshell, is gratitude. A grateful person is a prosperous one.

Live and Leave a Legacy

(I also include living a life of prosperity and helping others do the same.)

Collectively, your personal values help to define who you are and what you stand for in life. This culminates in how you live and what you pass along to the generations that follow. In that vein, I strive to both *live* and *leave* a lasting legacy. How do I go about such a thing?

First, I strive to *live* a legacy each and every day. I do that primarily through living a good life, working hard, and being a good person. That means being respectful, kind, and helpful to others. It also means doing the best I can, not the least I can. The legacy I live…

- Reflects that I'm a loving and supportive husband (chapter 10).
- Shows I've loved, mentored, and raised my kids into respectful, successful, and independent adults (chapter 11).
- Demonstrates commitment to family and friends (chapter 12).
- Is a life of service, not only to my country but also the community around me, and the greater world within which I live (chapter 12).

I do all of this while I'm alive. By doing so, it shows that I'm not all talk. I walk the walk each and every day. *That*…is the legacy I choose to live.

Second, I plan to *leave* a legacy when I die. We all leave this Earth, but it's nice if we pass along a little something to those who follow. In a perfect world, my wife and kids will survive me for years to come. The legacy I leave…

- Includes an inheritance: money, investments, real estate, and other assets.
- Far more importantly, passes along the mindset, behaviors, systems, and principles necessary to sustain the inheritance.
- Above all, conveys the *character* and *values* that lead to generational prosperity.

By leaving behind such treasure, my kids (and others) can benefit from the race that I've run. Ultimately, I'll hand off my own personal torch of life – this book will help with that. I hope *The Torch of Life* continues to bless the lives of my family and many others. In turn, they'll pass along *their* legacy to the next generation, and so on. *That*…is the legacy I choose to leave.

As icing on the cake, I sincerely hope my legacy (through this book) will benefit *you* in some way. After all, this book is for *you* as much as it is my own family. You are an active participant in your own prosperity and the generations that follow. It's *your* turn. Reflect on who *you* are, how *you* live, and what *you'll* leave behind. What will *you* contribute? How will *you* be remembered? What legacy will *you* leave? I hope you live life to the fullest and realize all of your dreams. I hope you leave an inheritance to family or loved ones. It may be money, a house, or even a family business that you've built through years of blood, sweat, and tears. More importantly, consider what personal values, family traditions, or cultural heritage you'd like to pass to the next generation. Perhaps you'll pass along an inscribed copy of *The Torch of Life* to your heirs. Whatever it is, do it like you mean it!

So, remember folks, values *matter*. They are foundational to your prosperity. Living by a strong value system will help you be a good person. Without the moral compass that values provide, many successful people go down in flames. People end up broke, lonely, imprisoned, debilitated, unemployed, and who knows what else…often due to a lack of values. The ten personal values I've provided are not all-inclusive; I'm sure you can think of many others. Ask yourself *who* you are and what you stand for. Live and leave a legacy that you're proud of.

CHAPTER 9

THE POWER OF INDIVIDUALISM

As I wrap up *Part I*, this is the final concept on *how* to achieve generational prosperity. My use of the term 'individualism' here is very focused when compared to its more conventional definition. I don't refer to it as some high-level philosophy or societal doctrine that prioritizes individual rights over that of the group or collective. Nor is it some type of lone wolf behavior used to tackle life all alone. For my purposes, here's how I define individualism…

Treat yourself and others respectfully as individuals. Take individual ownership of your life through a high control mindset.

Pretty simple, right? I know. Then why is this so complicated for so many people? Clearly, people can be labeled and grouped in countless ways: by nationality, race, color, gender, political party, religion, generation, education, profession, and many other things. I believe most people enjoy belonging to a calling bigger than themselves and contributing to the group in some fashion. That's great because people *should* belong to groups. Many people join others for a worthy high-order cause. They may join an association of engineers in an effort to rebuild national infrastructure. They may join a team of scientists hoping to cure cancer. They may even band together militarily to defend themselves against attack from a common enemy. Yes, people are social creatures and naturally associate with others. Belonging to groups and honoring our family or cultural heritage is wonderful!

Although a sense of belonging is great, we should **not** lose our *individual* identity in the process. Neither should we label, stereotype, and define ourselves (or others) by it. In fact, individual identity is what holds us accountable to others and to ourselves. So, where is this all headed? When we fail to treat others as individuals, it's a slippery slope; individuality gets blurred or lost completely in the collective. This can lead to many negative actions, some of which may even be a crime. If I may be blunt, I'll call these actions what they are – displays of stupidity, disrespect, and sheer ignorance. Here are just a few: labeling, stereotyping, prejudice, segregation, and discrimination. All of this amounts to disrespect, not only towards others, but mostly to yourself. Yet another true story from my own life…

My wife told me that she has personally experienced far more racism in her home country than here in the United States. However, there they called it 'colorism', where some people treated others differently because their skin tone was a shade darker or lighter than their own. Her personal experience with racism against her in the U.S. over the last 32 years and counting? Precisely zero, except for one colorist girl who disparaged my wife because her skin tone was darker than the girl's. Clearly, all of this amounts to ignorance on the part of racist or colorist idiots. Sadly, some people are petty and have no life. If you wish to have a life (and a *prosperous* one), then read on.

My wife's experience was just one example which happened to deal with skin color. But as you'll soon discover, individualism goes way beyond that. Folks, this is *much* bigger than race or ethnicity.

Why SELF- (Label, Stereotype, Segregate, Discriminate)?

At the risk of leaving anyone out, raise your hand if you're a…

Hetero/homo/poly/hybrid/black/white/brown/male/female/hispanic / italian/indian/pacific-islander/indigenous/latin/asian/anglo/TS/TG/ LGBTQ/ABC/XYZ/+/-/he/she/us/me/him/her/up-down/in-out/on-off/hairy/bald/catch-all…person.

Some, none, or all of the above?

Did I miss anyone? Good grief. Yes, we're all different. (Hey, never say I'm not inclusive.) And yes, it's great to know *what* you are. I kindly and whole-heartedly agree! I accept everyone's differences and respect what makes us all unique. I tell my kids to never be ashamed of what they are, but don't shove it in people's face. (Especially if you don't want to be labeled by it; don't label yourself.) But *pssst*...quite honestly, most people don't care. Why? Because most people care more about *who* you are. I know I do and I hope you feel the same. So, if you're building websites, writing books and blogs, posting on social media, and parading in the streets to emphatically proclaim *what* you are, I hope you devote that same effort and intensity to your education, career, volunteerism, character, behavior, and values. Right...? Good, that's awesome!

That's right. Sadly, too many people **self**-segregate into cliques and groups based upon superficial and low-order things such as race, color, ethnicity, gender/identity, and the like. Yes, unfortunately it still continues to this day. Are you one of them? There are many people who complain about being labeled or stereotyped and then commit the very same act they're complaining about. Wow. Is that hypocrisy, stupidity, or both? There are still some people who view 'commonality' through anyone closest to their own skin tone. Even though I challenged you in chapter 7 to line up 8 *billion* people from lightest to darkest and find two people with the *exact identical* skin color. Even though...some people will *still* try to associate with others who they believe are similar in color. "By golly, this is *my* race and I'm sticking to it!" You can't convince them otherwise. Never mind the fact that if you go back through the millennia, you'll discover their mixed racial genealogy. Never mind the fact that even in my wife's home country, some people *still* find a way to parse out the slightest variance in skin color and somehow label others as darker or lighter and treat them differently as a result. Wow is an understatement.

The funny part is they only do this when it's to their perceived advantage. They say things like...

"See, that person is poor and because my skin color is similar, that's why I'm poor."

"See, that person was arrested and because my skin color is similar, that's why I was arrested."

That's their excuse, anyway. But when do you ever hear them say…

"See, that person is a criminal and because my skin color is similar, I must be a criminal too."

"See, that person is a gang member and because my skin color is similar, I must be one too."

Hmm. Something to ponder. Just another example of hypocritical SELF-labeling and SELF-stereotyping. This is also a display of disrespect. In chapter 8, I talked at length about the value of respect. When you disrespect others (and yourself), it displays a lack of character. It's not a reflection of others, but rather a reflection of *you*. By disrespecting yourself based upon factors such as race, gender, and ethnicity, you **limit your own potential**. In other words, you mistakenly believe only *other* people can get promoted, earn a degree, follow the law, build wealth, or succeed in some fashion. It also manifests itself in how you behave and treat others.

How you treat others (and yourself) is part of *who* you are. Sadly, this type of disrespect is all too common. I'm sure you've seen it with your own eyes; in fact, it pervades virtual reality like a disease. Have you ever wondered if *you* are guilty of such actions? As you'll soon see, individualism is much bigger than skin color or gender. Much bigger. This is actually (or should be) common sense.

Well, if all of this is such common sense, why are some people still stuck on stupid? I mentioned how this is practically a disease in places like unsocial media, the tabloids, and other virtual reality spaces. I also asked if you believe you're guilty as well. Do you…

- Patronize (racial/gender-based) businesses?
- Read (racial/gender-based) magazines or books?
- Watch (racial/gender-based) TV channels?
- Listen to (racial/gender-based) radio stations?
- Promote (racial/gender-based) organizations?
- Label, categorize, and view things based upon race or gender?

I hope *you* don't, but I see it all the time. I often wonder to myself if these people have any clue as to what they're doing. Do they *consciously* label and segregate themselves and others, or do they not even realize it?

Do you know anyone who's guilty of this? Hey, it can be a hard pill to swallow, but your life will completely metamorphose when you break free from ignorance. This is a key part of intellectual health (chapter 5). Seemingly everywhere you look, people are disrespecting others or themselves due to racial, gender, and other biases. Sadly, this is to their *own* detriment. All things equal, these actions *limit* your prosperity – no exceptions! Self-labeling and self-exclusion only serve to isolate and pigeon-hole yourself. You end up becoming the very thing you claim you're against. Can you say hypocrite? Here's a question for you – which company below would *you* do business with?

Company ABC, a *self*-labeled (race or gender-owned) business.

Company XYZ, a business (that is owned by an *individual* of *any* race or gender).

If you chose Company ABC, consider yourself guilty! Ok, maybe not guilty of a crime, but guilty of self-labeling, self-exclusion, disrespect, and self-limiting your very own social development! Viewing life through a racial/gender lens leads to tunnel vision and biased perspectives. That racial/gender mindset and subsequent behavior will hold you back for the rest of your life. If you want to thrive in business and in *life*, remember to treat others (and yourself) as individuals. For example, if my wife or daughter started a business, it would be a "business", not a "female-owned business" or a "race-owned business" (fill in the race). The same applies if my son or I started a business.

News flash – business functions are race and gender neutral. *Everyone* must perform sales, accounting, payroll, marketing, and related tasks. I shake my head at people seeking 'business for women' or 'business for men'. What? Good grief. What happened to simply *business* (for everyone)? People should patronize a business because it's effective, competitively priced, responsive, respectful, provides prompt service, and inclusive…*not* because of the owner's gender or skin color. Sorry. Doing so, *by definition* is racial or gender bias, if not full-on discrimination, even if not in the legal sense. If I shop only businesses owned by people of 'my own race/gender', that's not only sad and pathetic, but biased, discriminatory, and ignorant. This is true not only of business, but also applies to sports, social clubs, universities, entertainment, government, and more. All individuals should be welcome, period. Whether in business or otherwise, respect yourself and others enough to succeed and participate on *merit* and *character*. Here's another example of how this has played out in my family's life…

One day, when my son was younger, he came home from school with a flyer that basically invited him to a race-based honors ceremony to recognize his academic excellence and that of fellow students with a similar racial/ethnic background. Needless to say, I sent an email with a few respectful but choice words to the principal and that never happened again. My basic message to the school was…

"How dare you label and segregate my son because of race, ethnicity, or skin color. Is it because you're patting him on the head patronizingly as if even he can achieve academic excellence? Or are you trying to give him and 'kids like him' extra-special recognition? Precisely how light or dark must someone's skin be for inclusion? Either way, don't ever send this racial garbage home with my child again. When the school decides to have an honors ceremony that recognizes ALL kids equally who achieved academic excellence, then invite us to attend. -Thank you."

Unreal. While they were at it, why didn't the school have another ceremony for males, one for females, and one for (…). Yes, the stupidity is unbelievable, especially and ironically from an institution of learning. Wow. I see more *self*-labeling, *self*-segregating, and *self*-discriminating today than I ever have in my life. Are some human brains regressing? Are some people incapable of intellectual growth? The lesson is simple – treat yourself and others as individuals. In some ways, individualism is the *opposite* of discrimination (of all sorts) – the anti-discrimination, if you will. Use it to your advantage.

As I began to write this book, I asked my wife, **"If you could give only *one* single piece of life advice to our kids, what would it be?"** Remember, only *one* piece of life advice on *any* topic. Without any hesitation, she firmly said to tell our kids…

"Don't ever let anyone hire, promote, or advance you in any way to 'check a box' (race, gender, or otherwise). You'll have an asterisk by your name

for the rest of your life. It's extremely disrespectful for anyone to offer that and extremely disgraceful for you to accept it. You want to earn your success in life – on character and merit." (Sonic boom!)

Wow! Amen. I couldn't agree more. So, you *earn* your seat at the table. Now, mind you my wife doesn't play games. She's had so much success in life, it's unreal. And not once did her race or gender *ever* factor in. She doesn't buy into excuses. She's not a self-created victim. Did I mention how much I love my wife?

So far, our kids have heard mom's message loud and clear. Our son is a successful software engineer and our daughter is a dean's list college senior, en route to medical school. Nothing whatsoever has ever held either of them down in the slightest way. Yes, folks, individualism matters.

In short, when you quit viewing life through a racial or gender lens, you'll learn to respect not only others, but also yourself. You'll quit playing *victim*...

- If you don't get hired or promoted, it might mean you were the least qualified candidate.
- If you don't get accepted to a specific school, you may not have had the highest grades or best overall credentials.
- If your business isn't thriving, you may not have the best products, services, value, or prices.
- If you get arrested, it might be because you broke the law.
- If you're suspended from school, it might be because your behavior warranted it.

Are there exceptions? Does racial and gender discrimination occur? You betcha. It sure does. I just showed many examples above how people stupidly *self*-discriminate nearly every single day. Sadly, there are also other losers in life who discriminate against others and they ultimately get rooted out and punished in some fashion. However, that's not an excuse to dumb yourself down to blame race or gender for anything that doesn't go your way. Don't be stupid enough to confuse the exception with the rule. Don't buy into the self-limiting misperception that you are somehow a perpetual victim. After all, why limit your own potential? Why handicap yourself?

My family lives by individualism and it has worked every time – every single time! I'm so proud that our kids are inclusive and accepting of all individuals; unless those individuals somehow don't deserve that respect. And clearly, not everyone deserves respect. I'm also proud our kids don't follow the sheeple and self-segregate into racial or gender cliques, clubs, and circles. It means my wife and I have taught them well. That's partly why they're so prosperous!

By the way, I hope I've been clear on my feelings around discrimination so far. However, allow me to now shift further forward in my broader concept of *individualism*. In fact, we're going to elevate much higher than discrimination around race or gender. The concepts in this book lead to generational prosperity; if you wish to perpetuate ignorance and pettiness, you're reading the wrong book. As you may have noticed, that's what I do here in *The Torch of Life* – I take things up a level or two (or three). I warned you in the introduction that some principles may reframe your entire way of thinking. Don't settle for ordinary, mediocre, or bare minimum, even in the way you treat others or yourself. If you're still stuck on the color of someone's skin (including your own) or the whole gender bias thing, umm…hold on to your hat because this book may revolutionize your entire life! Let's zoom wider by another notch.

Individualism is the gold standard for treating others with respect. You can believe it or not, but my family and I have lived it for over a half century with resounding success. Now, let's continue to pan back further beyond tunnel vision and a short-sighted focus on skin color and gender. Here are a few other ways to break diversity misperceptions…

Money

"I can't get ahead because I'm not privileged. People like me will never be wealthy."

That's right, with **self**-limiting beliefs like that, you'll never be wealthy! Opportunity is all around you. Not handouts, but *opportunity*. Change your mindset *and* behavior. You *can* do it. Every able-bodied individual in America can become wealthy. In fact, the principles in this book show you how but you must do the work. If you follow these principles, you'll succeed with money. In fact, you're likely to become a multi-millionaire!

Education

"People with my background are not educated. I can't get an education due to systemic inequality."

Once again, the blame game gets you nowhere fast! Who's stopping you? Take *individual* ownership and get an education. I don't mean graduate high school. I don't mean get a college degree. I mean do *all* of that and then some! Become a *lifelong learner* starting today! I covered this in chapter 2. Getting an education requires hard work. Be different – attend school, pay attention when you're there, take notes, ask questions, do your homework, study for tests, complete assigned work, attend school activities, and seek out study partners. Surprisingly, you'll start to succeed...*regardless* of any misperceptions about your background.

Home Ownership

"My family has always been renters. People like me will never own a home. The rich are holding me down. The system is rigged. The 1% own everything."

There you go **self**-labeling and stereotyping again. First of all, who are the rich? Second of all, how are they holding you down? Do rich people meet somewhere and compile a list of people to hold down? Exactly what system is rigged? Trust me, banks and lenders *want* to give you a loan, but you must not pose a credit risk. People *want* to sell you a house. I don't care who you are; if you're an able-bodied person in America, follow the principles in this book. Always grow your income, follow the wealth principles, pay your bills on time, be a lifelong learner, live by positive life values, and when the time is right...*buy a house*!

Are You a Victim or a Victor?

The list of self-imposed victimhood goes on and on. And on and on. So, you now see, individualism is about far more than race or gender issues. And we're just getting warmed up. Those are certainly important but it also goes way beyond that – it's an entire mindset. It includes your labels and stereotypes about money, religion, home ownership, careers, what part of town you're from, where you were born, what music you listen to, your relationships, your parenting, cultural background, your language, and a whole lot more. Heck, how many times have you heard people referring to the various generations: baby boomers, generation X, millennials, generation Z, generation this, generation that. Good grief. The principles here apply to *every* generation. Hard work applies to everyone. Character and values apply to everyone. Lifelong learning applies to everyone. The money principles apply to everyone. So on and so on. There's good and bad in *every* generation, no exceptions. There's good and bad in every race, gender, profession, sport, religion, and any other group you can conjure up. I can't stress enough the importance of taking *individual* control of your life – for your own benefit.

Once again, are you a *victim* or a *victor* in life? It's a choice. Folks, I believe in some of you more than you believe in yourself! I wrote this book in part because I want *everyone* to prosper. These principles are universal. Some of this may be difficult to hear. Some of it may be tough medicine, but you can do it. If you're not succeeding, remember this from chapter 7: **different input = different output**. Do something different. Break free from group think and group behavior. Break free from self-limiting sob stories that society tells you (or that you tell yourself). Be your own individual. Walk your own walk. Change your behavior. Change yourself and future generations. Change your entire family tree. Stand up and say, "Enough!" Quit worrying about what everyone else is doing. Quit following irrelevant sheeple, politicians, or so-called influencers. And for your own benefit…quit making excuses! Be a victor.

Achieve Inclusion and Equality

Sadly, some people lack an understanding of *diversity*, even people working in the field of human resources! Talk about irony. If you make racial or gender-based personnel decisions, you view diversity through a superficial and disrespectful lens of skin color or gender. Hello. You violate the very thing that promotes inclusiveness and equity if you select people based upon race and gender. Here's a wild thought – how about we seek diversity based upon character, values, education, experience, training, skills, and talents? Crazy, I know. True diversity in business is onboarding people (*individuals*) who can add value to the core business functions: engineering, marketing, advertising, sales, manufacturing, logistics, and others. (Not by the color of their skin or gender/identity.)

By the way, this isn't only a business or career issue. Far from it. Let's achieve diversity in sports through speed, strength, stamina, on-field IQ, sportsmanship, teamwork, coachability, athletic skills, and other relevant qualities. Let's achieve diversity in politics through experience, qualifications, articulate speaking, accomplishments, and effective policy. And so on. Notice that nowhere in here is skin color or gender/identity a factor. That is, unless you judge others by race or gender – isn't that sort of racist or sexist? Hmm. Folks, this is not a complicated concept. The power of individualism fully promotes inclusion and equality.

For those that want **inclusion**, *act* like it. Don't self-segregate. Don't label others by race, gender, color, religion, or some other stereotypical nonsense (i.e. the rich, the system, Wall Street, southerners, northerners, etc). If someone treats you unethically, illegally, or just plain wrong, it's *their* fault…not the democrats, not the republicans, not this race or that race, not this gender or that gender, not the police, not the teachers, not this religious group or that one, and not society…it's that *individual's* fault, period.

For those that want **equality**, *act* like it. If you want to succeed, then go to school, get a job, work hard, and obey the law – just like everyone else. If you want the same education, show up, study hard, do the same work, and get the grades. If you want the same pay, do the same volume and quality of work. If you want to be treated with respect under the law, act like it; don't act like a disrespectful animal when interacting with society or representatives of the law. (If one of my kids acted towards police the way I've seen some people act, they better *hope* they get arrested! And by the way, it has *zero* to do with their demographic.)

So, you see, if you want to be treated fairly, equally, and respectfully as an individual, then you must also act the same. You're not special, entitled, or privileged. Like it or not, it's a two-way street. That's what makes individualism so powerful. We're not wronged by groups or society – we're wronged by individuals.

For example...

- If I had a bad day, "the military" didn't treat me wrong – perhaps it was my *supervisor* at the time. Likewise, "the military" didn't assign me to trash detail, the *First Sergeant* did.
- If I pay higher taxes, it wasn't "the democrats" or "the republicans" who caused that, it was the specific *individuals* who voted on legislation to raise my taxes.
- If a girlfriend stole my money and cheated on me, it's not "women" who are untrustworthy, it was my *girlfriend*.
- If some sicko in the school system does an unspeakable act to a child, it wasn't "the school", but rather the *individual* perpetrator that should be held accountable. (And obviously any other individuals that may have been complicit, but certainly not the entire school system.) This holds true of any profession.

Here's an odd thought. How many people do you see protesting and rioting over some perceived issue holding them down: the system, the rich, billionaires, social justice, minimum wage, religious or ethnic issues, big corporations, etc.? Sure, people have a right to *respectfully* and *lawfully* speak their voice. Go for it. In fact, I believe they *should* do so.

However...just for fun, do these *same* people also devote that *same* energy towards their education, their jobs, their finances, their families, and so on? Where's their outrage over rampant drive-by shootings, gang violence, drug dealing, human trafficking, and other such issues? Where's their outrage over people *disrespectfully* attempting to immigrate *illegally*, as if they're privileged? Where's their outrage over minor-aged children walking the streets and committing strings of crime? Where's their outrage at the parents of such children? Where's their outrage over children who are abused, neglected, and discarded by *so-called bleeping parents*? This applies to others as well.

Why don't our "civic leaders" march the gang members, dope dealers, and juvenile delinquents to school and make them get an education? Why don't they clean up the inner cities where it seems like there are *multiple* killings *every* week? Why don't the parents who rail against teachers, politicians, and police do the same thing for their *own child* who dropped out of school and is committed to a life of crime, drugs, and guns? If people were as passionate about parenting, education, and lawful societies, perhaps we wouldn't have the former issues. Hmm. *Now that just might be social justice after all.* Imagine if *everyone* was accountable to get an education, work hard, serve their community, and obey the law. Something to ponder. When you break things down, these are *individual* issues. It's easy to label, stereotype, point fingers, and cast blame on someone or something else. Some people love to make excuses. Some people like to say, "It's not my fault." Sorry. Nice try. Each individual is accountable for their own actions (or inaction). And parents are responsible for their minor children.

Individualism Meets Principles and Values

In chapter 7, I emphasized the power of life principles, in particular 'different input = different output' and 'hand-ups help; hand-outs hurt'. These two principles often call for an entirely new way of thinking. Just like eliminating hunger requires a different approach, so do other issues such as poverty and social justice. If your rap sheet is five pages long, don't be shocked when you eventually crash and burn. You can only harass, steal, rape, assault, and/or kill for so long before you're finally confronted. Change the course of your life for the better. Do something different. These issues transcend *every* demographic and *every* generation.

If we also sprinkle in some values from chapter 8, we've got a recipe for true transformation and a wealth of prosperity. In particular, it's helpful to apply the values of respect, diligence, integrity, and generosity. (Yes, all of this stuff is interconnected.) We can use these principles and values to dig out hunger, poverty, and social justice issues by their roots! We start by eliminating labels and stereotypes of *all* kinds. Instead of taking the same old tired and ineffective approach (going nowhere fast), we must use critical thinking and try something new. See the difference…

Less effective:

- A top-down approach.
- Broad-brushed racial, gender, or other demographic labels (excuse-based).
- Lend a hurtful hand *out*.

<u>More effective:</u>

- A bottom-up approach.
- Apply individualism (accountability-based).
- Lend a helpful hand *up*.

By applying a new approach, we might begin to address the **root** of these issues…

- Determine *why* individuals are hungry or food insecure.
- Determine *why* individuals are homeless or living in poverty.
- Determine *why* individuals commit crime.

These are just three examples where individualism can make a huge difference. There are many more examples. How do we stop hate crime? By stopping *crime*. How do we stop political violence or domestic violence? By stopping *violence*. Individuals are not hungry or poor because of their race or gender. Individuals are hungry or poor because of their behaviors, values, and choices in life. This concept is fairly straight forward. We must quit obfuscating everything behind labels and bureaucracy. Doing so wastes time, money, and other precious resources. It also costs lives! Instead, we must get to the root of the issues.

Coincidentally, solving these issues involves resources for education and employment opportunities. For example, if a person is hungry, we feed them but also find out *why*, in order to help them become independent. If a person is homeless and lives in poverty, we help house them but also find out *why*, in order to help them become financially stable. Parents may require social service support on parenting skills. If a person requires mental health help, then resources must be made available. It seems not enough people want to ask *why* because it requires time and effort. It's easier to paper over problems by throwing money at them or using labels to obscure the issues.

By the way, an individualistic (bottom-up) approach also involves a new and magical ingredient called *individual ownership*. Wait, what?! Yes, that's right. If an individual violates the law, they're held accountable. If they refuse to work, get an education, or pay their bills, then guess what? It means that individual's struggle is *their* fault – they own it. It's not their race, gender, or political affiliation…it's *them*. Sadly, not everyone will do the work required. Sadder still, some deflect accountability. In that case, the problem is theirs and theirs alone. No one else is to blame. All you can do is wish them well. Sad but true. Prosperity cannot be forcibly poured into someone; they must want it and be willing to do the work. People end up in these situations for many reasons having nothing to do with their demographic, but rather their *individual* actions or inactions. Just a few possible root causes…

- Lack of education. Did they drop out of school? If so, why?
- Lack of parenting. Do they have a parent or guardian? If not, why?
- Lack of employment. Do they have a job? If not, why?
- Lack of money. Do they save and budget? If not, why?
- Drug addiction. Are they hooked on drugs and/or dealing drugs? If so, why?
- Mental illness. Do they require professional help and follow-on care?

This book is not focused on solving broader societal issues – that's an entirely separate conversation altogether. Therefore, I limit my discussion here to the effects on individual and generational prosperity. As you can see, the principles contained herein cannot possibly be ignored. They're absolutely critical. These principles do work and will work, period. Solve the root, solve the problem. By the way, this playbook is also a bottom-up approach, so the more people that follow it, the better it works. *Individual* prosperity feeds into *family* prosperity which feeds into *community* prosperity. Again, bottom-up! We have the ability to change entire **generations** if only we would apply these principles. Entire **generations**. As for me and my house, we're well on our way! We're part of the solution, not part of the problem. We're doing our part. This involves education, financial security, home ownership, values, family, healthcare, and that's right…individualism! The vision is a playbook for *everyone*. But remember, you can only lead the horse to water.

Individualism at Scale

By the way, this concept is true at scale as well. That's why individual rights and freedoms have continually improved in the United States over time. Centuries ago, some individuals believed in limiting women's rights. Some individuals believed in slavery. As time would have it though, enough individuals (of **all** races and genders) fought against those disrespectful and demented ways of thinking. Many individuals (of **all** races and genders) fought and even died to advance those freedoms. I'm proud to have been one of the individuals who has served to protect and preserve those rights – for *everyone*. So has my wife, I'm proud to say.

When I was assigned to military bases in Germany, Japan, and other countries, the people were not my enemies. We were not hateful towards each other. Why? Because we didn't label or stereotype each other. Yes, we could say Japan once attacked the United States or we were once at war with Germany (each their own collective *country*). That's true. And what's *also* true is that most people have a brain and realize that acts of war committed by other individuals in the past do not define events and individuals of today. That is what allows us to grow, progress, and prosper. We don't remain stuck on stupid. At least, most of us don't. I had many good friends while serving in those countries and my life is better because of it. I only wish more people in the world would open their eyes, minds, and hearts in a similar fashion. Instead, too many remain stuck in time and wallow in hate and divisiveness. They carry labels and stereotypes from the past and perpetuate them in the present. We only ever have *today*. The lesson here, at least in my playbook, is to lead the way and be the example.

Once again, this proves and reinforces the entire concept of *individualism* – all throughout history, there have been *individuals* who have done right and *individuals* who have done wrong. Good *and* evil. This continues today. Many people (of **all** demographics) continue to commit crimes and unspeakable atrocities, even within our own cities. And sadly, some remain stuck in *self*-perpetuating misperceptions that hold themselves down. However, thankfully there are many more individuals who are committed to advancing equality, justice, and prosperity – I'm proud to be one of them. How about you? Are you part of the solution? It's time to break free of this disrespectful ignorance and think of yourself and others as *individuals*.

I could go on, but I hope you get the idea. Sadly, some people never will. There are bad apples in every bunch; don't be one of them. Be an individual, not a sheeple. The concept of individualism can practically give you super powers. By the way, I have a special place in my heart for politics regarding this because things can be so divisive to so many ignorant or disrespectful people. All you have to do is accidentally glance online to know what I'm talking about.

Political Individualism

First of all, not all politicians are the same; like all people, they too are uniquely individual. However, a common theme for many politicians is to label, group, and divide people in an attempt to advance their own self-serving political interests. I call this herding the sheeple. Are you a sheeple?

Some imply that you're too lazy or stupid to pay off your student loans, so they pander for your vote on forgiveness (shifting the debt).

Some imply you're too lazy or stupid to get a voter ID card (for a fair voting process), so they pander for that vote as well.

Some imply that you're too lazy or stupid to succeed on your own, therefore you're promised some kind of paltry hand-*out* in exchange for your vote.

Some imply that people are too lazy, stupid, or privileged to follow a *legal* immigration process, so they label others as racist and encourage *illegal* immigration. Which, ironically by the way, if our country is so racist, why do *millions* of people of *all races* risk their lives trying to immigrate here? *Sigh.*

Yes, these political ploys are intended to incite herd mentality, group think, and garner votes, mainly due to voter ignorance. This is why some people vote for a particular party or individual *regardless* of how horrible their track record is. Sadly, uneducated and sometimes racist or sexist sheeple buy right into it. Self-created victims buy right into it. How about you? Do you consider yourself lazy or stupid? If you vote for such things, maybe you do. I surely hope not…for your sake. I think you're smarter than that. I think you're better than that. Something to ponder. Either way, an education and a strong intellect are the best antidote.

Don't be a sheeple or a self-created victim. It's worse than being a Bumbling Dumbledorf.

Part of this pandering and herd mentality leads us dangerously astray as a nation. Since too many politicians spend too much of our money on too much nonsense, our country as a whole is in danger of economic collapse if we continue down this road. Here's a thought – why is the richest nation on Earth drowning in **tens of trillions** of dollars in debt? Hmm. I thought we were supposed to *lead* the world. We should actually have a budget *surplus*! Silly me. So, what happens when the next major natural disaster strikes? And the next? What about future pandemics? What about a large-scale military conflict? How do we afford upgrades to major infrastructure? The answer (apparently) is that we *can't* afford to pay for *any* of this! If we could, then why is it always funded with *more* debt? How utterly embarrassing. Talk about a threat to national security. Good grief.

Anyway, I choose to pick on politicians here because, as a group, there are enough of them (and complicit sheeple) to continue digging us into a financial abyss with group think, labeling, segregating, and sheer stupidity. Balancing a budget is grade school math – spend less than you make. Congress clearly needs help with this concept. *Pssst…*if you wish to build wealth, please don't operate your own household like this. It's deeply hypocritical that some people criticize reckless government spending, yet their own household finances are a disaster; they don't budget, they're deep in debt, and invest nothing for retirement. Remember, critical thinking goes a long way, even when voting for government officials. Some politicians forget they're *public servants*. I'm not a political pundit and I don't care who you vote for. My only request of you is the following – please apply critical thinking. And please, please…regardless of party, vote on *policy*, not popularity, personality, race, or gender.

I'll end my mini-rabbit hole on politics by saying that no President or Congress has ever changed my life. I've never relied on government hand-*outs* for anything. When I've received a tax break, it wasn't the government being nice and giving me money; it is and always has been, me keeping more of *my own* hard-earned money. Any military benefits I've received were *earned*, not given to me. When I've received any pandemic stimulus money, again, it was *my* tax money to begin with. I simply invested any stimulus money wisely instead of blowing it. Sadly, we're all still paying for it anyway because it only gets added to the debt pile with all of the other trillions. However useful, no stimulus money has ever "changed my life." I've never relied on student loans; if I had, I would have paid them back. So, while some sheeple melt down and bleed out of their eyes over elections, I continue controlling the controllables in my own life. The principles in this book are far more relevant to me and my family than empty political promises. Regardless of who's in office, I'll continue living and helping others along the way. I hope you do the same…regardless of who you vote for <wink>.

You vs. You?

This is where I give you **bad news** and **good news**, in that order. Are you ready? Ok, first the bad news. There are some people who will drag you down. They tell you lies, waste your money, make you fat, hinder your career, ruin your marriage, and a lot more. They usually do so unintentionally. In other words, they don't *intentionally* set out to hurt you, but they do. And that's not even the bad news. The bad news is that these people are *themselves*. You may even be one of them! That's right, many people are their *own* worst enemy and sabotage their *own* lives. By perpetuating group think and blaming others, they incorrectly convince themselves that it's always someone else's fault. As I've said earlier, there are many targets to blame: parents, teachers, coaches, bosses, police, corporations, politicians, the rich, the man, or society at large. It may even be someone or something from the past. Who really knows. Either way, now comes the good news – you have a mirror. Yay! That's right, always start by looking in the mirror. The good news is that if you're one of those people who hold yourself back, *you* are also the same person who can change your situation!

A core component of individualism is to take ownership of your life. It's a high control mindset. You decide which direction you're headed. By taking *individual* ownership of your own life, *you* are in the driver's seat. Some people refer to this as agency or locus of control. But don't get lost in details. The terminology is not what's important here, but rather the concept that all things equal, *you* have more impact on your life than someone or something else. Here's how this mindset works…

A *high* degree of agency or control means you believe your actions matter more. For example, if you're stuck in life, it's *your* fault. If you're broke and in debt, it's *your* fault. By owning the situation, you can decide to make a change for the better. This puts *you* in the driver's seat and empowers you to steer your life in a more positive direction.

A *low* degree of agency or control means you believe your actions matter little. If you can't lose weight, it must be a genetic thing. If you don't get promoted, the system must be rigged. If you're poor with money, it must be a racial thing. By casting blame on someone or something else, you give yourself an excuse for not succeeding. With rare exception, you'll never have success unless someone hands it to you.

This is also where the principle of 'control the controllables' fits in nicely. No, you can't control everything but you should control what you can. Remember, "What you believe, you can achieve." Your beliefs feed into hope. As you'll see in chapter 14, hope is powerful.

You decide how prosperous you want to be and then begin the work to get there. And let no one or nothing stop you! It's a battle of you (the victim) versus you (the victor). Who will win out? Here's what this 'victim v. victor' mindset looks in real life...

"I'm heavier than I should be and wish I could lose weight."

> **Low Control (victim):**
> My parents never taught me how to exercise. My work hours don't allow me time to cook or eat healthy. My kids keep me so busy that I don't have time to work out. There's no gym nearby. And besides, I'm just big boned or it's genetic...I love my curves. There's not much I can do about it.

> **High Control (victor):**
> I'm proud of my body, but I've realized that obesity is not a *vanity* thing, it's a *health* thing. Starting today, I'm going to prioritize my health. If necessary, I'll consult a qualified professional to build a healthy diet and exercise plan. Then I'll make time to actually follow that plan. I don't need fancy or expensive gym equipment. All I need is some space for rigorous exercise (indoors or outdoors) and a pair of sneakers to walk, jog, or run. I'll buy

only healthy groceries to avoid the temptation of eating junk food at home. Following my doctor's advice, I'll steadily lose weight and monitor it weekly or monthly to hit my targets. My plan will not be a passing fad or a fleeting trend. Over time, a healthy diet and exercise routine will become a permanent part of who I am. I'll follow the principles in *The Torch of Life*, especially chapter 5.

"I struggle financially and wish I had more money."

Low Control (victim):

I *have* to go to work. My job stinks and pays poorly. They don't care about workers. There's no opportunity for promotion. My boss is a jerk. They need to raise minimum wage. I have no idea where my money goes. Inflation is to blame. I'm a single parent. I'm just stuck.

High Control (victor):

I *get* to go to work. My current job is only a stepping stone in my overall career. I've realized I'm not entitled to a promotion just for showing up. Therefore, I'm going to upskill my education, training, and experience. I'll earn more money, either at my current job, a different one, or by starting my own business. In addition to earning more money, I'll start following a written budget. My budget will include managing my expenses, paying off debt, saving money, and investing for my future. I'll follow the principles in *The Torch of Life*, especially chapters 2, 3, and 4. I'll work towards millionaire status.

"I want to go to college but don't have the time or money."

Low Control (victim):

Going to college means taking out student loans. Only the privileged can afford college. I don't have the money. I don't have time. It's too hard. Maybe I'll do it one day.

High Control (victor):

I realize there are many ways to earn a degree completely debt free. I'm going to stop making excuses and start making time! A college education will boost my career, my income, and my life. I'll follow the principles in *The Torch of Life*, especially chapter 2. I'll start today.

Wow, what a difference! We could go on and on because this mindset applies to *so many* things. I don't know about you, but I'll take the *victor* mindset any day! That's the power of a *high* control mindset. Folks, this is individualism at its finest. Transformative. Life changing. And when you combine this concept with all of the others in this book, you'll start to notice your life changing for the better. I can assure you it won't be perfect. I can assure you bad things will still come your way. It happens to all of us. Trust me, life is not all rainbows and bluebirds. However, by controlling what you can and by taking *individual* ownership, you'll stack the odds in your favor. Take a moment to reflect on your own mindset and how applying individualism can transform *your* life.

In closing, treat yourself and others respectfully as individuals. Take individual ownership of your life through a high control mindset. That's individualism. However, although we're all individuals, we should work together and support each other. We should be kind and accepting of others. We should lend a hand-*up* whenever possible. Please join me because in the end, our prosperity is greatest when we *all* prosper.

PART II (WHY)

So, we've covered a lot so far and if you thought that was the good stuff, just wait. It gets even better. To recap a bit…

Part I included principles on *how* to achieve generational prosperity. However, *why* are you doing so? Why get an education? Why grow a career? Why build wealth? Why tend to your health, unplug from virtual reality, follow principles, live by values, be a victor, and do all the other things?

This is where *Part II* comes in. The following chapters uncover *why* you should live like you mean it and be intentional in life. Broadly speaking, you should do so *in order to…*

- Have a rich and meaningful life.
- Respect and honor prior generations. You walk in their footsteps, stand on their shoulders, and benefit from the sacrifices they made.
- Serve future generations. Pay it forward and provide a helpful hand-up.

Life should overlay things such as education, career, and wealth. They are a means to an end, not an end unto themselves. We do those things *for* our loved ones, not in lieu of them. As you may recall, that's why I don't live to work; rather, I work to live! Oh, and by the way, living these principles is just plain fun! You'll soon discover more, but here are just three specific reasons *why…*

- We get an education not to stare at our diploma and say, "look at this" but *in order to* apply that knowledge, grow our career, and have a better life.
- We grow our career not just to keep busy, check a box, or collect a paycheck. Rather, we work *in order to* provide for our family, add value, and serve others. Our work (the means) provides a sense of purpose and meaning (the end).
- We build wealth not to be greedy or selfish, but *in order to* achieve security, comfort, freedom, and independence. Wealth

provides a fun, dignified, and generous life. We are selfless with our excess and leave an inheritance to those who follow.

There are many reasons *why* people do what they do. In the following chapters, I'll share my own personal reasons – my five why's. In doing so, I hope you'll realize that life is far more than a big house, fancy car, or a pile of money. My reasons 'why' energize and renew my spirit each and every day. They are what drive me to live *Part I* so intensely. Here's a small overview of my five why's…

First, per my mission in life, is my **marriage**. Being married to my wonderful wife gives me meaning, purpose, joy, and fulfillment.

Second, and also part of my personal mission, is **fatherhood**. My two amazing kids are core to my life and fill my heart with immense pride and joy. They are part of the next generation.

Third, and final part of my mission, is **life** itself. How wonderful. How amazing. I view this as the core of prosperity, where all things occur in life as we know it. My life is fun, exciting, adventurous, fulfilling, rewarding, and more. This is also where I lend a helpful hand-*up* to others along the way.

Fourth, is **death**, which provides urgency. If life is where all the action happens, then death is the ticking clock that provides the impetus to do so. Tick tock, tick tock. Death motivates me to live!

Fifth and finally, are my **beliefs** about spirituality and what lies beyond life here on Earth. Our beliefs about the future and other things heavily impact how we live in the present. How best to spend our time here on Earth? What's next? What's beyond? My hope and beliefs around these profound questions lift my spirit in *this* life.

In the pages ahead, I'll expand upon these five why's and what they mean to me. Most importantly, I'll also include some thoughts and advice on how they can benefit *you*.

For me, I've lived *Part I* of this book for so long, it has become mostly second nature. This has come with practice, experience, and time.

Nowadays, I spend most of my focus on *Part II* things. *Part II* is essentially *next level*. Make no mistake, the two parts are synergistic and both are critical. I truly hope you find this next part even more rewarding than the first.

To reiterate, I did not write this book for my own benefit. I wrote it for the benefit of my adult kids and anyone else who wishes to benefit from it. It's my sincerest desire that *you* (and others) will benefit in some way from the contents of its pages. And again, the takeaway is to apply these core principles and concepts in your own life – in your own way. Do not try to walk the exact steps that I've walked. Each person is completely unique in their own way and in their own life…as it should be. Make your own path in life; that in itself is rewarding.

However, we can all apply certain universal principles that will help us on our journey. Just like in football, there are countless strategies and ways to win. Each team is composed of individual players with unique talents and styles. However, mastering the playbook of blocking, tackling, passing, and catching will help *any* team achieve victory – they are universal to all football teams. So too, will the concepts in *Part II* help you achieve your own victory. They will help you prosper but only if you live them.

CHAPTER 10

MARRIAGE

(LASTING LOVE)

It's true that a single person can enjoy the radiant warmth of a bonfire in life. However, a strong and healthy marriage can fuel a raging *inferno* of sizzling heat!

In chapter 1, I discussed the importance of *intentionality* and *critical thinking*. There, I also shared my 3-part personal mission statement in life. A core component of that mission is my role as *husband* (reiterated below).

"As a *husband*, to love and support my wife with all my heart and ability."

Being a husband gives me purpose. It adds meaning to my life. It's icing on the cake. It's also my firm belief that a loving and lasting marriage plays a huge part in my (and my wife's) prosperity. I believe it can do the same for you. I take my role seriously. If you're already married, please read on; perhaps you'll discover a few plays in the playbook that can make your marriage (and life) even better. If you're not currently married, maybe you'll be inspired to search for your true love. Or, perhaps you've already found that special someone but haven't yet put a ring on it. Who knows, we're all wired differently. Either way, I absolutely *must* share the very foundation of why I'm so happy. I would be grossly negligent if I did not include one of the *most important* components of my life – my marriage.

For me, being married is *beyond* the intellectual growth of lifelong learning. It's more *rewarding* than a successful career. And it's far *richer* than financial success. I realize that marriage isn't for everyone; it hasn't always been for me, but thankfully I've found it (or it found me). I've been happily married for over 21 years now and hopefully many more to come! That said, I must caveat my idea of marriage and the part it plays in a relationship. So, here's my two-point caveat…

First point – my idea of marriage is NOT two people saying, "I do" and then throwing their marriage certificate in the drawer to collect dust. It is NOT a marriage of convenience. It is NOT two people living separate lives as roommates. It is NOT an unhealthy marriage or one that involves abuse of any kind. No, I don't believe an unhealthy marriage leads to prosperity. In fact, I'd argue that it's actually *counterproductive* and will only hold you back in life. So, if your marriage is an unhealthy one, I'd suggest you start with a marriage counselor and remember the universal principle 'different input = different output'.

Second point – I respect *all* relationships and family units. Marriage may not be for everyone. You can certainly live a prosperous life without being married. However, I share what has worked for me. Having lived on both sides of the fence (single & married), I choose marriage hands down! Why? I hope the reasons become clearer as you read.

Caveat over.

To me, a life without the love of your life is like a fire without the heat. A heart without the beat. As part of my health wealth, I enjoy being *relationally* healthy. Finding that magical someone is different for everyone. In my case, it's the love of my life, my beautiful wife. In fact, this is where I get to humbly boast a bit, so please bear with me.

Have you heard of a stun grenade? It's also called a flashbang. It's a small hand-held grenade. However, it's not intended to injure or kill, but rather temporarily stun an individual and disorient their senses. When detonated, it produces a flash of blinding light and a very loud bang, thus the name flashbang. Sometimes, the military or law enforcement will throw one into a room to disorient the bad guys before entering. So, what does a stun grenade have to do with my wife? Well, for one thing she's absolutely *stunning*! When I first met my wife on February 13th, 2004, the day before Valentine's Day, I felt as if I'd been hit with a flashbang…boom! My senses were instantly disoriented. All I could focus on was her beauty and mesmerizing smile. I tried not to be too obvious but I'm sure she sensed me melting. Talk about sight at first love, I mean love's sight first, I mean…oh, you know what I mean. Yes, she had me tongue tied! More than 21 years later, she's more stunning than ever and I still melt on occasion. Every year, we celebrate the day *before* Valentine's Day because that's when we first met. How does one get so lucky?

I struggle here because I don't know how to fully convey this awesomeness in writing. I know of no principles, techniques, or steps to finding the love of your life – to even try would be a grave injustice. I admit I must have just gotten lucky in this area. Sometimes, I even feel guilty. I feel guilty that I'm so blessed. How can anyone ever find such a love since my wife is already taken? I don't know, but I'll wish you the best of luck. It may be helpful to read other books on the topic of love and relationships. Perhaps you should seek advice from marriage therapists or relationship experts. You might try your hand at dating apps. Maybe consult a crystal ball, psychic, or Ouija board. Frolic through a field of 4-leaf clovers? I don't know, but whatever you do, I beg you to try. Please, try your hardest. Because more important than money, houses, yachts, careers, and material things is finding someone that you *truly love*. It's challenging to find that special someone; to do so, you must follow your heart. But when you do find that someone, go all in and all out. Wide open, full-speed ahead. Love that person with all your heart and ability. To do anything less is a disservice to you both. How you do that is up to you.

Since there's no right way that I know of, allow me to share a glimpse into my marriage and why I love my wife so much. By doing so, I hope you'll become eager to find your own love. If you've already found that special someone, perhaps you'll have an even greater appreciation for them. You may be inspired to show your love in new ways. In short, marriage is finding that true love and then living by certain principles that continually strengthen your relationship and spiritual connection. Let me share how this has played out in our lives and can in yours too.

Commit.

No commitment, no marriage – no duh! By definition, this is *required*, else you don't have a marriage. Don't half-step it. That's why my wife is my *wife* and not my girlfriend, roommate, lifelong fiancé, or mistress. Be faithful and committed. I've gone *all in*, from ordinary to *extra*ordinary! I've gone from 90% to 100%. My wife and I are our own individuals, but in our relationship, we are *one*; don't dare try to come between us. Don't give up when the ride gets bumpy; those are the times to double down and hold each other tight. Don't be emotionally shallow, flighty, or temperamental. Anyone can love when times are good but true love perseveres even when times are tough. Through thick and thin, through ups and downs. From young and beautiful to old and wrinkly.

I've briefly shared some health issues that my wife has experienced. The real lesson is that we have battled and continue to battle them *together*. Trust me, she hasn't been the only one to get sick. I recall times when I fell violently ill; fever, cough, congestion, chills, and vomiting…lots of vomiting. One night in particular, I barely made it to the bathroom and got sick all over the toilet, the floor, the rugs, and whatever else was nearby. Vomit bombs are real. After crawling my way back to bed and shivering under the blankets from severe chills, I saw the bathroom light on at about 2am – it was my wife cleaning up the mess I had made. She's been there for me too many times to count and I love her for it. (I've also had the opportunity to return the favor many times.)

Another time, my back pain flared up (again). When this happens, the pain is so severe, I'm barely able to dress myself. In particular, my socks and shoes are impossible to get on or off by myself. Guess who's been there to help? That's right, my super wife – putting on my socks and shoes for me. There were times she did this for days on end so I could make it to work. A small but loving act of commitment. I could go on, but the takeaway is to love and support each other in sickness and health, in good times and bad. We chose not to allow our collective health issues to tear us apart. Rather, they've brought us closer together and made our marriage even stronger. We don't discard each other on a whim. Because if you think the grass is greener, guess what? There will be issues with the next person, and the next, and the next…get the point?

In addition to the ups and downs of health, you should commit to your spouse in other ways as well. Be faithful to each other and do not commit infidelity. You should also commit to each other financially. No secret spending or hiding money; lying about money is financial infidelity. We have *our* bank accounts, not his and hers. You should also commit to each other's goals, dreams, and desired futures. For example, when we got married, my wife committed not only to me, but she also committed to relocating our entire household wherever the military sent us. Likewise, I committed to supporting my wife's career transition from military to civilian. Therefore, when her new career began, I retired from active duty in order to provide her with career stability. We worked as a team, pulling in the same direction (forward).

So, it may be health issues, fidelity, money, career goals, bankruptcy, addiction, death in the family, layoffs, a car wreck, or even a simple argument that temporarily gets overheated. A *committed* marriage will weather life's storms. Be strong. Be faithful. This is not to say you should remain in an abusive or unhealthy marriage – you certainly should not. However, road bumps in an otherwise healthy and loving marriage should be tackled *together*. Your shared values, common bonds, and mutual love will persevere and make it worth it. At the end of the day, you love each other and are committed to each other. That said, the foundation of your commitment is built upon shared values.

Shared Values.

It should be common sense, but sometimes I'm not so sure it is, so I'll say it anyway. If you're going to marry someone, it's vital to have shared values. This doesn't mean you think alike, talk alike, look alike, and act alike. No. A strong marriage is built upon a bedrock of shared values; both of you agreeing on things that are important to *you*. For example, my wife and I are very aligned on parenting, education, career, and money, among other things. In fact, chapter 8 listed a host of values that we both share and how they form the foundation of our prosperity. Likewise, we're both military veterans and service is an ongoing part of our life. We walk the walk on generosity and volunteering. Above all, no drama and no chaos. We keep things simple. Those values are great but clearly, they're not for everyone.

People are entitled to their own value systems. I just know our system works so we stick with it. The question is what do *you* value and how do *your* values align with your spouse's. So, as beautiful as my wife is, I value *who* she is even more! What kind of marriage do *you* want (if any)? Ask yourself how it's working out. In theory, it may be *possible* to have a successful marriage with polar opposite or conflicting values. However, I believe that's the rare exception rather than the rule. I also doubt it would be a very deep and meaningful relationship. So, it's not that you like blue curtains and she likes red ones. Rather, I'm referring to core interests that are important to both of you. This includes but is not limited to where to live, whether to have children and how to raise them, career aspirations, views on drugs and alcohol, and of course, religious and political beliefs. By the way, you should discuss all of this *before* getting married. Although not necessary, some couples may find pre-marriage counseling helpful. Yes, we're each unique individuals, but a couple should pull in the same life direction through a set of shared values.

Communicate.

Open communication is a key ingredient to a happy and healthy relationship. Communication builds trust. My wife and I talk all the time and keep no secrets from each other (except why there's so much air freshener in the bathroom). Our lives are an open book, including phones, laptops, emails, voicemails, etc. I know her passwords and she knows mine. We don't go snooping around, but what do we have to hide? I advise open dialogue. When times are tough, use your ears to listen. When advice is sought, use your voice to provide it. Always communicate from the heart.

It's nearly guaranteed that couples will disagree at times. Knowing that, it's wise to have a way to work through your disagreements. That's the magic of communication. Although we're all different, it's important to understand how your spouse communicates. Let's call it your communication protocol. Effective communication requires you to be on the same wavelength. Don't guess or assume. In our case, my wife is normally the quiet thinker. Conversely, I can get impatient and start talking too much. I've learned to give her distance and use questions to ask how she's feeling about an issue. In turn, I've become more patient when we talk. Another thing that helps is to remain focused on the issue you're discussing. Deal in facts and specifics, not hyperbole and drama. When my wife and I disagree on something, we keep the conversation on the thing (topic at hand) and not personal affronts. We can agree to disagree on things, but always respectfully and in each other's best interest – always. Lastly, say, "I love you" often…and mean it.

Love Selflessly.

Love is a verb. Don't ask, "What's in it for me?" Rather, ask, "What more can *I* do?" Ask yourself how *much* you can do, not how little. Don't base your relationship on quid pro quo. Just do. No keeping score; that's a loser's game (regardless of score). Loving selflessly is your opportunity to act. There are many ways to show your love and they don't have to be expensive or elaborate. It's not one-and-done, but rather an integral part of life.

Every so often, I surprise my wife with small things that I know she likes; flowers are one of her favorites. On the flip side, I enjoy it when she makes me a hot cappuccino at night. Small but thoughtful. Doing household chores, so the other can relax is another easy (and free) way to show your love. Run errands. Cook dinner. When our kids were babies, there were plenty of other 'opportunities' to show love: give baths, fill bottles, clean messes, and of course...change diapers! You get the idea – there's no shortage of ways to selflessly love your spouse. Be creative. Big money not required.

As you can see by these few small examples, there are many ways to show your love. I enjoy showering my wife with many acts of love and most of them are inexpensive. Remember, it's the thought that counts. Do I love my wife any less than the billionaire who buys his wife a million-dollar diamond ring? Hardly. In fact, my wife and I agree that the opposite is true; if big money is required, then it must not be true love after all. Something to think about.

I make an effort to love my wife with the same intensity as when I was first courting her. Too many people allow time to erode their relationship. They become complacent and slowly begin to take each other for granted. It takes work to continue fanning the flames!

Be Spontaneous.

Don't fall into a rut. Be playful. Laugh, smile, and joke with each other. Try new things together. Push the boundaries in a positive way. Be fun and adventurous. Hold this thought because as you'll see in chapter 12, my wife and I have done (and continue to do) many exciting things together. We certainly have our spontaneous side and travel all over the country!

Grow.

Be a hot-air balloon, not a boat anchor. In other words, strive to soar your relationship to new heights, not drag it down into the abyss. Always be growing. You and your spouse should not be the same people today that you were 5 or 10 years ago. You should grow emotionally, spiritually, financially, mentally, and relationally. You should grow in the same direction.

Since getting married, my wife and I have both completed our graduate degrees. We have both earned a number of professional certifications. We both continue to learn new languages together (amo a mi esposa). We've steadily grown our financial security. We've both read countless books. Together, we've guided, mentored, and parented our children into successful adults. We've traveled the country together and experienced so many new things. And most importantly, we've grown closer to each other than ever before. We've done all of that (past tense) and will continue to do so today and tomorrow (present & future tense).

Quality Time.

Make time for each other. Intentionally. Don't become strangers passing in the night. Quality time is **not** scrolling on your phones together. Spend time doing things that you both enjoy. Focus on your individual hopes, dreams, goals, fears, or concerns. Have deep and meaningful conversations. Actually, *listen* to each other. My wife and I spend lots of time traveling and dining out, which affords us plenty of time to talk without distraction from kids, errands, appointments, and life. If you're unable to travel, simply go for a walk together. Quality time is important for a strong relationship.

Lasting Love

Looking back, I can't even imagine life without my wife. We've been through so much together and have accomplished a lot – we're also both better for it. I could not have done what I have all on my own. More importantly, I never would have wanted to. The key takeaway is the resulting benefits of a loving marriage. Allow me to share just two small things that I love about my wife and how they've strengthened our relationship.

First, I think the best thing I love about my wife is how great a mother she's been (and continues to be) to our two children. Without my wife, I would not have the two amazing kids that I do. That alone makes me feel like the most blessed person in the world. Our kids love their mom, but I know from experience they won't *truly* appreciate how much she's done for them until they're much older. That's just the way it is. She's epitomized parenting as I outline in chapter 11. From diapers to college graduates and beyond. Not only talk, my wife has walked the walk as a mother and I love her for it.

My advice is to find someone on the same page as you regarding parenthood. It's very important. Do you both want kids? If one does and the other doesn't, that will eventually be a problem. And remember, adoption is an option for anyone unable (or unwilling) to biologically have children. If you both want kids, be sure to talk about your beliefs on raising them. This includes the importance of education, discipline, diet/exercise, values, dating, and all of the things discussed in chapter 11. Yes, it all ties together. You can use this playbook as a conversation starter. For my wife and I, kids are great but they're a big responsibility and not for everyone. For us, we wouldn't have it any other way. Our kids are the greatest blessing in our lives – the next generation! Whether you wish to have kids or not, be sure to discuss things with a potential life partner. Parenthood can be a divisive make or break issue in a relationship. So far, it's been all *make* for us and we're so grateful!

The second thing I really love about my wife is how strong she is – army strong, as they say! Her strength is contagious and drives me to move forward in life, even when the going gets tough. I shared how she immigrated to the United States when she was 14 years old, quickly learned English, and joined the U.S. Army after graduating high school. Suffering from severe back pain, shin splints, and pelvic pain, enduring boot camp and the physical rigors of military life was tough. But for her, failure was not an option. In spite of her pain, my wife soldiered on to not only complete boot camp, but also to excel in her military career. Times were not easy. Her plan was to become an officer one day. Unfortunately, my wife's health issues solidified her decision to honorably separate from the military sooner than she had hoped. It was ultimately in the best interest of both her and the military. Ironically, it was in *our* best interest as well. Her military separation is what allowed us to be together. At that time, my wife and I had been dating for a while, so we decided to get married that summer.

The years following my wife's military separation proved again and again how strong she is. After giving birth to our daughter and still battling health issues, my wife started her civilian career. She worked her way up to becoming a certified contract specialist for the federal government. Her work ethic impressed her supervisors, who were pushing to promote her again. However, after some years, her health issues became more severe. She was forced to leave the workforce in the interest of her health and her life. It's impossible for me to convey just how bad things were for a number of years, but it was very bad. I shared in chapter 5, how my wife suffers from debilitating migraines. Those excruciating migraines led to her laying her head on my lap with tears running down her face due to the pain. She spent hours of each day in a dark, quiet room, laying under the covers. We spent hundreds of hours in hospitals, grasping at anything that would lower the pain. Needless to say, she persevered. Things are still far from ideal, but her pain has somewhat leveled off a bit. She currently takes an infusion every 3 months for her migraines. She has also found other medications and therapies to help manage other health issues, some of which were severe.

In short, my wife's battle (*our* battle) has been a long hard road and is still a work in progress. My thoughts are simply, 'wow, what a woman'! All in all, my wife has twice the strength I do. I have no choice but to walk beside her and support her in every way I can – she simply does not give up! I'm thankful to have such a strong woman as my wife. I want us to hold hands in old age, knowing we supported each other every step of the way. I do not take a single day for granted and look forward to many more years together.

Yes, it may simply be luck that brought my wife into my life. I wish I could claim credit for intentionally seeking her out, but that would not be true. What is true is that our paths did cross and we did get married. As a result, I've experienced so much happiness, fulfillment, and prosperity as a result. My wife has given me two kids. She has displayed more strength and resilience than I could ever imagine. Her career, as short as it's been so far, has contributed greatly to our financial stability, security, and comfort. As if that wasn't enough, she's been my co-pilot on the journey of life, including countless travels and road trips all over the country. As I'll share in chapter 12, we've done the best that we can and continue living the fullest life possible.

In a world of photo filters, virtual relationships, chat-bots, sexting, plastic body parts, twerking, and reality show drama queens, I've beaten the odds. My wife is classy, intelligent, hard-working, strong, beautiful, humble, and so much more. I'm so blessed.

As much as I rave about my wife, I'll slip in a quick note here to mention that I'm the best husband she could ever ask for. How do I know? I have the trophy to prove it! My wife bought me the "Best Husband" trophy while we were visiting Gatlinburg, TN one day. The trophy sits on the nightstand beside our bed as a reminder <wink>.

Boasting aside, I know the success of our marriage has not been an accident. My wife and I have both followed the principles in this book, lived by the values, and continue to grow alongside each other with each passing year. The importance of our value system in chapter 8 cannot be emphasized enough; it is the bedrock of our marriage and ultimately our family. Who knows how long we'll live, but each day will be lived to the fullest…together!

It may sound corny or cliché but my wife is my partner, my friend, and the love of my life. Without my wife, I have the propensity to go off the rails. She's my rock and counter balance. My wife brings me calm, warmth, inner peace, and love. If this isn't love, I simply don't know what is. She's my butter bean (my nickname for her). Yes, I'm lucky to have such a wonderful wife. However, I didn't write this solely to boast about how lucky I am or how great my wife is.

Seek Out True Love

If *you* wish to have a prosperous marriage (and life), seek out that special someone to fall deeply in love with. If you succeed, all else will pale in comparison. Having that special someone to walk by your side is love at its finest. The heat in your fire and the beat in your heart. When you do find that special someone, be sure to do your part to take your relationship to *next* level. Elevate your marriage to new heights each and every day. Focus less on what they can do for you and more on what you can do for them. The advice I've provided here echoes the importance of relational health in chapter 5. In fact, I'd argue that a strong and loving marriage is the very *pinnacle* of relational health! This is all to your benefit. By working at your marriage and following these concepts, you'll be richly rewarded in many ways…

First, and most importantly, you'll have someone in life to walk beside you. A friend, confidant, and partner – someone to love. You can support each other when times are tough and celebrate with each other when times are good. Somone to live *life* with.

Second, if you choose to have children, a loving spouse will be a caring and supportive co-parent to your kids. Raising kids can be tough, so having two parents to share the load is helpful for not only you, but more importantly for your kids.

Third, depending on your careers, a spouse can help you achieve financial success far easier than doing it alone. When two people pull together as one, they can achieve twice as much. In fact, if you believe in synergy (which I do), you can achieve *more* than twice as much!

I sincerely hope you find your own true love; it will turbo boost your life! Be intentional, identify what you're looking for in a partner, and go find that special someone. Don't settle. Your search will be difficult, but it will be worth it. When you do, don't tip-toe and don't hold back. Don't go half-way; go all in. Get *married*. Crush it. When you find someone worth loving…love like you mean it!

Finding true love is perhaps the most important part of *The Torch of Life* – it adds meaning, purpose, and fire to life. You'll never truly know the feeling until and unless you experience it for yourself. Sure, you can live a happy life alone, but wow, can you live a *happy* life with someone you truly love. In other words, you don't know what you're missing until you find that special someone. I don't *need* to be married; I *choose* to be married. It takes life to that *next* level. It takes work and time, but remember – anything worth doing is hard. And this is worth it!

To My Wife:

Thank you for walking by my side for over two decades and counting. I'm double-blessed; you're an awesome *wife* and amazing *mother*. Your continued love and support have taken our marriage to new heights with each passing year. Your exceptional strength, commitment to learning, exemplary values, and hard work have fueled our prosperity. This book, largely a reflection of our life, could not have happened without you. I love you.

CHAPTER 11

PARENTING

(THE NEXT GENERATION)

So, chapter 10 revealed how my role as husband adds meaning to my life and how it can do the same for you. Here, I share a second component of my 3-part personal mission. That is, how the role of *father* gives me great purpose and promotes generational prosperity (reiterated below).

"As a *father*, to love my children and raise them to be respectful, caring, and successful adults."

If you so choose, I believe parenthood can add meaning to *your* life also. Whether you're a parent or not, this principle affects us all in some way. I'm convinced that much of today's crime, poverty, and other societal woes are a result of inadequate parenting. Look around at the consequences of child abuse, neglect, and dysfunctional broken homes. Contrast that with the benefits of a loving, organized, and healthy family life of proactive parenting. Take a moment to reflect on how *your own* character, values, and behaviors have been influenced by *your* parents. Now, I'm not a child psychologist or behavioral specialist of any kind. I'm just a simple dad with two adult kids. However, I'll bet you a ham sandwich that **parenting** is the most impactful thing in a child's life. Taken to the next level, those children become the next generation in our society. Raising children is the very essence of *generational* anything. The quality and caliber of our children and, in turn, our society at large is mainly determined by *parenting*. Yes, the courts, the schools, the police, and the church play a role, but parents are the key. And I vote we take our job seriously. Hear me out as you read along and I'm sure you'll agree. If you disagree, that's fine too – I'll be ok. And as a parent, I'll also say that active parenting (the verb) is one of the principles closest to my heart. Before discussing parenting as a verb, allow me to clarify two things…

Thing 1. Obviously, there are many types of family units; too many variants to list here. There are also many variations of parental custody, guardianship, and legal rights associated with said family units. This includes biological, step, adoptive, foster parents, and more. Also, each parent or guardian may have partial or full custody. There are single moms and single dads. Yes, things can get complex. So, allow me to simplify. Here, I merely refer to a parent as *someone who has parental (guardian) responsibility for one or more children.* That's it. If you're a parent, you know it. (If you're unsure due to legal custodial proceedings, then seek professional counsel.) This is not a judgment on which types of family units work best; life is rarely cookie-cutter. I applaud ALL parents and guardians that actively protect, guide, teach, mentor, and love their children. Here, I simply share what has worked for me and what I believe can work for you.

Thing 2. The world is not all rainbows and bluebirds. All parents are human, just like the rest of us. Therefore, some parents may suffer from addictions, severe health conditions, physical or mental abuse, trauma, legal troubles, or other significant issues that affect their ability to parent. However, this is not an acceptable excuse for neglectful or abusive parenting. In such cases, the parent should seek the appropriate help they require. Depending on the situation, this help may come from other parents, church leaders, teachers, therapists, counselors, doctors, attorneys, social workers, and other qualified professionals. Additionally, various levels of government can offer resources to help families in need (parenting classes, food security programs, financial aid, housing assistance, and more). So, if you're a parent struggling with an issue, seek help and **fix it** – a child depends on you!

That said, I love kids, but I love *my* two kids the most! I hope all parents feel the same way about their own kids. Yes, mine are adults now but let's be real, regardless of age, your kids will always be your kids. They are curious, innocent, and full of imagination. Kids are the future…the next generation. As I've stated in the introduction, that's my key motivation for writing this book. As I've also stated, fatherhood is core to my personal mission in life. What better way to promote and achieve *generational prosperity* than to actively parent?! I wish all kids had the privilege of being raised by loving parents; I believe the world would be a better place. Perhaps I'll have grandchildren someday. If so, I hope I'm around to help their parents out. If I'm not still around, I hope the advice here in this book will help them in some way. I hope this advice helps *all* parents. Whether my kids have a family of their own is their choice. I just hope they realize how wonderful it's been for me being their father. I also hope they know I did the best job I knew how and will continue to do so for as long as I'm alive. Far from perfect, I've learned many lessons along the way and have adjusted as necessary. I've also been blessed with my wife, who has been the best mother our kids could ever ask for. We've learned many things *together*.

One of the biggest lessons we've learned is that 'parent' is more than just a noun. Raising kids into successful adults is hard work and requires action. *Where you focus, you prosper.* And have no doubt, my wife and I have *focused* on parenting. That's where the principle of parent (as a verb) comes in. So, what does it look like to actively parent?

If you're blessed to be a parent, you've probably already realized that it's hard work. And hard work is not an excuse to neglect parental obligations. If you're *unable* or *unwilling* to be a parent, first of all…stop having kids. Then, choose a loving option for your child (adoption, foster care, etc). Outside of that, parents should go *all in* and fulfill their obligations to love and raise their child to the *best* of their abilities. Remember, anyone can be a biological father or mother; that only takes sperm and egg. However, it takes love and commitment to be a real *dad* and a real *mom*. It also takes time and there are many ways to get there.

In my experience, the role of a parent is to do three key things. Just three? Well, like I said, my mind is pretty simple, so I like to keep things…simple. Plus, it works. Now, these three things are hard work and they encompass a lot. What are they, you ask? Well…you should *protect* your children, provide *structure* for your children, and provide *guidance* to your children. Allow me to elaborate on how these three things have allowed my wife and I to raise our two kids into successful adults.

Provide Protection

The first (and most important) role a parent has is to *protect* their children: physically, mentally, and emotionally. It's a scary and dangerous world out there. There are countless ways a child can be traumatized, injured, or killed. Just hearing about a child being hurt brings me pain; writing about it is excruciating. The sad truth is that you can be the most careful, attentive, and loving parent in the world and bad things can still happen. Call me old-fashioned, but my heart aches for those stories of a child dying before their parents. I've witnessed too many tragedies and will not share them in this book. However, here's a story I heard about 20 years ago that seared into my memory…

A mother was driving down the road with her child in the back seat of their car. They saw a turtle in the road and didn't want it to get run over, so the mother pulled the car over to the side of the road. I don't remember what state they lived in, but I see this done all the time here in Florida – we have many turtles. Kind people with good intentions carry the turtle out of the road and onto the grass. I've done it myself a time or two. However, in this instance, the young child acted quicker than the mother anticipated. Before the mother even realized or could react, the child quickly opened the car's back door and eagerly jumped out to save the turtle. As you may have suspected, the child did not look for traffic and was hit and killed by a passing vehicle.

Now, I have no possible way of imagining how that mother can process such a horrible tragedy. So sad. I only hope she received professional therapy and found a way to carry on through life. I'm sure you've heard of other situations where a child was harmed, even in the care of someone who loved them deeply. It can happen in an instant. We've had a few close calls with our own kids, but nothing quite so scary. I don't care to write about such things. I shared this one story above simply to highlight that dangers are all around us. It's not always lions, tigers, and bears that pose a threat to children.

You can (and should) think about things that can be dangerous to your children and how to mitigate those dangers. There are resources and checklists online that highlight dangers to children of all ages – if you have kids, do your homework. Keep in mind, those things change as the child ages. You must tailor your protective awareness and actions to your child's age, environment, and situation. For example, sudden infant death syndrome and small choking hazards may pose a threat to an infant. However, not so much to a teenager who, instead, may be at risk of reckless driving or sexually transmitted diseases. Likewise, installing child-proof locks on cabinets may be appropriate for infants and toddlers. However, teenagers may require a deeper conversation about how to navigate peer pressure, bullying, body image issues, dating, and more. My, oh my. Yes, protecting your child involves many things and it gets more difficult as they gain independence and spend more time outside the home.

Whether we like it or not, our kids will encounter bad people in life as they start to leave the house. It's our job to balance how much help and protection we provide against allowing them to figure things out on their own, thus gaining their independence. It's a delicate dance. I've found it works best to give them slack gradually instead of all at once. For example, call me mean, but I purposely ensured both of our kids fell while learning to ride their bikes. A gentle nudge from behind at a slow speed taught them that falling hurts. I didn't want their first fall to be at full speed where they'd be at risk of a much bigger injury. It also taught them to dust themselves off and get back on the bike. They learned caution and resilience instead of being an entitled snowflake unable to overcome the slightest adversity. Life can be cruel and dangerous.

Besides bike riding, they learned more resiliency lessons at school. Any time they had problems in class, we had them work it out with the teacher on their own. If that didn't work, then we'd step in and help only to the degree necessary. That taught them to solve problems within their control without mom or dad doing it for them. They've carried those traits into adulthood and have navigated life well so far.

Sometimes, things were beyond our kids' control and that's when my wife or I would step in to help. Just like a mama grizzly bear protecting her cub, a snarling growl would usually ward off a potential threat to our kids. Other times, you may have to rip someone to shreds. It just depends. Your children will interact with other kids, teachers, neighbors, family, and friends; potentially bad things are bound to happen on occasion. The more exposed your child is to their environment, the higher the probability of encountering dangerous things. Chapter 6 highlighted a laundry list of dangers that virtual reality poses to children, especially mentally and emotionally. So, not to beat a dead horse, remember that your children can be at great risk from online threats.

In our house, *parents* set the rules. When it came to our kids' safety, those rules were rigorously enforced. We kept in tune with their use of phones, computers, laptops, and gaming consoles. Every so often, my wife or I would conduct a 'random check' of their electronic devices: apps, browser history, cookies, text logs, etc. Did we micro-manage their lives? No. Were we overbearing or invasive at key times? You better believe it! We wouldn't let our kids hang out with pot heads on the street corner or child molesters down the road; why the bleeping-bleep do you think we'd let them do it online?! Come on, now – *know* what your kids are up to, whether in actual reality or virtual reality. *You* set the rules. Also remember, being protective of your children doesn't always mean from physical or virtual bad guys. There's also a subtler protection that can be just as important.

If you're a proactive parent, it's a good idea to protect your children from self-inflicted damage such as poor health and hygiene. A child who eats a bag of candy every day is likely to have rotten teeth and other health issues. A child who overeats is likely to suffer from obesity and many other related poor health conditions. A child who doesn't bathe regularly or change their bedsheets often is likely to smell nasty and catch something creepy. Neither my wife nor I are doctors or dentists but overall, we've simply followed the principles in chapter 5. Yes, kids, you *will* bathe and you *will* diet and exercise. Protect your kids from their own (mis)behavior. Once again, you set the rules and rules are worthless unless you *enforce* them!

Now, admittedly, you can do aaaalllll of that for 18 years and your kids will *still* do whatever they want when they leave the house. (Notice I said when they leave the house. Until then…our house, our rules.) We hope most of it sticks when they leave home. One of our adult kids, who will remain nameless, temporarily fell off the wagon with flossing their teeth and dental hygiene. A gentle adult-to-adult reminder was all it took to get them back on track and (hopefully) keep them there. Hey, we all fall off various wagons from time to time – guilty as charged. Anyway, we can't control what our kids do when they become independent adults. At that point, they make their own choices and live with their own consequences. However, we are *obligated* to protect them as best we can while they are minors and dependent on us. The *best* we can.

Provide Structure

The second role a parent has is providing *structure* for their children. This is where the principle of 'order>chaos' applies (chapter 7).

For example, school systems have an academic *structure* in place (degree programs, course syllabus, class schedules, etc). Teachers require a structured course curriculum; spit balling it is not exactly effective (no pun intended).

Most of us drive our vehicles within a transportation *structure* (roads, highways, bridges, signs, signals, etc). Drivers require a structured transportation system; driving chaotically and zig-zagging across open fields with no roads, highways, signs, or traffic lights doesn't work very well.

Likewise, it's tough to guide kids without having a parental structure in place. Lacking structure, nearly all people (especially kids) will flounder around and swim in circles; there's no path in front of them. Kids should have order and routine in their lives; they need to gain traction and make progress. Does this mean they march around in formation like boot camp recruits? No. Children should have ample free time to play, run around, laugh, have fun, and do "kid stuff." Kids should be kids. However, there are a few areas where parental structure will benefit your kids. Luckily, *The Torch of Life* has already shown you various structured paths that provide consistent and repeatable processes. In case you forgot, here are just a few…

- Chapter 2 includes a model on learning how to learn (and earning a *debt-free* education).
- Chapter 3 includes a structured approach to a rewarding and lucrative career.
- Chapter 4 includes proven principles for growing financial wealth.

So, without reiterating what's already been covered in previous chapters, there are additional parental structures that help you raise your kids. One caveat – it's important not to be *overly* structured. Being too rigid or overly complex can be counterproductive. Flexibility and latitude are essential. Bend but don't break. Think of guard rails on the highway or kiddie bumpers in the bowling lanes. The basic concept is simple – provide your kids with a structured path and they will follow it. What are some basic ways in which parents can do that?

Sleep

Our kids had a consistent sleep routine and they stuck to it. They weren't up until 2am playing video games. They didn't sleep until noon all day, either. On school days, they woke up in time to get showered, dressed, eat a decent breakfast, and get to school on time. On weekends, they were allowed to sleep a bit longer, but not all day long. A good sleep routine was very beneficial to their success. Consistent sleep is healthy for kids and keeps them on track.

Diet

Kids will benefit from consistent meal times. Aside from healthy eating (chapter 5), a structured routine provides predictability and efficiency. Kids can focus better in school with a full stomach. They also know the difference between dinner time, homework time, and play time. Kids eat a better dinner if they haven't been snacking all day. And they're not getting up in the middle of the night eating midnight snacks.

Exercise

Just as it's important to protect kids' health as mentioned earlier, they should also have a regular exercise routine (chapter 5). A boot camp fitness regimen is not necessary. However, our kids exercised at home consistently at least 3-4 times per week. By the way, gym class does not count – most of it today is a joke. Our kids were also active in many sports over the years. Exercise was not an option in our house. Fancy equipment was never necessary, just time and love. If you don't have money for organized sports, go for a walk or jog with your kids. Throw a frisbee around in the backyard. Go for a swim in the community pool or at the beach. Take a bike ride. Do jumping jacks and calisthenics. It doesn't really matter, but make it fun and do it. Make the time. And did I mention – put. the. phone. down.

By and large, most kids have plenty of energy – you just have to funnel it in the right direction. We tried to make exercise fun, which is what it should be anyway. Kids don't *have* to exercise; they *get* to exercise. In their toddler years, they got to sit on dad's back while he did push-ups; then it was their turn to try their own push-ups (without dad on their back). Even in diapers, I'd hold their feet wheel-barrow style and let them walk around the house on their hands. They couldn't stop laughing. I often wonder who got more tired – me or them. Chasing them around the yard with water guns was also fun. Parent Tip: if you want some quiet time, wear your kids out on the playground…they'll sleep like babies!

As our kids got older, it was soccer, baseball, dance, gymnastics, martial arts, wrestling, track, swimming, and anything else we could squeeze in. Hundreds of hours of sports and activities. It's amazing what you can do without stupid phones. Keep in mind, mom and dad led the way; we were always outside running and doing our own workouts around the house. We still do today and I'm proud to say so do our kids. Of course, we all have our health issues that limit things, but who doesn't – we just do the best we can and keep active on a regular basis. When in doubt, ask your doctor what exercise you're able to perform without risk of injury and then…do it. Our message to the kids is that exercise is non-negotiable; it's a lifelong consistent habit just like brushing your teeth. Build a routine that works for your family and stick with it.

[Again, chapter 5 provided advice on diet, exercise, and overall health. Here, the focus is on having a structured approach for your kids.]

Education

As mentioned above, the school itself provides structure. However, parents should also provide structure at home in support of academics. Parents must ensure their kids go to school, learn while they're there, and do their homework. This includes scheduling time for homework, studying for tests, and completing assigned projects. If your kids are taking online classes, ensure they're actually doing schoolwork instead of playing video games. When kids are young, it helps to provide them with a clear and simple focus. For many years, our kids followed three academic priorities that we had them write on a sticky note…

1. School work.
2. Responsibilities.
3. Everything else.

Now, obviously, these priorities were not literal. Clearly, things such as health, safety, people, religion, life, and other stuff are far more important than school work or responsibilities – no kidding. We discussed these in more detail with our kids to provide clarity. They knew the intent behind these priorities; they provided an academic time *structure* to help them prioritize their after-school activities…

First, they did their school work for the day. If they had a question that we couldn't answer, their job was to write it down and ask the teacher in class the next day.

Second, they fulfilled whatever responsibilities they had that day: exercise, laundry, take out trash, vacuum their room, care for their pets, clean their bathroom, etc. It usually wasn't much on weekdays – most chores fell on weekends, when they had more time.

Third, and finally, was everything else: watch TV, video games, sports, play, practice driving (when they had their driver's permit), etc.

It's funny how our kids had ample time for 'everything else' when they set their mind to it. Homework and chores always got done. Then it was time to play, relax, and have fun. It's all about priorities.

By the way, we always preached to our kids that school is a privilege, not a punishment. Just like exercise, you don't *have* to go to school; you *get* to go to school. My wife and I have been 'lucky' – our kids worked very hard in school and we're very proud of them!

Money

As with many things, we took a gradual approach to teaching our kids about money. I've detailed specific principles in chapter 4, but here is another area where *structure* is beneficial when it comes to parenting.

Once our kids were old enough to grasp the concept and value of money, we had them track it on what we called a money log. Their money log was simply a notebook where they tracked their money – nothing fancy. Any time they received money for birthdays, holidays, or report cards, they wrote it down in their money log. The same was true when they spent money (pet supplies, toys, or gifts). Simple, fun, and uncomplicated. This built habits and muscle memory around being *intentional* with money. Somewhere around high school graduation, we formalized it to a more structured budget by using a spreadsheet. By then, the kids could forecast scholarship money and budget for college tuition, car insurance, gas, social activities, and other expenses. It brought their budgeting skills to the next level and set them up for full independence when they left home. It wasn't about *how* they budgeted (money log, notebook, spreadsheet, or digital app) – rather, it was about providing a basic *structure* to their finances. It's in contrast to the haphazard and chaotic normalcy that many kids follow.

As you can see, these are just a few examples of structure. Take a page from this playbook and use it for your own family's benefit. I'm sure you can also think of other examples. Just don't go overboard; things should not be overly complex. Taken too far, excessive structure can be counterproductive, taking more time and energy than necessary. It should make things *easier*, not more difficult. Whatever you do should have the goal of helping your child – and perhaps making your life as a parent a little bit easier. If something works, stick with it. If it doesn't, then change or eliminate it. Don't reinvent the wheel.

Provide Guidance

The third and final role of a parent is to provide *guidance* to their children. Guidance sits on top of structure.

To illustrate with a small example, new drivers (typically kids) require *guidance* within a transportation structure. This guidance comes from driver education instructors, driver handbooks, and…parents. We shouldn't just toss them the car keys when they're 16 years old. Instead, we should provide guidance. I spent a number of years in the passenger seat of the car while teaching my kids how to drive.

Besides getting gray hair, here are just a few examples of guidance I provided them…

- Proper following distance from the vehicle in front of you.
- Following road signs, traffic signals, rights-of-way, and parking protocols.
- How to safely respond to emergency vehicles (police, firetrucks, ambulance, etc).
- The dangers of impaired driving (alcohol, medication, sleepiness, etc).
- How to handle engine failure, avoid road debris, and/or tire blowouts in traffic.

Teaching your kids to drive is just one small, but very important thing you'll do as a parent. As I'll soon share, there are many other ways to guide your kids towards adulthood. It doesn't happen by accident. And by the way, guidance should be tailored to the child's *age* and *circumstances* in life. For example…

Age: A toddler will obviously require different guidance than a teenager.

Circumstances: A teenager who plans to attend college will require different guidance than a teenager who plans to join the military or go into the trades.

Here, as a guiding parent, your role is multi-fold: teacher, coach, mentor, butt-kicker, cheerleader, and much more. All of these roles contribute in some way to guiding your children from point A (birth) to point B (independent adult). Actually, guidance can (and should) extend into adulthood, but it occurs at a different level. Ok, so how do we guide our kids?

My idea of parental guidance requires being proactive; it requires intentionality and action! I also believe in a spectrum of guidance, from very little to non-negotiable (remember balance?).

An example of providing little guidance includes not necessarily dictating *how* your kids clean their room, but simply ensuring that they *do* clean their room.

An example of non-negotiable guidance is enforcing hygiene. They *will* properly brush and floss their teeth daily. They *will* clean their room. In other words, put up some 'guidance guardrails' and foster as much independence as possible from your kids.

A parent should guide a child the way the child is pre-disposed or bent, not dictate the daily minutiae and raise a little robot. Everyone has their own personality (thank goodness), including children. So, remember to tailor your guidance to your child's unique behavioral tendencies, likes, dislikes, strengths, weaknesses, and personality.

In what areas do children require guidance? In the beginning, pretty much everything! After that, you'll tailor things to their age and circumstances as mentioned earlier. There's no standard answer. You'll adjust as your kids develop and mature. Use the below guidance as a baseline and fine-tune as needed. You'll recognize some areas as also structured – that structure helps facilitate the corresponding *guidance*. Following the small example of new drivers, below are a few major areas where my wife and I provided guidance to our kids. They include values, education, health, discipline, praise/reward, and adulting. Things have worked out quite well (so far).

Values

Trying to instill values in your children is an uphill and never-ending battle. Parents are competing with the world. Your kids will be exposed to friends, neighbors, classmates, teachers, and the ever-so-alluring Internet (unsocial media, tabloids, videos, etc). Your kids will undoubtedly be influenced by the world around them, so be alert to this and talk with them often and candidly (age appropriate).

It's imperative that you teach kids values from day one and never let up. Since I've discussed baseline values in chapter 8, there's no need to rehash them again. Here, the focus is on parents acting to instill the desired values in their children. While teaching kids a positive value system, it's important to differentiate between a value behavior and your child's personality. For example, you may be teaching diligence, aiming for behavior of thorough and persistent hard work. One child may demonstrate that by doing their chores in the morning while another may do so in the evening. The time of day doesn't matter, only that the child is working hard. Another example may be teaching gratitude. There are many ways to express gratitude, so be careful not to dictate only one possible way.

Regardless of the values being taught, becoming too rigid or over-bearing can be counterproductive and sour the mood around values. This is not bootcamp, so be sure to have fun with it! Encourage kids to bring their own personality to the table – we're not trying to raise automatons. The goal is simply to teach healthy, positive values to our children…don't overthink it. And don't forget the golden rule which is to walk the talk and live by the very values you're trying to teach!

Some years after formalizing my own personal mission statement, we had a family discussion about personal values with our kids. They each gave input on what's important to us as a family and our general mission in life. In other words, what do we stand for as a family? As output from that discussion, we all agreed on our family's overarching mission statement. Here it is…

"To live & leave a legacy of hard work, education, and teamwork. To help & support each other and the community around us. To lend a hand up, not a harmful hand out. To be part of the solution, not part of the problem."

We all acknowledged it could be tweaked over time. While it's not formal, legalistic, or binding in any way, it does serve as a sounding board for our family's values and mission in life. As our kids continue to grow and form their own lives, my wife and I hope they remain true to these basic values. It's nice to think they'll continue being the wonderful, helpful, and caring people that they are today. It's also possible they'll have their own family some day; ideally, *their* kids will continue the same generational value system.

So, if you're a parent, what guidance have you provided to your kids on values? What do they stand for? How do they behave? Do they walk the talk? Values matter. A lot.

Education

In the instance of academic structure, the overlaying *guidance* comes from staff, faculty, and of course…parents. As part of that guidance, we also preached a mindset of lifelong learning. I devoted an entire chapter emphasizing the importance of being a lifelong learner. It's crucial to guide your kids through their education. In our case, the teachers taught, but my wife and I took *ownership* of our kids' education.

For example, due to our military and career relocations, our kids attended *seven* different schools from kindergarten to 12th grade. We encountered good teachers, great teachers, and hmm…other teachers. Our kids had to adapt to new environments, navigate new hallways, adjust to new policies, make new friends, and a whole lot more with each new school. Yet, they thrived in each and every school. We had a portable system in place (structure) and *guided* our kids to follow the same model in each new environment. I covered the learning model we used in chapter 2. Both kids were very successful in high school – all because we guided them and they did the work. I encourage you to use that same model to make things easier for you and your kids. Why? You guessed it…because it works.

A parent (noun) sends their kid to school and waits for a report card. When you actively parent (verb), you attend parent-teacher meetings, understand course requirements, purchase school supplies, ask about homework, and help as needed when your kids are struggling. Be involved and know what the heck is going on. You don't do the work for them, but you ensure it gets done. Some days you're a butt kicker when your kids are slacking off. Other days you're a forceful advocate for your child when you encounter *that* teacher on occasion…yes, you know the one.

The formal education goal is a simple one, but it's surely not easy. Get your kid from day one of pre-kindergarten to walking in cap & gown for high school graduation. Rest assured, there will be ups and downs along the way. Stay engaged. Stay involved. Your involvement should be on an arc; be more involved at the start and less involved at the end. Once our kids entered high school, we only focused on the big picture. At the start of high school, we guided them onto a path for honors and advanced placement courses. Towards the end, we set their focus on SAT/ACT preparation and their transition to college.

All throughout school, our kids also completed community volunteer hours. Their volunteer programs were a case study in all three parental responsibilities in action (protection, structure, and guidance)…

Initially, mom or dad attended the volunteer work with them. We did this to ensure the environment was safe and free of 'creepy' chaperones (*protection*).

We also worked side-by-side with them to model work ethic and acceptable behavior; in other words, "this is how you volunteer" (*guidance*).

Once they got the hang of it and we confirmed the environment was safe, we'd simply drop them off and pick them up when they were done. They fulfilled their volunteer requirements, logged their hours, and submitted everything to the program administrators (*structure*).

Yes, it was hard work, but looking back now, all of these school activities flew by! Keep it simple in all areas; tell them, show them, then step back and monitor their progress.

When it comes to providing guidance for your child's education, I suggest one final thing. A key parental role at this stage is to help your child navigate smoothly from high school to that *next thing*. Chapter 2 described the many educational opportunities available to our kids as they transition out and leave the nest. The next thing may be college, trade school, internships, military service, entrepreneurship, or something similar.

As our kids will attest, we never tried to dictate the path they should take. In fact, that would be a travesty. I hear stories of parents enrolling their 4-year-old in a certain sport and driving them in some tyrannical fashion. The poor kid never had a chance to voice whether they even liked the sport or not. Stealing your child's youth and dictating their career is extremely sad. And no, the "pay-off" is not worth it. Even if my kid turned out to be the world's best superstar – I could not live with the guilt and regret that it was *my* choice and not theirs. No, thanks. Then we act surprised to see professional athletes' lives go off the rails because their 'success' was achieved at the expense of character, values, and the freedom of thought to pursue their own path in life. Once again, this highlights the difference between success and *prosperity*. This also sometimes happens with the family business as well; mom and dad indoctrinate junior into working the family business at any expense. Also, some military parents will brain wash their kids to follow in their footsteps by joining the service after high school. My wife and I never once did that. Our kids each received *guidance* on their options and they made their *own* educated decision on *their* career paths. If you love your kids, I strongly suggest you do the same. It's great and wonderful if kids *choose* to walk in your footsteps. That's fine and admirable, just don't force it. In either event, ensure they're educated and prepared for their transition into adulthood. Remember, providing guidance is *your* job.

Health

Chapter 5 covered health in more detail; that is the structure. Here the focus is on the parental guidance and enforcement. Along with diet and exercise, you must instill good hygiene habits in your kids. Brush the teeth, comb the hair, trim the nails, and scrub-a-dub-dub each kid in the tub. In addition to their personal hygiene, our kids lived by neatness and organization, courtesy mostly of mom. At the end of the day, toys, books, and clothes were all put away 'nice and neat' where they belonged (order>chaos). The basics are great, but don't forget sleep hygiene. In general, kids need more sleep than adults. Also, when they were young, bed time was usually story time so that made it enjoyable and something to look forward to for the kids (and us). Later on, during the teen years, we simply recommended a consistent sleep schedule and let them learn the hard way if they went to school tired. As they grew up, we added to their hygiene routine: cleaning their rooms, doing laundry, washing dishes, and more.

Discipline

Sometimes parents feel like big meanies. When it comes to disciplining your kids, it shouldn't be personal. The goal is simply to correct undesired behavior. Discipline can take many forms, but you should use the least amount required to effect the desired change (aka progressive discipline). Progressive discipline means you start small and slowly increase as necessary, never to exceed a certain point. There's never an excuse to permanently injure or traumatize a child in the name of discipline. My wife and I must have been lucky because we rarely had to use physical discipline for our kids. (It's funny how we seem to be so lucky.)

When our kids were toddlers, their main discipline was sitting in 'timeout' (a soft couch with cartoon characters on it). If they acted up in public, we may have threatened them with a pinch (pinching their leg).

Sometimes, a firm grab on their ear would suffice. Very rarely would our kids get a swat on the bottom, but it did happen on occasion. Anything disrespectful to mom or anyone else would result in an instant swatting and timeout session. Also, anything dangerous would result in the same. I'd rather have my child receive a swat on the backside rather than get run over in traffic. It was all for their well-being. Those years were few because once they were old enough, it was far simpler to take something away. Taking away toys, snacks, games, or TV usually did the trick. Later in life, it was their smartphones or tablets. With rare exception, that was pretty much the extent of discipline tactics (how to) in our household. However, the tactics of discipline is the small picture.

The real takeaway (the big picture) is to use appropriate discipline as part of an overall parenting strategy to raise your kids into successful adults. It's only one piece of the puzzle but an important one. You're trying to correct misbehavior and further prepare them to be productive, law-abiding citizens one day. Keep in mind, if you don't succeed in discipline at home, it only gets worse outside of the home. Either *you* discipline your children or *life* will.

I shake my head at some of the (mis)behaviors I see in schools today. Wow. And sadly, there are some parents who think their kid can do no wrong. If *our* kids ever got in trouble at school, they were even *more* afraid of mom and dad finding out. School should be an institution of structured and orderly learning and socialization. Fighting, stealing, bullying, and other such behavior should not be tolerated. If left unchecked, the misbehavior (and consequences) only gets worse. One day your kid is facing discipline in the school system and the next day they're facing discipline in the civil or criminal justice system.

Your kids can go from classroom detention to police detention, the court room, or worse, to a jail cell. Just look around – there are plenty of entitled people who feel the laws don't apply to them. They're special. They speed down the highway, cut people off, steal, threaten, intimidate, and then fight and resist police when they're confronted. Yes, they're entitled – entitled to be prosecuted by the law. Society has rules for a reason and there are consequences for breaking the rules.

I can't stress how important it is to fulfill your obligation as a parent and discipline your child. If *you* don't, someone else surely will. If children can break the rules at home, they'll feel entitled to break the rules in society. By the way, kids are *lucky* if they receive discipline at home. Why? Because while it's never guaranteed, parental discipline nearly always avoids societal discipline. Even if your child evades school discipline, they'll be at constant risk of criminal discipline (probation, jail, prison, etc). If they evade criminal discipline, they'll face civil discipline (lawsuits, restraining orders, etc). If they evade all of that, there's a very high chance they'll end up in the hospital or the graveyard (drug overdose, gang violence, stabbing, shooting, car wreck, etc). Even lack of discipline while driving a car can lead to fatalities. So on and so on. Folks, unchecked misbehavior only gets worse; there's no such thing as "getting away with it." Here are a few key discipline areas to focus on…

- Chores and responsibilities.
- Bed times.
- Diet.
- Exercise.
- Manners.
- Dress code do's & don'ts.
- Schoolwork.
- Driving.
- Values (yes, they matter).

Unfortunately, it appears some kids receive no parental discipline at all. I see kids cursing teachers, flipping off police, bullying others, and simply acting like wild animals. Have you ever seen the way some of them act on police bodycam footage? Wow. Entitled and spoiled. Much of it stems from ignorance, lack of values, and no parental discipline at home. Don't be *that* parent.

Here's a news flash regarding discipline – it's not only about correcting misbehavior. You should gradually teach kids to discipline *themselves*. Therefore, discipline is a gateway to *self*-discipline. Self-discipline in education leads to intelligence. Self-discipline in diet and exercise leads to a healthy and fit lifestyle. Self-discipline in your career leads to job security and higher salaries. Self-discipline in personal finance leads to wealth. So on and so on. Parental discipline is a pre-cursor to *self*-discipline. It's wise parenting to promote self-discipline in your children.

Praise & Reward

Whereas discipline serves to correct misbehavior, praise and reward serve to *reinforce desired* behavior. Just as you may use the figurative stick to discipline your kids, more importantly (and more commonly) you should use the carrot. Plus, praising and rewarding your kids is just plain fun! My wife and I have consistently praised and rewarded our kids for three main things: efforts, accomplishments, and values. How so?

Efforts

Effort is the underlying behavior or action to praise. This is actually *more important* than the accomplishment, which is the end result of effort. The effort will build the long-term habits, techniques, and muscle to achieve the results over and over again. A simple example is our learning model from chapter 2, which outlined repeatable behaviors.

Perhaps our kids had an upcoming test. I told them, "If you put in the effort (behaviors), you won't get in trouble if you bomb the test." Ironically, if they *did* put in the effort, they didn't bomb the test…simply amazing. They never got in trouble for a bad grade if the effort was there. Please note the emphasis here is not on the model, but rather the *effort* put into it. Did they actually *do* what they knew how to do? If so, they were praised for their effort, not their grades. Grades were *accomplishments* (icing on the cake). Because if you do the work, the grades will follow. Imagine that. It has worked nearly every single time for their entire life. Perfect? Absolutely not. Like we all know, no one and nothing is perfect. But even with a very difficult exam, our kids still scored well above average. Not because they're special, privileged, or better than anyone. Nope. Because they simply followed the process and did the work. Crazy talk, I know. Obviously, this applies to many other areas of life as well.

If your kids play sports, praise their effort, not just winning. This includes, but is not limited to, training, practice, following the coach's directions, and getting back at it when they fail. Here again, if the kids actually do all of that (effort), the winning will follow. Integrity, good sportsmanship, and effort are more important than winning through cheap shots, cheating, unethical behavior, or illegal moves.

You can also praise effort in household chores, hobbies, diet, exercise, personal hygiene, and a whole lot more. Be creative. The goal is to motivate your kids to continue working hard at whatever the thing is. Reinforce desired behaviors (effort). Long term, this builds *diligence* (remember that?). Yes, this all ties together.

Accomplishments

Praising effort is fun, but rewarding accomplishment is even more fun! Our kids accomplished a lot over the years and we're very proud of them. In school, they've earned excellent grades, honor rolls, awards, scholarships, and more. In sports, they won trophies, ribbons, tournaments, and the like. In turn, my wife and I would justly reward them in an age-appropriate way and commensurate with the accomplishments. Sometimes we'd take them out to dinner. Other times, it was simply ice cream or pizza. They earned their fair share of money, toys, or other gifts. The dollar amount varied over the years, but for most of high school, they earned $50 for report cards with all A's and B's and $100 dollars for straight A's. We gave each of our kids a relatively sizeable cash gift for high school graduation. The biggest tangible gift we've given was for their 18th birthday – they each got their own car. Granted, it was one of our hand-me-down used cars, but a nice car nonetheless. Mom and dad upgraded their own cars and the kids got what would have been the trade-in. Our son's car was 8 years old when he got it. Our daughter's car was 6 years old, but it had more mileage, so it evened out.

A point of emphasis here is that our kids got such nice gifts *because* they worked their butts off to earn them. They accomplished what they did *because* they followed the principles in chapters 2, 7, 8, and others. No hand-*outs* in our family. It certainly was not *expected* on their part or *owed* on our part. And we could afford it *because* we followed the principles in chapter 2, 3, 4, and others. Folks, this **Torch of Life** stuff works wonders – if you apply it. By the way, *none* of these gifts would have occurred had our kids not lived by our values. It's important to reward effort but so are the concepts of humility, balance, and providing context to a given situation – which brings us to values.

Values

I've already shared the importance of values in chapter 8 and instilling those values through *guidance* above. Here, the emphasis is on praising and rewarding kids when they exemplify those values. Of all our kids' many life accomplishments, *this* is what I'm most proud of – the truly *good* people they've become. Their *values* supersede their success in academics, sports, money, and career. Mistakes can be corrected. Failure can be overcome. Money will come and go. However, values are the foundation of *who you are* and I'm super proud of who my kids are…dad proud! They've walked the walk in many ways.

Granted, our kids are not angels and they're certainly not perfect. Once again, if you ever find the elusive perfect person, there will be no need for the rest of us. However, they've worked hard to earn good grades; cheating, plagiarism, or 'artificial intelligence' not included. They've worked hard to earn their money, theft not required.

In fact, our daughter made us proud in middle school by exemplifying integrity. She found $20 in the gym locker room one day and reported it to her coach. The coach said, "thank you" and gave her a big smile (I'm sure one of affirmation).

Then it was our son's turn – he exemplified respect. He told us about a particular kid in school who was a little different from others and consequently ridiculed or teased at times. Instead of joining the ~~stupid~~ thoughtless bullying behavior of others, our son had genuine conversations with this classmate and got to know him a little better. By being kind and respectful, our son built another friendship with a good person who was otherwise alienated by ~~idiotic~~ immature classmates. (I like to think the kid appreciated this and will remember my son for doing so.)

These are simply two small examples of countless ways our kids have exemplified positive values. It doesn't matter the scenario or how big or how small the act. The message here is for parents to reinforce values through praise. It matters. I've praised my kids verbally (aka dad speeches), physically (hugs/kisses, high fives, fist bumps), and with money or gifts when they exemplify positive values. I sincerely hope all parents do the same.

One final note on praise. Remember to praise and love your kids just for being. It's not a requirement to achieve something in order to earn praise. You should praise and love your kids because you're their parents – and because they're your kids. Make them feel loved and worthy because they *are* loved and worthy.

Adulting

Lastly, in terms of guidance, parents must prepare their kids for what I call adulting. This includes advice on relationships, intimacy, love, socialization, and anything required to be responsible adults (work, bills, taxes, car maintenance, and more). This happens gradually and in age-appropriate fashion, but it really picks up steam in the teenage years.

Guiding teenagers is both challenging and rewarding. It helps to remember that we've all been there ourselves. I think it's fair to say the bulk of our adulting guidance has fallen into two main areas: relationships and independent adulthood (leaving the nest).

My wife and I have never had the need to get down in the weeds with our kids regarding relationships. Not yet, anyway. That's because neither one of them chose to date while in school. We told them it was always an option and they could date if they wanted. When asked if they wanted to date, the answer was always 'no'. That could have been because they were always quite busy with academics, sports, hobbies, traveling, and many other activities. Either way, we've been fine with their decisions. That said, we still talked to our kids about the benefits and pitfalls of dating and we still do today. Each of them has decided not to date in their particular season of life, but have expressed interest in doing so when the time is right for them. Smart decision. Overall, my advice to my kids is to feel out relationships in a responsible manner. There's no right or wrong time. Have fun, communicate openly, but watch out for pitfalls along the way: values mismatch, illegal activities, sexually transmitted diseases, abuse of any kind, lack of ambition, lack of education, self-stereotyping cliques, victim mentality, and general soap opera drama. I'd prefer them be in no relationship rather than an abusive or unhealthy one. They know more advice is coming when they start a serious relationship. In the meantime, we continue guiding them on building their independence.

Most kids can't wait to become independent adults, leave the nest, and make all of their own decisions. We started a bit early on some of that – especially the decision part. As I started to sense that our kids were eager to make their own decisions, I gladly fulfilled their wishes. One day, I lovingly conveyed the message via a dad speech…

"You kids are free to make your own decisions. You always have been. Everyone gets to make their own decisions in life. The catch is, you also get to live with the consequences of your decisions. Like it or not, everyone follows rules or risks the consequences. These are not only house rules, they're life rules."

What did I mean? Here's a few examples they were given. You can decide to…

- Not obey house rules. You're free to leave and pay your own rent, your own phone bill, buy your own food, health insurance, dental insurance, and… (Needless to say, they happily followed house rules.)
- Not have car insurance. You're free to pay fines, get sued, have your license suspended, or face jail time.
- Not finish school, earn a valuable degree, or learn a skilled trade. You're free to remain ignorant and live paycheck to paycheck for the rest of your life.
- Not diet and exercise. You're free to get fat, lazy, sick, unfit, and unhealthy.
- Not obey the law. You're free to face fines, penalties, or prison time.

Yes, mom and dad were serious about the freedom to own your decisions and the accompanying consequences. Not obeying house rules had consequences. Why is that? Because *life* has consequences. Our job was to prepare our kids to be successful adults. Our job was to prepare them for life and we took our job very seriously! It's true, you can always do what you want…but remember the consequences. On the flip side, here are some other decisions and resulting consequences. You can decide to…

- Earn a valuable degree or skilled trade. You're free to have a rewarding and prosperous career.
- Follow a budget, live debt free, invest, and follow the wealth principles. You're free to achieve financial security and become a multi-millionaire.
- Build a strong and healthy marriage. You're free to experience

love, support, and happiness like you've never imagined!

Oh, the fun of choices and consequences. We all get to simply *decide* how to live our lives. Why do so many choose to their own detriment? I don't know, but our kids received crystal clear guidance on this concept. What they do from here is their choice (and consequence). They can never say they weren't told or didn't know. And to their credit, our kids have been very thoughtful and deliberate about their decisions – so far. I hope it stays that way. Time will tell. So, yes, we provided advice on the bigger adulting picture of decision making, consequences, and personal accountability. However, we also taught our kids practical and tactical skills essential for independence.

As your kids grow, be sure to teach them useful life skills. This includes things such as how to maintain their vehicle, maintain their home, cook and prepare meals, budget, pay bills, file taxes, perform a change-of-address, organize files, navigate various insurance plans, and all the fun things we adults take for granted. Above all, it's wise to teach them that the only dumb question is the unasked one. When doing something for the first time or two, it's wise to ask questions and seek competent advice.

Also remember, guidance comes in different forms. *Telling* your kids what to do is good; *showing* your kids is even better! Don't be a hypocrite; talk the talk, but also walk the walk! Kids will internalize *what you do* and *how you act* far more than what you preach to them. While there are no guarantees, being proactive in these areas will stack the odds in your parental favor. When it comes to guidance on adulting, be a role model worth modeling. It will pay off in the end.

Memories & Milestones

Most of us are busy in life, especially parents. Don't ever get so busy that you fail to appreciate the moments along the way. Some of my most cherished memories in life involve my kids. Many of these moments flash through my mind like a collage of heartfelt memories. They also make my eyes sweat…

I remember many nights of holding my baby girl in my arms while she fell asleep on my chest. I remember my toddler son lovingly feeding his baby sister apple sauce from a plastic spoon. I remember many years of birthdays, ice cream cake, presents, smiles, and laughter. Opening presents around the Christmas tree, watching fireworks on the 4th of July, hunting for Easter eggs, and enjoying Thanksgiving turkey. My young son dressing up as a ninja and my little girl dressing up as a princess for one Halloween of many. I remember offering baby teeth to the tooth fairy one moment and not much later nervously waiting while my teenagers underwent surgery to have their wisdom teeth removed. Clicking them into car seats one day and handing them the car keys not soon thereafter. I cherish the hundreds of hours spent with my son while he played numerous sports. The pride in his smile when his hand was raised in victory on the mat or when he scored a home run in baseball. My heart broke with my kids when their pets passed away – the pets that they cared for with much time, energy, and love. My heart melted when I saw my beautiful teenage daughter dressed for the prom. I could probably go on forever and I hope to make many more memories with my kids. Time is precious. I've been so fortunate and I'm so grateful for the opportunity to be their father. The takeaway is to cherish the moments. Parenthood adds so much to life.

One of my favorite gifts from my son is a key chain. Attached is a mini B-52 bomber, a U.S. Air Force emblem, and a charm that reads…

> *Take pride in how far you come.*
> *Have faith in how far you can go.*
> *But don't forget to enjoy the journey.*

How true! And I cherish the thought he put into it. So, not only is it great advice, but he also tied the gift to my military service. A memorable keepsake.

I also have a particular gift from my daughter that I treasure. It's an engraved plaque that reads…

TO MY DAD
Always remember

you hold a special piece of
my heart forever
NO MATTER HOW FAR I GO IN LIFE
I WILL ALWAYS BE YOUR
LITTLE GIRL
AND YOU WILL ALWAYS BE
MY DAD and MY HERO

How could a dad *not* love that? Before she gave it to me, she dropped a hint that I was going to love it…and she was right!

I keep both of these gifts on my office desk right where I can see them. If you're not a parent, perhaps you will be one day. I encourage you to give it serious consideration. It's truly a blessing.

Generational Prosperity

Being a parent has been deeply rewarding. If I died today, I'd die a very happy and proud father. However, I cannot possibly write about the love of parenthood without reflecting on my own parents. I was blessed to have both a loving mother and father. Parenting is a two-way street and, as such, I must express my gratitude for all that my parents have done for me. I would not exist without them. I would not be where I am today if not for my parents. My father has passed but I was able to help him in every way I could during his final years. Likewise, I will do the same for my mother. What I must emphasize here is to care for your parents in the same way they cared for you. I was fortunate. I understand there are exceptions. Clearly, some parents don't deserve their title. However, where applicable, we must extend grace, understanding, and compassion. Under normal and healthy circumstances, our parents should be loved and honored. Loving children will remember, support, and care for their parents as they age. Let it come full circle…all the way through.

A parent's job is to complete the hand-off of security, stability, values, love, and prosperity to their kids. As such, it's my personal goal to continue the chain with my own two kids. As covered in chapter 4, an estate plan is the financial and legal link to generational wealth. My wife and I *made the time* to complete our estate plan because we love our kids.

And far more importantly, we've mentored our kids on the other concepts and principles in this book with *their best interest* at heart. This includes the mindset and values necessary for true prosperity – the entire package. Neither my wife nor I know when we'll die, but we'll surely live and love until we do.

As the torch of my life continues to burn down, I'm prepared for the generational hand-off to my kids. I hope they take it and run like the wind! It's my wish that the flame will burn even brighter for them as they carry it through their own lives. In turn, I hope they pass along their own torch of life to their next generation – whatever that may look like. I'm a grateful and blessed father.

Final Thoughts

The playbook for parenting is certainly not *easy*, but it really is quite simple and effective! In a nutshell, parents should give their kids *protection*, *structure*, and *guidance*. Parents should *love* their kids always. Hard work and execution pay off. Oddly enough, all of this has worked quite well for us as parents. Far more importantly, it has worked extremely well for our kids. This is not a humble brag, but rather wholehearted insight on what has worked for us. By and large, kids will follow whatever structure and guidance is in place at home out into adulthood. Not always, but it does stack the odds in their favor.

Like many things, parenting should not be approached from a 'holier than thou' high-horse view. Many things can go sideways (or worse) despite our best efforts. Every parent should give their very best – even in the toughest of times. After all, you're responsible for another living human being…your child. I try not to, so forgive me, but I get disgusted with stories of neglectful or abusive parents. They allow their kids to run wild with no love, no discipline, and no accountability for their entire lives. Then…when the kid is held accountable by society in some way (teachers, police, supervisors, courts, etc) those same parents suddenly love their kid. They're filing lawsuits, protesting, rioting, and who knows what else. Perhaps we should file lawsuits against *them* for lost tax dollars, child neglect, crime victims, courtroom costs, property damage, and a whole lot more. Hmm. Something to ponder. Where were those same parents all of those years? Where were they when their child needed them? Where were they when their kid was skipping school, talking back, acting out, running the streets, assaulting others, breaking the law, and having unwanted babies? Sadly, that part is forgotten. That part is never talked about. Raising kids into successful adults doesn't happen by accident; it takes many things and *active parenting* is one of them. For society's sake, for your own sake, and most importantly for your children's sake…parent like you bleeping mean it!

Secret Sauce:

Don't focus on raising kids into successful adults. Rather, focus on the *underlying behaviors* that raise kids into successful adults. That is, you should perform the three key parental roles (provide protection, structure, and guidance) and instill positive character traits and values in your kids. Successful adults will follow.

I end this chapter on parenting with some heartfelt acknowledgements.

To All Parents:

Thank you. Your job is highly honorable and extremely critical – raising human beings. I encourage you to take your job very seriously. Don't just *be* a parent (the noun), but rather *actively* parent (the verb). Protect, guide, praise, discipline, and love your children. Surround yourself with a team: family, friends, neighbors, teachers, classmates, co-workers, counselors, therapists, doctors, and more. Lean on your team as needed to help raise your children into successful and responsible adults – collectively, the *next generation*.

To Parents Who Have Lost a Child:

Losing a parent is sad, but that's the way of the world. I cannot possibly imagine losing a child. You have my condolences and sympathy, times one thousand. My heart aches for you and with you. Sadly, there are many uncontrollable things in life that can bring about tragedy, no matter how hard we try to avoid them; nothing, not even life itself is guaranteed. It's my sincerest hope and prayer that your child is at peace and you somehow find brighter days ahead.

To My Children:

You give me meaning, purpose, happiness, and fulfillment. I'm unbelievably proud of not only what you've accomplished so far in life, but most importantly who you've become. You're both intelligent, hard-working, respectful, caring, humble, responsible, and so much more. I wish you a life of prosperity and, if you desire, a family of your own. I'm so excited for your future. Although I'll be gone one day, I'll be with you eternally in spirit – that's a promise. Live each day to the fullest because tomorrow is never promised. Whatever you do…do it like you mean it! I love you.

To the Mother of My Children:

I'm so grateful to have you as my wife and mother of our children. You have nurtured them with a loving heart. You have protected them and guided them with a firm but caring hand. Through countless hurdles, military service, career changes, job relocations, living in nine different houses, and battling severe health issues, you have *never once* failed our children. I can think of no stronger mother than you. Our kids are truly blessed. I love you.

To My Parents:

Thank you for all that you've done. Thank you for always being present and loving me. Thank you for changing my diapers, cooking my meals, washing my laundry, and cleaning up after my messes. Thank you for kicking my butt when I deserved it and thank you for hugging me the rest of the time. I always felt safe and loved. I apologize for the dumb things I did as an immature kid when I may have acted irresponsibly or disrespectful. Only as I've grown and matured can I now truly appreciate all that you have done for me and I am forever grateful. I also thank you for the adult advice and guidance over the years. I love you both. To my father (Dad-o), may you rest in peace…I hope to see you soon.

CHAPTER 12

LIFE

(MEANING & PURPOSE)

We all get one of these things called a life. That is, if we're one of the lucky few to have ever lived at all. As I stated in the opening introduction, some are not so fortunate. I feel lucky, blessed, and ever so grateful for the many decades I've lived so far. I don't take a single moment for granted. After all, what are the odds out of all infinite space and all eternal time that we're alive at the intersection of right *here* and right *now*? Perhaps it's just some random, cosmic coincidence, or pure happenstance. Possibly. Many people answer these questions through the lens of their religion; I hold that thought for chapter 14. For the moment, allow me to focus on this life, as we know it, and why I believe it's the pinnacle of *why* we should live the best one possible. For those blessed and privileged enough to be given a life…we only get *one*. Our life may be short, long, or somewhere in between. In the big scope of things, our life is but a mere instant – a microscopic fraction of time. That is, our mortal life here on Earth. Where does that leave us?

The Meaning of Life?

What about our life? What's the meaning? Are we supposed to do something specific? Do we have a purpose or an assignment? If there is a purpose, what is it? What should we actually *do* all day? Why are we here and why now?

I'm sure humanity has pondered these same questions over many millennia. Countless books have been written on the meaning of life. *This* book's aim is how to achieve generational prosperity. A critical part of that is finding meaning and purpose in life. Therefore, as you read, I encourage you to reflect on your own views and your own life. And if I may be so bold as to respectfully challenge you, I'd ask that you do so with an open mind. Read and think as if your mind was a clean slate. Don't be locked into any specific views, preconceived notions, or beliefs that you may currently hold. Don't worry…you can always get back to that later if you wish. I'm certainly not trying to change anyone's views or beliefs. But for now, just allow your mind to be completely open. Aks yourself…

- What gives me meaning and purpose?
- What would make my life prosperous?
- How do I define prosperity?
- If I had unlimited money, what would I do all day?

To begin with, we never truly know how much time we have here on Earth. For me, that's all the more reason not to take a single day for granted. On the pages that follow, I'll expand upon what gives me meaning and purpose in life – the third and final piece of my personal mission statement. In doing so, I'll trace my own personal path as it has aligned with the principles in this book thus far. You'll see how the principles integrate with each other and how they're mutually supportive of one another. By showing how it has all come together for me, it's my sincerest hope that you can benefit the same.

As I conclude my own journey, it will then be *your* turn. I encourage you to reflect on *your* own life's meaning and purpose. After all, my kids (and *you*) are why I wrote this book. I share pieces of my own story only to provide you with inspiration, motivation, context, and a visual of these principles in action. Here we go.

My Personal Journey

What's my own life's meaning and purpose? In my younger years, I went full speed ahead in life without much focus or direction. I worked hard and played hard, running all over the world, primarily engaged in my military career and enjoying social activities with friends. Unfortunately, I lived stupidly and aimlessly for a while, as many of us do. My recreation involved 3-wheel and 4-wheel ATVs, dirt bikes, snowmobiles, fast motorcycles, and plenty of partying with friends. By and large, a fun but unproductive lifestyle with little direction, meaning, or purpose. In the beginning of my career, I worked hard but seemed to go nowhere fast. I was a rat in the wheel…a Bumbling Dumbledorf. However, as my life progressed, I started to learn more, read more, and grow more. I matured my way of thinking and acting. Eventually, I took my education seriously which began to fuel my career and, consequently, my finances. A key turning point in my life was meeting my wife and, in turn, raising our two kids and building a life together. Being a husband and father has turbo-boosted my life. All of this, over time, has led me to solidify my life's meaning and purpose in my personal mission statement.

In chapters 10 and 11, I explained how my roles as husband and father give me meaning and purpose. Here, I expand upon the final component of my mission – my role as a *person* in life (reiterated below).

"As a *person*, to succeed through hard work, education, and teamwork & help others do the same."

Collectively, these three roles provide me with deep meaning and a crystal-clear purpose in life. So, in addition to husband and father, my mission as a *person* is to succeed and help others in any way possible – at least those who are willing to help themselves. In short, to live a life of service. The very essence of service and generosity is lending a hand-*up* to the generations that follow. Admittedly and unapologetically, my family is first in my heart. However, the interconnected generations of humanity are what unite us all. As such, we should support each other in as many ways as possible. In life. Yes, this very life, right here and right now. This is where it all fits together like the pieces of a puzzle. Like the gears of a well-oiled machine. Here's where the principles of *The Torch of Life* culminate into the most prosperous life imaginable. Here, I share my journey as it has mapped to this playbook up to this point. As you follow along, reflect on how these principles can apply to you…

My mission in life grew out of many years of *intentionality* and *critical thinking* (chapter 1). My life *prior* was a candle; my life *after* has been a flame thrower! My written personal mission statement provides a clear sense of adding value to myself, my family, and others. It's my north star. My purpose is service oriented (to my wife, my kids, and the world around me). As such, the principles in this playbook have guided me on *how* to achieve my mission and *why* I should do so.

Why do I subscribe to lifelong learning (chapter 2)? Admittedly, it took me until about age 28 before the academic lightbulb started to flicker above my head. Up until then, I worked hard like many others. However, I began to notice more advanced professionals around me and that education was a common denominator to their career progression. At least, it certainly didn't hurt. A switch flipped and I was off to the races. While working 40-60 hours a week, I completed a 4-year degree in 3 years (1 year was earned through college level exam testing). Upon completing my bachelor's degree, the military relocated me from Japan back to the United States. Approximately 6 months after settling in to my stateside job, I enrolled in my master's program. Between learning my new job, buying a house, testing for promotion, a deployment to Kuwait, and getting married, I finished that degree in about 3 years.

All said and done, that education helped me to advance within my military career and also transition seamlessly to civilian life upon my military retirement. To make an educated guess, it has earned me over six figures of income *more* than if I did not have that education. Aside from the financial benefit, I've also learned many valuable lessons and skills that have helped me immensely in life. Just a handful of those skills include team building, communication, resource management, organization, and critical thinking. Looking back, those years would have passed whether I went to school or not. In the end, I'm loving the fact that I did…it's still paying off today! Much of it fed into growing my career.

Why grow my career (chapter 3)? Why did I *serve* on active duty for over two decades? Why did I then go on to work a civilian career in IT? It would have been easy to remain stagnant and *not* take on any additional responsibilities. It would have been easy to *not* study for promotion. Heck, it would have been easy to *not* constantly up-skill and earn multiple professional certifications. But alas, as luck would have it, I did grow my career and by choice. Yes, it was hard work…but it was worth it! Again, those years were going to pass regardless so, would I rather earn *more* or *less* money during that time? To me, the answer was (and still is) obvious. My resulting income increased and allowed me to earn even more over the years. No, I haven't earned as much as some others, but again, it was never a competition. I'm extremely proud of my service and the value I've provided to my nation. The sense of contentment and accomplishment make me feel very prosperous – not *just* financially. At risk of sounding corny, allow me to call it a 'job well done'! And not by coincidence, those career earnings have fed into my personal finances.

Why do I follow my financial principles for building wealth (chapter 4)? Like most people, I've worked hard for my money. However, unlike most people, I've grown to follow a system for managing it. How you manage money matters. By following a budget (principle 1), I intentionally decide how to spend my money. I just mentioned how I grew my income through my career (principle 2). Living debt free (principle 3) has given me financial security and options to spend my money freely without stress or obligation to debtors. My emergency fund (principle 4) lets me sleep well at night knowing I can cover most reasonable surprises in life. Investing for retirement (principle 5) allows me to steadily build wealth for myself and my family. Owning my own home (principle 6) *really* lets me sleep well at night; I'll always have a home, it will steadily appreciate in value, and I can put even *more* into retirement. Overall, I went from being haphazard and broke to walking a path of financial wisdom and intentionality. Without rehashing chapter 4, let's just say this has led to a bountiful harvest. It's not complicated, secret, or reserved for a special privileged few. This path is available to *every* able-bodied American – but you must make a *choice* and then *do the work*. I implore you to do so as well...for your *own* benefit.

Why do I promote health wealth (chapter 5)? Why not, right? After all, we only have one body and one life, so why not make the most of it. Today, I'm focused on my total health. I've been physically active my entire life. Unfortunately, my diet has not always been up to par, but I've made many changes for the better over the years. For my age, I live with a few health issues, but I consider myself above average in terms of fitness. By following these principles, I'm able to live a fairly active and healthy lifestyle. Now, I realize that I can die tonight from a heart attack. I can get a cancer diagnosis at any moment. I can be shot or run over by a bread truck tomorrow. There are countless ways to die. We rarely know when our time will come but it *will* come. So be it. However, you want time on your side; stack the odds in your favor through health wealth. I would not be able to enjoy *any* of my life if my health did not allow it. I accept that I will die someday, but in the meantime, I will (within reason) control what I can through diet and exercise. Proper diet and exercise give me the stamina, energy, and strength to live each day to the fullest. Additionally, I focus on my mental health. This includes making time for relaxing, thinking, resting, and an attitude of gratitude. So far, it has worked, meaning that the days that I've been given so far have been very good ones. Mental wellness has enabled me to be emotionally present for my family, appreciate what I have, continue lifelong learning, and reflect deeper on my spirituality. In other words, all things equal, my health (and life) have been better because of my relatively healthy lifestyle. In short, live a healthy life!

Why do I unplug (chapter 6)? Why do I live in ~~virtual~~ actual reality? Well, because actual reality is awesome! Life is awesome; not virtual life, but actual life. Remember, a prosperous life is where all of this leads. Don't flush it away in front of some stupid screen. Sadly, I still encounter people all stressed out, anxious, and wrapped around the axle over some irrelevant nonsense in the tabloids or unsocial media. I politely shrug my shoulders and say, "Hmm, is that so?", as I continue having fun, succeeding, helping others, and living my life. It's not a 'better than' attitude. I simply refuse to waste precious life on some petty thing posted online somewhere. Yes, there are billions of things going on all over the world at all times and I rarely need to know about *any* of them, never mind *all* of them. Geez.

I've discovered that the most interesting and relevant moments are those that are happening right here where I am at this moment. After all, did people decades ago have any less fun without smart phones, tablets, and computers? The answer is "no", they actually had *more* fun. How do I know? Because I was there. Most of us were busy enjoying time with family and friends instead of worrying about what some troll was doing on the Internet. Some may say, "Good for you...you're special." No. Hardly. I'm certainly not special. I simply *decide* not to get sucked into the virtual vortex; it's a *choice* that anyone can make. Part of the reason I wrote this book was to convey a path to prosperity. I could not possibly feel it was complete without sharing the power of unplugging. The sheer power of living in actual reality. The freedom, happiness, and joy are simply too amazing. I wouldn't have it any other way! I hope you join me – for *your* sake.

Why do I follow life's rules of the road principles (chapter 7)? Because they work, plain and simple. Life is so much easier when you have some guiding rules to live by. Certain principles in life are as universal as gravity; follow them towards success or don't and suffer the consequences. I value *order* over chaos, which gives me more time *and* more money. I practice the principle of *balance* whenever and wherever possible. I've also learned to focus on areas that are important to me because *where you focus, you prosper* – and I often do this in writing. Above all, I devote much of my time to offering helpful hand *ups* to others in need, but only if they're willing to help themselves. Principles are surely important, but let me tell you…values are *vital* to a truly prosperous life!

Why do I live by values (chapter 8)? My personal values define who I am and what I stand for in life. Without rehashing all of my values, the predominant idea is to be respectful, kind, and help others. In other words, share what works. That's why I wrote this book. I sleep well at night knowing that I'm part of the solution, not part of the problem. I treat others with respect and have donated hundreds, if not thousands of hours volunteering all around the world. That volunteerism alone has been more rewarding than I could have ever imagined. I've seen the tears of joy, appreciation, and gratitude in others (and in myself). Far from perfect, I consider myself a good person and strive to do good in any way I can. I intend to live and leave a legacy – one that will contribute to following generations and the world around me. If I could pass along only *one* thing to my children (or anyone else), it would be a strong value system. I hope I've been successful at that so far. I also respect myself and others as individuals.

Why do I promote individualism (chapter 9)? Simple, because I respect *you*. That is, unless you do something to lose my respect. I also respect myself. I don't label, stereotype, or discriminate against people based upon *what* they are. However, I do judge them by *who* they are. Likewise, I treat myself the same way. This has helped me in many ways.

First, I'm politically non-partisan. Aside from voting for an *individual,* I don't worship any *party* or the other. I know it's bizarre, but I vote on an individual's *policy*, not their personality, gender, or race. This keeps me open-minded and informed on objective facts. Moreover, I rely on what happens in *my* house more than what happens in the White House. As a side benefit, I avoid all the half-baked, opinionated drivel on unsocial media and heated arguments with family or friends that go absolutely nowhere. Pretty simple.

Second, I don't participate in or condone any type of discrimination, period. Neither do I view everything in life through the lens of race or gender. Again, pretty simple; at least to me, it is. If you haven't caught on yet, the theme here is simplicity and common sense. People will prosper (or not) based upon their own *individual* actions (or inaction).

Finally, by surrounding myself with other like-minded individuals, my life has become even richer and more rewarding. I've adopted a high-control mindset. Subsequently, I gravitate towards *victors* who help themselves and others soar to new heights. I avoid self-created *victims* who drag themselves and others down. This includes family, friends, professional colleagues, and people I do (or don't) associate with. Overall, no discriminatory judgement of others. After all, if I judged and treated others negatively based upon their race or color, I never would have met and married the love of my life!

Why do I believe a strong and healthy marriage is core to prosperity (chapter 10)? It's because of my awesome wife! Hey, you don't know what you don't know, right? Before meeting my wife, I was doing well and feeling happy. I thought I was living the life. However…after meeting my amazing wife, I've realized that I can be truly *wow happy* in a thriving and healthy marriage! My wife has been by my side for over 21 years now and I couldn't imagine those years without her. She's been the master key to unlocking my most meaningful life possible. We've been there for each other during good times and bad times. We've cried tears of sadness together when we lost family members. We've also cried tears of joy together to celebrate the many successes of our family and friends such as new babies, weddings, graduations, promotions, birthdays, and more! Loving and supporting my wife gives me purpose, meaning, and energy. For over two wonderful decades, my wife has been my friend, confidant, accountability partner, cheerleader, travel companion, and a whole lot more. As if that wasn't enough, she's also been a superstar mother to our two wonderful kids.

Why do I love parenthood (chapter 11)? *Because my kids will inherit the torch of my life.* They are the 'generation' in my generational prosperity. They bring me pride and joy. I love them with all my heart. My kids give me meaning and purpose. They bring my life full circle. I'm a proud and grateful father. There's something very rewarding and comforting about having a strong family unit. Although we certainly aren't perfect, our family strives to live each day to the fullest. There will be ups and downs, but we support each other along the way. How could I possibly have lived a full life without my two awesome kids? Luckily, I'll never have to find out! I know life is never promised. Mortality will take me from my kids one day, but no matter what…I've already been blessed. Each passing day is simply icing on the cake.

So, yes…*this* is life and *this* is generational prosperity. I've been blessed with an advanced education, a rewarding career of service, a path to wealth, a happy home, great family, and so much more. But the best part? **A life lived to the fullest, a wonderful wife to share it with, and two amazing kids to carry the torch when I'm gone.** Live a legacy, leave a legacy. My cup continues to run over in many ways. I hope yours does, too. Speaking of cups running over, up until this point, I've written a lot about hard work, education, diligence, budgeting, saving, and the like. By now, you may be thinking it's all work and no play – this *Torch of Life* stuff is hard work. That's true. Lest we forget, I've also reiterated that it's important to have *fun* every step of the way. This is even *more* icing on the cake (icing on the icing, perhaps).

Have FUN!

I want to talk about *fun* for just a minute. At risk to my humility, the principles in this playbook have allowed me to have fun in life…*lots* of fun! In fact, I strive to have at least *twice* as much fun as I do work. Fun is not a comparison game and my version of fun may not be yours. As I've stated before, *you do you*, which includes having fun. My point is that this stuff works!

I don't know about you, but I love to travel and experience new things. I've been to 9 other countries, 39 states, and counting. On average, I probably spend at *least* 60 days a year on travel, fine dining, and experiences. Road trips galore. If you like to travel, then travel like you mean it! The country is big and the world is even bigger. Immerse yourself in new cultures and environments. Each travel experience is an opportunity to see new sights, try new food, and meet new people. Get outside of your bubble. Enjoy life.

Now, some people may not care for extensive travel. Perhaps you're into scuba diving, car racing, fishing, hunting, opera, boating, flying, sporting events, or any number of other things. Those are all great! I've done plenty of that, too. Life is *full* of wonderful and exciting things to do and experience. The point is, whatever you choose to do, be intentional about it and then get out there and do it! In my opinion, fun should not be reserved for some later date. I hear too many horror stories…

- Now that I'm retired, I can withdraw from my retirement account and enjoy the fruits of my labor! I've sacrificed so now I get to *live*.
- Once I'm a millionaire, I'll be happy.
- Now that I'm an empty nester, I can have fun and travel.
- Now that I'm finished with school, I can do what I want.

Wow, talk about the horror! Please don't ever have this mentality. Please live life to the fullest *today* and every single day. Live in the present and enjoy the moments. Don't wait for some elusive thing in order to be happy or have fun. Find some degree of happiness in even the darkest of days. This goes back to the principle of *balance*. There are plenty of hours in each day to work hard and still have plenty of fun. Be grateful. Be happy. Choose the glass half full. If it helps, try using a gratitude journal – after a while, it becomes automatic. Work hard so that you can play harder! Whatever your idea of fun is, do it. **You should have some sort of fun every single day.** I sure do.

Smell the Roses

In addition to having fun, it's also important to slow down and savor things on occasion. It shouldn't always be run, run, run. I pity people who are so busy they don't take time to smell the roses. Although roses are great, I also enjoy many other simple pleasures in life. For example, the smell (and taste) of bacon. I also love the aroma of freshly brewed coffee or freshly baked hot apple pie. There are many ways to slow down. Take a hot bubble bath. Get a massage, manicure, or pedicure. Enjoy a cold beverage. Relax for a moment. Breathe in, breath out. Pamper yourself. Watch a good movie. Just as you might savor a great wine, so should you savor life.

I'm also a big fan of nature and love being outdoors, especially on a beautiful fall day – cool, crisp air and colorful autumn leaves. Be aware of your surroundings and the bigger world within which you live. Nature. Take a moment to learn about nature and other living creatures; humans are not the only life on this planet. Far from it. This is a way to remember we're all a smaller part of a larger whole. We should do our part to protect and conserve the planet we live on and the other living creatures we share it with. This is the essence of life. It's not the shopping mall, bumper-to-bumper traffic, city smog, junky electronics, or polluted landfills. Spend the night by a campfire gazing up at the stars. Walk barefoot in a mountain stream. Lay on the warm white sand of a beautiful beach, listen to the waves lapping at the shore, and smell the salt air. Hike into the woods after a fresh snowfall and simply sit still; listen to absolute silence, minus the occasional song of a spirited and gleeful bird. Mother nature is beautiful if only you'll see her. Absolutely beautiful. The proof is all around us.

I've visited amazing natural wonders including Yellowstone National Park, the Great Smoky Mountains, Petrified Forest National Park, Carlsbad Caverns National Park, Ruby Falls (TN), Anna Ruby Falls (GA), Pike's Peak Cog Railway, Mount Washington Cog Railway, Zion National Park, Antelope Island, Garden of the Gods, and countless other destinations. It doesn't really matter where you go, but go. Get out and see the wonderful world we live in. Travel is a blessing. One last area of my life that's also been beautiful is the opportunity to help others.

Generosity & Helping Hand-Ups

It's possible that I'm hard-wired to serve and help others. I don't know. I like to think it's a choice that I make. Perhaps that's what drew me to serve in the military. I hope I've thoroughly conveyed this by now, but a *selfless* mindset is far more rewarding than a *selfish* one. Prosperity is far more enjoyable when it's shared with others. There are countless ways to help people. Out of all the fun I've had in life, some of the most fun (and emotionally uplifting) has been volunteering. Aside from serving our nation, I've had the honor of helping thousands of others along the way. In addition to what I've already shared previously, here are a few more things I've done…

➢ Visited veteran's homes to provide comfort and companionship to aging, lonely, and ailing military veterans.

➢ Volunteered time helping food banks to reduce or eradicate hunger and food insecurity.

➢ Raised charitable donations for the Combined Federal Campaign and Air Force Assistance Fund organizations.

➢ Supported American Red Cross and Salvation Army with donations, fund raising, and blood drives.

The list goes on, but the point is simply to demonstrate small but meaningful ways to help others around you. It doesn't require creating a $50M philanthropic non-profit. Find a cause that's near and dear to your heart. Find someone in need. Find any reason to help. Donate your time, money, knowledge, or talents. You may not change the entire world, but you may change an individual's world for the better. On a personal level, I've provided meals for a co-worker's family while they battled cancer. I've gifted money to family members who have lost loved ones and were hit with financial need. I've performed *thousands* of hours of personal care giving. My wife and I helped a young couple whose house was destroyed by fire; she cooked a ton of food, invited them for dinner, and packed plenty of leftovers in meal-ready bowls. We offer advice on success and prosperity to anyone who cares to ask. Folks, the list is endless. Please look around you and lend a hand up! You won't regret it.

So, in conclusion of my life's meaning and purpose, I'll end by saying it won't last forever. My fun and generosity won't last forever. My life won't last forever. Nothing will last forever. All of this fun, generosity, and abundance of love will eventually end. All the more reason to cherish and live each day to the fullest. All the more reason to pass this along to the next generation! I hope this inspires *you* to do the same. Live *your* fullest life. Now, it's *your* turn.

Find *Your* Meaning & Purpose

So, have you thought about what gives *your* life meaning and purpose? What would make *your* life prosperous? Remember, everyone's path is unique, so don't get hung up on the details of *my* path, but rather the concepts and ideas behind the principles. My intent is to provoke thought and inspiration. This playbook gives you a guiding framework — customize it to *your* life. That's why I emphasize that *The Torch of Life* is *a* way and not *the* way. My aim is to show you a path that works and to inspire you to think (intentionally) about your own path. Be yourself and follow your own passions. People find prosperity in many ways, including through…

- Careers. Even then, which career do you choose? As we know, there are thousands of careers to choose from.
- Volunteering. Again, there are thousands of ways to volunteer.
- Parenthood, arts, sports, hobbies, learning, exploring, traveling, or a million other things.

The point is to be yourself and walk your own walk. Use this playbook as a foundation, a guide post, or a north star of sorts, but be sure to tailor these principles to your own life. That said, I believe there are certain paths that work better than others.

Choose a Path

Choosing a path in life that *helps* others will stack the odds greatly in your favor. It's hard to go wrong when you help others. It's hard to go wrong when you add value. It's hard to go wrong through a life of service. In short, be a good person. I'm sure it's easy to think of countless good people throughout history. You may have some in your own family. You yourself may even be one of those good people. I encourage everyone to choose the kind and generous path.

Conversely, living a life of harm, destruction, cheating, lawlessness, theft, killing, and hate will *not* lead to prosperity. I challenge you to think of a single dictator, gang member, bully, abuser, tyrant, hardened criminal, or other such person who has lived a truly good life. You must scratch them from your list if they lived in the shadows, hid from the law like a roach in the dark, ended up in prison, or otherwise led a hate-filled and negative life. Some people think they've "made it" because they momentarily have millions of dollars from, say, some illegal activity. Why must they look over their shoulder every day of their life, attempting to avoid justice? Why can they not come out into the light? Why can they not live an open and transparent life, free and without guilt? No…they have never truly prospered.

So, fulfill your own purpose in life and do so in a *good* way. This is where it all comes together – the pinnacle of prosperity!

In Summary, Live Life!

Yes, life is where the rubber meets the road – where it all happens. So, by now, I hope you can see how *The Torch of Life* can certainly lead to a rich and rewarding life. You have a playbook on not only *how*, but also perspective on *why* you should live like you mean it. A strong and healthy marriage and children of your own can be the cherries on top of a truly rich and meaningful life. A life with purpose. But remember to have *fun* – not only when the work's done, but each and every day. Have lots of fun. Travel, relax, savor the moment, and learn about the living natural world around you. As an added bonus, have some of the most fun you'll ever have – be generous! Find a way to serve others and lend a helpful hand up. I've shared a glimpse into my own personal life merely to highlight the power of the principles in this book. Whatever path you choose, please live your *own* life – whatever that looks like for *you*. Be intentional and live your life with meaning and purpose. Everybody dies, but not everybody truly lives. Live as if your life depends upon it… because it does!

Thank You:

I am so blessed for all that I have. A great many people have contributed to my prosperity and I am forever grateful. A big THANK YOU to all who've shared this life with me, including *you* for taking time to read this book. There are **way too many** people to thank individually and each has impacted me in their own special way. Life is good. But alas, all good things must come to an end. I hope what's *beyond* is even better. Until that time comes, I've still got some living to do, so please…join me!

CHAPTER 13

DEATH

(ACCEPTANCE & ANTICIPATION)

Life is great but along comes death. Death is the curtain call to the encore. The subject of death can be very emotional. I respect everyone's thoughts, feelings, and emotions surrounding the topic. Now, mind you…I'm not a grief counselor, therapist, or death expert of any kind. What follows are merely my thoughts and personal experiences with death. The message I convey is the exact message I share with my own two kids.

First off, why even think about death? After all, we're striving to *live* a life of prosperity, right? Well, death is part of life and as such, it's a package deal. As it currently stands, if you're born, you will die. So, not only are we likely to experience the death of loved ones in our life, but of course we'll encounter our own death one day. We can choose to bury our head in the sand. Or we can prepare for it. Besides, preparation generally works out better in the end. This is true in many of life's rites of passage including birth, marriage, graduation, retirement, and more. If it's wise to prepare for those events, then why not prepare for death? Yes, I'm weird. I don't obsess over it, but I do prepare for it. Oddly enough, I tackle it head on by walking directly towards it. I've chosen to turn the lights on, harness death, and make it my ally instead of a monster in the dark closet. I suggest everyone do the same. I suggest *you* do the same. Why? Because it contributes greatly to *this* life. That's right. Allow me to share how I prepare for death and how you can do the same. In the process, you'll see how it's beneficial in this life and beyond. After all, that *is* what this playbook is about, right?

You may have noticed this chapter is sub-titled 'acceptance & anticipation'. These two go together like yin and yang…

The first way I prepare for death is through *acceptance*. As part of acceptance, there are two practical things I do. The first is *estate planning*, which I covered the tactics of in chapter 4. You'll recall that your estate plan is the legal and financial link to generational wealth. The other practical thing I do in pursuit of acceptance is *mental preparation*. The act of mental preparation can 'soften the blow' of death, thus aiding in acceptance.

The second way I prepare for death is through *anticipation*. Whereas acceptance is a bit more practical, anticipation is purely emotional and spiritual. As you'll see, my anticipation of death is sort of an on-ramp to life *beyond*. So, let's begin by looking at acceptance.

Acceptance

As it currently stands, death is guaranteed. It's one of the *uncontrollables*. Knowing that, it's logical and even healthy to accept it. I'd argue that acceptance is *necessary* in order to have the best life possible. Fighting the inevitable is rarely beneficial and usually counterproductive. Living in denial and refusing to accept inevitable and uncontrollable events (especially death) can lead to mental health issues. Remember *The Serenity Prayer* from chapter 7. A better option is to build the muscle of acceptance. There are many ways to exercise acceptance in life. However, as it relates specifically to death, I'm a little odd. That's right, I approach this uncontrollable with two *controllables*: completing an estate plan and practicing mental preparation.

Estate Plan

Accepting that I will die has led me to my first practical and tactical way of approaching death. That is, completing my estate plan. I covered the specifics of an estate plan in chapter 4 and will not rehash that material here. **However, know that death (and acceptance of it) is the very essence of why you should complete your estate plan.** Think about it – if you were never going to die or become debilitated, you wouldn't need such a plan. Agreed? Agreed! Like I've mentioned, this stuff all ties together. As it relates to my death, my estate plan gives me peace.

My plan is current and complete. I sleep well at night knowing that if I die before my wife, she won't have *unnecessary* stress over financial or legal documents. Notice I said unnecessary. That's right, if I wasn't prepared, she'd be left in a financial bind. Also, she'd struggle to find important documents to wrap up my final affairs, transfer ownership of assets, carry out my burial wishes, and a whole lot more. All because I was too *lazy* to do some darn paperwork? Not happening on my watch! I want my wife surrounded by loving family after I'm gone…not stressing over how she's going to dot i's, cross t's, and pay bills. Good grief. I love my wife far more than that!

If you're not married, the same concept would apply to a loved one or significant other (fiancé, girlfriend/boyfriend, life partner, etc). You *do* love them, right? Here's a scary thought. What if you're the sole caregiver for someone else and you die with no plan?! You could be caring for a disabled family member, special needs child, or ailing parent. Yikes! That person would be left helpless upon your death. Folks, this stuff is serious. Do yourself a favor, accept your eventual death, and complete an estate plan…please. As if *that* isn't reason enough, there's one more reason to do so.

My estate plan not only protects my wife in many ways, but it also protected our kids when they were minors. If my wife and I died together (or close in time), our kids would have received the same benefits as I just mentioned for my wife. Our plan included legal guardianship documents as well. Therefore, our kids would have been cared for by a trusted family member instead of letting the courts decide what happens. It would be painful enough for a child to lose both of their parents. It would be even worse for that child to also become homeless and have no parental guidance. My wife and I don't operate that way. In other words, we don't neglect our kids' well-being. No, we love our kids far more than that! I hope you love your kids just the same. Fortunately, my wife and I are still alive and our kids are now both in their twenties. So, instead of our kids being dependent children in our estate plan, they have since transitioned into adult beneficiaries.

Nowadays, the *real* benefit is that our estate plan financially and legally transfers our assets to our kids upon our death – the next generation.

Seamless. Now *that* is a huge step towards generational prosperity. Having this plan in place allows me to exhale. I spend my days enjoying life with my family, traveling, and helping others. I raise and love my kids and help them build their own value system; a system that will also contribute greatly to *their* prosperity, even after I'm gone. So, it's not a matter of only helping me *when I'm dead.* No, no, no. The estate plan component of acceptance also helps me *when I'm alive*…here and now. It's not just the documents themselves that matter. The true value lies in the sense of peace that it provides me. The icing on the cake? My wife and kids *also* have peace. They know my funeral wishes will be taken care of upon my passing. They also know my health wishes in the event I become incapacitated. Likewise, they know they'll each be okay financially. I love my family too much *not* to complete my estate plan. Folks, this is why *The Torch of Life* matters! Love your family enough to follow a playbook that brings it all together: career, money, planning, family, life, and yes…even death. The total package. Boom. As you can see, the relatively simple and practical act of completing an estate plan has huge implications in life *and* death. In addition to estate planning, the other thing that helps me accept death is mental preparation.

Mental Preparation

When I was younger, time and age seemed distorted. As a child, I thought 40 was old. At 18, I thought military retirement was a *lifetime* away. I thought only old people died. Then I blinked. My military retirement is now over *15 years* in the rearview mirror! My 40th birthday is a distant memory. And sadly, I realize it's not only old people who die. As time continues to fly by, I now fully appreciate just how *precious* it really is and how *quickly* it actually goes. My perspective on life and approaching death has evolved significantly.

Nowadays, it seems as though I truly feel my age. Granted, I'm not ancient, but body parts are beginning to sag, wrinkle, and turn gray. I've come to realize that I'm not bullet-proof or invincible. My body now creeks, cracks, aches, hurts, and takes much longer to recover from injuries. Perhaps I'm in the fall season of life. I move slower. I eat less. My kids are now adults. I see celebrities and pro athletes on TV who are in their 70s and 80s?! Wait a minute, weren't they young, strong, popular, and sexy just yesterday? At the peak of their careers? I've grown to realize we're all headed in the same direction. That direction inevitably leads to the same place…death. And sadly, I've lost family who have died over the years. We all do.

If you live long enough, you'll experience the loss of a loved one. Perhaps many loved ones. This can be tough. From what I've witnessed, certain circumstances can make it *especially* tough. A sudden and unexpected death can be tougher to process than an expected one. For example, you'd expect a 90-year-old with heart disease to die before a healthy 20-year-old who gets killed by a drunk driver. Likewise, losing a relatively young person can make you feel somehow cheated; that the person died before their time. Death of a child is so sad. Infant mortality is heart breaking.

For me, personally, age matters a lot; not only the age of the person who died, but my own age at the time of their passing. For example, I have distant and vague memories of my great grandparents from when I was very young. I was so young that I honestly don't even recall their passing. Fast forward to recent times (my mid 50's), and I have lost other family members whose passing I remember extremely vividly and very emotionally. As of this writing, the most recent and closest loss I've experienced was that of my father, over 2 years ago. We were very close but it's not my intention to share that relationship here. Rather, I use his passing as a frame of reference for how I've learned to deal a little better with death. About how I've grown and reframed my thinking over the years to be more accepting of death.

My father passed at age 82. At the time, I was 53 years old. I was obviously very sad to lose my father and I still miss him to this day. However, I know if I had lost him 20 or 25 years earlier, it would have been far more devastating to me. I would not have been as emotionally prepared or as psychologically mature. The older I get, the more *accepting* I am of his passing and death in general. No, that doesn't erase the grief and sadness. Acceptance doesn't diminish my father's passing or my loss in any way; it simply helps me to move forward in life. Both the sadness of loss and the gradual movement forward can be *true at the same time.*

I move forward in honor of my loved ones; in this case, my father. I want to honor my father's memory and make him proud by living the fullest life possible. I move forward out of respect for my wife; I don't want to rob her of her husband. I move forward out of love for my kids; they still need a father in their life. And I move forward for myself; I too will die one day, but until then, I will live. I respect precious life far too much to squander it.

From that mindset, how do we process the death of a loved one?

Everyone handles death differently. It's certainly wise to consider professional counseling to help process your emotions. I'm certainly no expert – this is only my own experience. It's fairly common to process loss when and after it occurs. However, what is *not* as common is to prepare for it in *advance*. In that light, what I've chosen to do is progressively continue preparing myself *before* the time comes (again). In short, *mental preparation*.

I've grown to take a proactive approach, rather than a reactive approach. My idea was triggered by the passing of another close family member who died unexpectedly a few years prior to my father. That loss hurt and I vowed to prepare myself better for future loss. I started to play those thoughts and emotions forward in a sort of 'what if' scenario. So, I was able to practice this mindset for a few years before my father passed away. My only regret? I wish I had started sooner. That led me to now practice what I call mental preparation. I consider mental preparation a fairly practical technique for helping myself accept death – especially the death of a loved one. It is, however, clearly more psychological and emotional than estate planning, which is merely transactional.

The way I practice mental preparation is simply to imagine a hypothetical loss and the corresponding emotions that will likely unfold. In other words, *what if* (so-and-so) died tomorrow? Perhaps you could call it exercising my grief muscle. In the case of my father, I found that doing so helped me *greatly* to process through my emotions both leading up to and after his passing. I had mentally cushioned the blow as it were. I was far more *accepting* of his death than I would have been if not for this mental preparation. For me personally, I've discovered valuable benefits to this approach. In the case of my father…

> ➤ It allowed me to live more 'in the moment' when he was alive. Today, this allows me to better appreciate the time that I have with family and not to take those moments for granted.

> ➤ It prompted me to tell him things while he was alive that I would have regretted if he had passed before I had the chance. As a result, my father and I had many meaningful conversations and spent many quality years together while he was alive. Even today, I imagine the last words I would have said to someone if they were to pass away tonight. I don't want to regret my words (or

lack thereof), so I'm extra attentive to what I say.

> I was extra mindful of being patient and kind. In the final years of my dad's life, things such as grooming, dressing, eating, and other daily activities took extra time for him. That was okay. Being prepared for that made things easier. Ever since, I've been more mindful of people's limitations and adjusted my own pace to meet them where they are.

All in all, by better preparing for the inevitable, I've enjoyed a more meaningful relationship with my father (and subsequent other family members). This is all part of emotional and relational health in action from chapter 5. Here, as it relates to death, I feel more relationally *intentional*. I've also been able to avoid many potential regrets as noted above. I continue to work on this mental preparation in the interest of living the best life possible and preparing for death, especially close family. I hope to be even better prepared when I experience another loss. Surely, this doesn't eliminate heartache altogether. I'll never totally avoid the sadness and grief (nor would I want to), but I will have built enough grief muscle to process through it in a healthier manner. Tomorrow is never promised. As such, I will live today and have come to better accept death when it arrives. I am honestly at *peace* with it. Who knows, maybe I'll be next...?

Yes, death can be hard but sticking our heads in the sand only makes it worse. Denying the inevitable is unproductive and unhealthy. I've chosen to face death head on, eyes wide open, and headed *into* the wind. As I've just described, the way I do that is through acceptance. Acceptance has helped me process the loss of loved ones and emotionally reconcile my own eventual death. Let's take this mindset to the next level and go from acceptance to anticipation.

Anticipation

Accepting your own death and the death of a loved one is one thing. But why just accept it? Why not embrace it? It's counterintuitive, I know. I'd argue that many (most?) people don't even think about death, especially when they're young. I'll take it a step further; I believe you should *not* think about death when you're young. Why would you?

First of all, kids don't have the fully developed brain, intellect, maturity, or life experience to fully grasp the concept of death like an older adult can. This is the same reason we discuss the birds and the bees in age-appropriate fashion.

Second, I believe kids should simply have *fun* when they're kids! Ignorance is bliss. Let the adults worry. There will be plenty of time for work, paying bills, repairing the car, and all sorts of other adult things. Don't get me wrong, kids should start to learn about death as they get older – the same way they learn about anything else. No, we should not hide the topic from them or lie to them. However, kids should learn about death gradually in due time. As kids mature into young adulthood and beyond, I suggest an evolving view towards anticipating death. So, what are my thoughts on anticipating my own death and how can this possibly be beneficial?

When I say I anticipate death, I'm not trying to be macabre. It doesn't mean I'm trying to guess when or how it will occur, as if I were trying to "anticipate its every move." It doesn't mean I dwell on it or obsess over it. Neither does it mean I'm trying to rush it along. I'm in no hurry to die. To the contrary, I want to live each day to the fullest.

However, it *does* mean that I've not only accepted the inevitable, but am also curiously and expectantly anticipating it. When it's my time, I welcome death and what lies beyond. There's a sense of curiosity. After all, people have wondered and hypothesized for all of humanity about what happens to us when we die. Where do we go? What's it like? When it's my turn to die, I'll join the billions of others who finally have the answers. I welcome the transition from temporary mortality to eternal spirituality first hand. That sense of welcoming provides benefits in *this* life.

A key benefit I get from anticipating death is the emotional peace I can offer my family, especially my kids. By speaking of death as a natural extension of life and embracing it, I want my kids to know that it's coming. I want them to know I'm okay, even after I'm gone. In essence, "Dad will be fine in the great *beyond* – I shall see you soon." And the same applies to them. I want them as prepared as possible (age appropriate) for death in general. **I want to hand down my acceptance and anticipation mindset to the next generation so they can benefit from it far sooner than I did.** That will enable them to be more financially, psychologically, and emotionally prepared than not. You may think this is all overkill (no pun intended). It's obvious, right? But of course, "people already know this", you say. Yes…in the same way they *know* of education, careers, money, relationships, and parenting, right? Who *actually* ever teaches people and guides them on the topics discussed here in this book? Sadly, the answer is found in…

- ✓ A national student loan debt crisis.
- ✓ Entire generations living in poverty or paycheck to paycheck.
- ✓ Millions of neglectful and abusive relationships.
- ✓ Countless kids abandoned to foster care or living in broken homes.
- ✓ Crippling addictions to virtual reality, opioids, gambling, pornography, and more.
- ✓ Mind-blowing levels of incarceration.

And yes, the answer is found in innumerable families left in a financial and emotional lurch when a loved one dies. These answers scream loudly that *The Torch of Life* is long overdue! The proof is blinking in neon lights.

That is the sad and unnecessary reality for far too many. So, to think that everyone will intentionally and proactively plan for death is virtually a pipe dream. Some will, but too many will not. This is yet one more reason I have these conversations with my own family. And yet another reason why I've chosen to write this book. Death will always be sad and these principles are certainly not a magical cure-all. However, please use this knowledge and experience in your own life. Discuss the acceptance and anticipation of death with your own family and loved ones. Do this for their benefit *and* yours. Please, please…pass it along.

One final and inspiring benefit that anticipation provides, as I said in the opening of *Part II*, is that death provides me the *urgency* to live. Knowing that my days are numbered makes me get on with it…right now! I anticipate dying; therefore, I live. I'm not suggesting that you panic, but neither should you sit on the couch, eat potato chips, and scroll your life away on a stupid phone. Tick tock, tick tock. Don't take time for granted. We learned about the cost of procrastination. Just think about this. If you were never going to die, why would you bother doing *anything?* You could always just say, "Nah, I'll do that later." *The finite time we have is precisely what makes life so precious – death provides that finitude.* This is true of many things: money, gold, diamonds, land, etc. If everyone had unlimited amounts of these things, they'd have very little value. We could burn cash in the fireplace to keep us warm. We could literally pave the streets with gold. **Life is precious** *because* **of death**. What will you do with *your* limited time? The anticipation of death leads me to appreciate life even more and get on with living!

In closing, our life here on Earth is but a mere blip on the radar. I used to be scared of death, even the word itself. No longer. Yes, it's a time for sadness, but *also* a time for celebration and gratitude. It's natural to grieve the loss of a loved one. However, be sure to also celebrate their life and be ever so grateful for the time they were given. Death is an integral part of life. The more I talk about it, the more accepting I am of it and the more I expectantly anticipate it. I work acceptance just like a muscle, making it stronger by the day. Even writing about death here in this book has been cathartic and enlightening. I hope you find the same reading about it. The anticipation comes from finally finding out what happens to us when we die. Yes, I'm curious. After all, in the big scheme of things, we're alive for only a short period of time, but death…who knows how long that lasts. Anticipation about death and *beyond* dove tail right into my belief system.

Chapter 14

Beliefs

(Spirituality & Beyond)

The following is nothing more than my beliefs and ideas. Why do I include my personal beliefs in a playbook for generational prosperity? Better yet, why would I not? I hope the reason becomes clear as you read. I'm positive that my beliefs play a very big part in my prosperity. However, my intent is **not** to convince you of my beliefs. No, not at all. Rather, my intent is to spark critical thought and deliberate reflection about *your own* belief system. What do *you* believe? More importantly, how does it impact *your* life?

Whatever your beliefs are, *have* some. After all, we're each a smaller part of something bigger. As such, it's important to think things through – *all the way* through. I challenge you to open your mind…wide open to something bigger. I've already shared many factors that elevate life from *successful* to *prosperous*. This includes such things as personal values, marriage, parenthood, family, love, and more. Let's add one more grand layer of icing to the cake!

As we know, human beings are composed of skin, bone, water, blood, hair, and other biological goodies. However, we're more than just carbon-based creatures. Let's face it, what really makes us uniquely who we are is our spirit – let's call it our *soul*. As such, our soul is comprised of our feelings, emotions, beliefs, hopes, dreams, passions, and desires. And while many people find success in life, these magical ingredients are the secret sauce to the spiritual bonds of humanity.

How could we ever be *truly* prosperous without a soul? Without a soul, we'd simply *exist* as a single-celled organism, somehow eating, drinking, and reproducing. We'd have no thoughts, imagination, emotions, free will, or control of our own destiny.

Furthermore, must our soul be confined to earthly matters? Is our spiritual energy bound to mortality? Does it simply *end* when we die? I believe not. My anticipation of death guides me to my beliefs about spirituality and beyond. Not the end, but the next. So, what are my beliefs regarding such matters?

Beliefs (Criteria)

I form my beliefs through purposeful and critical thought. Therefore, my beliefs evolve as I learn new information and refine my thinking. My beliefs are also paired with humility; they are my *beliefs* and *opinions*. As such, they are **not** fact-based, scientific, proven, or known truths. Have no doubt, my beliefs may be thoughtful, but they also come from the heart. I concede and accept that this is not logical or scientific, but it's vital to embracing hope. As you may already know, hope is extremely powerful, motivating, and uplifting. I'll share more about hope shortly. I also enjoy discussing beliefs but I don't *argue* over them; that's pointless and childish. I don't pound my fist and say "I'm right and you're wrong!" To the contrary, I love to hear new opinions and even welcome them. The topic is intriguing and intellectually stimulating. My belief system is premised on a few foundational criteria as follows…

- ❖ I remain **open minded** to new information that may influence my beliefs, either for *or* against. This is to my benefit. I'm not closed-minded, petty, stubborn, or obstinate.
- ❖ My beliefs should be **good,** not bad. They should promote **love,** not hate. They should **help,** not hurt.
- ❖ My beliefs should have **integrity.** If a concept is true, then it's true *all the way through* – no cherry picking. My beliefs should not be hypocritically self-serving. That is, they shouldn't lead to *my benefit* but to *others' detriment.*

As basic as it seems, these criteria are important to respecting others. There are billions of people in the world and I am just one of them – the world does not revolve around me. I encourage you to spend some time quietly reflecting on your own beliefs.

What are your beliefs? How were they formed? What criteria do you use? If you were born on a remote island with no family, church, or societal influence, what would you believe today? There are many people who answer these questions through the lens of their religion. I have my own thoughts on religion.

Beliefs (Religion)

Right up front, I respect your religious beliefs. Full stop. That's right…provided you don't believe in killing or harming the innocent, I appreciate your religious convictions. Likewise, I enjoy learning about people's various perspectives, but I don't like things 'shoved down my throat'. I perceive some people as preaching so forcefully, it's as if they're trying to convince *themselves* of their own beliefs. It's best to remain humble and not a know-it-all. Just as I wasn't born with my current beliefs, neither were you born with yours. Our beliefs evolve over time.

That said, I'm fairly agnostic when it comes to religion. So, 'fairly' means I'm convinced there is a higher power, spirit, creator, or energy. There certainly *is* something or someone beyond this life. However, 'agnostic' means I'm not yet fully convinced of the specifics of that something or someone. I'm open-minded and continue learning. I understand my stance may be fairly countercultural. Again, I'm not *against* religion. It intrigues me very much. In fact, you and I may believe the very same thing – I just take time to process deeper thoughts. If you have a specific God or values that you pray to, I fully respect that. Just understand *why* you believe what you do. For example, if you had been born and raised in a (Christian, Hindu, Islam, other) family, would you subscribe to a different religion? What if you'd been taught that from birth and that's all you'd known your entire life? Here's a thought exercise: imagine an alien traveled across the galaxies and landed here on Earth. How would you explain your religion to the alien? Did your God create the galaxy where the alien lives? Perhaps the alien has its own God. Who would be right? We don't know. This concept can be extremely tough for many to accept. Religious food for thought.

Some people may view religion and spirituality as one and the same. While I respect that view, I do not agree. I view religion as a sub-set of broader spirituality. There are many religions in the world. If spirituality was analogous to 'sports' overall, then the various religions would each be a specific sport, such as baseball, football, soccer, etc (Christianity, Hinduism, Islam, etc). And without knowing the details of each, logic dictates it's possible for each religion to be righteous, true, and proper in its own way. In other words, one doesn't have to be wrong for another to be right. Or does it? It depends on what you believe. Being ignorant on the matter, I'll simply continue living a life of goodness, service, and generosity. Without the highest faith, would a God punish me for living love and kindness? I sincerely hope not.

So, we've established that I'm *totally ignorant* about the specifics of any religion. That's why I continue to read, listen, and learn; perhaps a better understanding will continue to shape my beliefs. I'm way out of my league and I would be way out of line if I chose to write about it here in this book.

This is where I digress from my limited focus on religion. I encourage you to pursue what aligns with your beliefs. That is the point. Your religious beliefs should lift your spirit in this life. Wherever the dust settles, I advise you go all in. Adhere to your faith. Until then, I stay focused on a broader spirituality. I widen the lens and pan back as far and as wide as possible. My thoughts and beliefs go much, much bigger than any single religion. Allow me to share.

Transcendentalism (Spirituality & Beyond)

As I shared in chapter 13, I view death as simply an end to our earthly life. More specifically, it's an end to life as we know it. I have some admittedly wild and far-fetched ideas about what life may be like in the future. More on 'life as we know it' later. Ok, so when we die, our body will likely get buried, cremated, or put out to sea. It remains here on Earth, which is why it's common to refer to our body as *remains* when we die.

However, what happens to the rest of us – our *soul?* If our soul doesn't *remain*, where is it? Where does that energy go? That's the age-old question, right? Rumor has it that energy is neither created nor destroyed, but simply changes form (the law of conservation of energy). True or false? Does this apply to our spiritual energy? Hmm. What happens to our soul? Ultimately, what's *beyond* death? For the answers, we must look to our spiritual beliefs.

The highest spiritual concept in my modest mind is *transcendentalism*. The term has many definitions and variations to many people. I'm sure the meaning is much bigger and far more complex than what I present here. Entire books have been written on it. However, as I'm sure you know by now, I like to keep things simple.

To me, this concept is simply what *transcends* life as we know it and everything else. *Everything* includes, but is not limited to, beliefs about life, death, humanity, spirituality, and all religion. It spans our planet, our solar system, our galaxy, and the entire universe. It spans eternity and infinity. All of that and then some. In other words, it's a set of profound questions…

- What is *beyond*?
- Where did humanity come from?
- Where are we going?
- What happens to our soul when we die?
- What *transcends* our mortality?
- Is there a God?
- Was there a 'big bang'?
- Does our spiritual energy extend across the entire universe?
- Where do we fit in time and space?

These are big questions. *How* do we answer these and similar ones? *Who* answers them? *When* will they be answered, if ever? People are presumably working on it. Perhaps we're all working on it in our own way. I don't believe in group think. I also don't believe that consensus or popularity equal fact. After all, the world was once flat, remember? And many 'witches' were burned at the stake. I also know there are things we simply don't understand *yet* – perhaps we never will in our lifetime. Let's take a deeper look at this concept in the following pages. All of these concepts and questions fall under the umbrella of transcendentalism.

There are religions that tell us that essentially, God made the heavens and stars. That may be true and I can respect that notion. If so, how and when did God come into existence? I've also heard of the so-called 'big bang' theory that's said to have created the universe. I can respect that as well. However, what's *beyond* all of that? Way, way beyond. What's beyond the heavens and stars? How vast is the *entire* universe? This is where my mind starts to wander wide open, specifically on the subjects of *space* and *time*. Join me – let's see where this leads us.

Infinity (endless space)

The science of infinity is way outside my lane and far above my paygrade, as they say. I'm sure there are brainiacs who study such concepts in-depth; physicists, mathematicians, cosmologists, astronomers, astrophysicists, and other big-head intellectual academic genius thinkers…whew, I'm getting dizzy! I guess there's solace in the fact that even *they* don't know exactly what exists in the far expanses of our universe.

[Side bar on the term 'universe'. When I say universe, I mean *everything*. Some people may view our universe in the same way they view our solar system or our galaxy, implying it has boundaries or that there's more than one. I say this because I hear estimates on how old the universe is. Perhaps 'our' universe has an age. I can buy that. However, our universe is ultimately a part of something bigger. That something is what I'm referring to – all of it. So, the universe I refer to has no age or bounds; it's been around for *eternity* (more on that soon) and extends in every direction forever (*infinity*). Yes, it's quite possible that more than one universe exists, but to me the *uni*verse (one) is **everything**.]

The idea that space is *endless* intrigues me to no end and boggles my mind. The universe extends in all directions…forever! Even if it could 'warp', as some theories posit, and curve back on itself in a sort of loop – there's still something outside (beyond) that loop! And something outside of *that* something. Now, I don't know the first thing about the scientific makeup of nebulas, plasma, black holes, matter, anti-matter, and all of that fancy stuff – it's not necessary. The point is, you can go in a straight line forever. Forever. You may travel through an *atmosphere*, such as here on Earth. You may traverse a *vacuum* of empty space, such as between our atmosphere and the moon. You may pass through a soupy mix of *matter* or *anti-matter*. You may encounter something that you're unable to travel through due to the physical makeup and/or gravitational pull of the thing. If you travel far enough in a straight line, you may even hit a *brick wall* like in a cartoon. You may even hit *nothing*. And guess what? Nothing is still something! Forever and ever, and ever. And ever. So, what *is* out there? What cosmic material exists that may prevent us from traveling or seeing beyond it, but yet is still present? Perhaps it's the *dead end* of the universe. No outlet. But even beyond that, yep…there's something else. So, how does infinity affect my beliefs?

First of all, if you never spend any time thinking universally, you'll never get any benefit from it. The biggest you can think is universally; *everything* (time, space, spirituality, life, death, and things not yet known). It actually leads to more questions…

- Where does humanity fit within the entire universe?
- Are there other human beings (or other life forms) out in the universe?
- How far will humans eventually be able to travel within the universe?
- Will other life eventually reach us here on Earth?
- How would other life affect our beliefs around religion?

You may think, "Who cares, what does it matter?" Well, that sentiment can be both true *and* false at the same time (relativity). Sure, it's not *necessary* to reflect on infinity at all. However, the same was true of electricity, vaccinations, nuclear power, antibiotics, computers, satellites, and countless other things that have significantly transformed our way of life. These advancements and others have occurred gradually over time, each one starting first with a single seed of thought. Good minds think about the present; great minds also think about the future. So, what does it matter? You decide for yourself.

When it comes to infinity, I'm reminded of my place here on Earth and how we fit into the larger universe. Will our species spread throughout the universe? After all, humans have already ventured to the moon and are now eyeing Mars. Logic dictates that if we do not find a way to live someplace other than Earth, the human race will surely become extinct one day. Our planet *will* become uninhabitable someday. Is humanity destined to die a slow and gradual death? Or will our planet simply explode due to some cosmic action? The thought is not merely the plot in some sci-fi movie; Earth's transience is a *reality*. If we look far enough into the future, there will come a time when our planet will cease to exist. That may be millions, billions, or trillions of years from now. Who knows. It doesn't really matter how long. One day, Earth will no longer exist. **So, how important is it to preserve the human race?**

The scope and scale of the infinite universe provide perspective. I understand that I'm the weirdo and few people think of such matters. I got it. Many are simply trying to decide what movie to watch this weekend or if their favorite beer is on sale. And for the most part, I agree – that's a controllable and we *should* think of those things. However, make some time to *also* stretch and expand your mind for your own benefit. You may be surprised at how your views, your vision, and your spirit all grow in the process. The vastness of infinity keeps me grounded, humble, and content. Sometimes, I see people drooling over a mansion, a diamond ring, or a private island. They worship some so-called celebrity with a fancy car that will be junk in a few years. News flash – in the big scheme of life, those things are but a tiny grain of sand on the beach. Even planet Earth is a single grain of sand when compared to the entire sandy beach of the universe.

So, we *should* enjoy a movie this weekend. We *should* enjoy an ice-cold beer, if that is our wish. We *should* continue to work hard and strive for better. We *should* live our best life possible. Having and enjoying nice things is great! We simply shouldn't *worship* them. We should *also* keep them in perspective and have one eye on the future. It's not either-or. Both are true. We must allow our minds to wander wide open. We should also remain humble and content. I suggest we think and act big, but remember we're also very small. I view the Earth as if I'm out in space, looking down at it. It can make 'big' problems seem awfully small. It also helps me reframe what's important in life. If you've never thought about infinity before, give it a try. I find it empowering and rewarding. But don't stop there because next up is the concept of eternity.

Eternity (endless time)

Whereas infinity can describe endless space, it can also refer to endless (infinite) time. However, I prefer the word **eternity** to describe endless time – it has a more peaceful ring to it. And time *is* endless, at least conceptually, right? Depending on your beliefs, religion, and possibly physics, some people argue that time has a beginning. If so, does that imply it has an end? Maybe the big bang gave us time. Perhaps it was God, or *a* God that gave us time. I don't know and I keep my mind open to all possibilities. However, I believe time has always *been* and will always *be* – forever. Tick tock, tick tock. The idea of eternity invokes awe and wonder beyond imagination. Even if there was a big bang or Godly intervention, there was time before that. In other words, how long was it before time came into existence? Even *that* was time. No, I don't believe that time has a beginning or an end. It has existed for, well…eternity. For me, eternity is even more amazing than infinite space. I think about how much the entire universe has changed (and will change) over the course of time, eternal time. Forget billions or trillions of years – let's multiply that by trillions and trillions more. Think about this – suppose that our universe did come from some big bang. And suppose it is billions of years old. In the context of eternity, our universe could have already expanded, collapsed, and been reborn *gazillions* of times in the past and can continue to do so…*forever*. Is all of that energy (including our spiritual energy) being recycled in some fashion? Are we in some gigantic replay loop? Is the universe merely a microscopic cell in some enormous living creature? Are we a science experiment? Is this endless random happenstance? Too many questions, right? So, how does all of this feed into my beliefs and why does it matter?

Like infinity, the concept of eternity provides broader and deeper *perspective* to our humanity. After all, our entire life is but a mere ticking of the second hand relative to the clock of eternity. This concept, more than any other, *drives* me in life and leads me to *cherish* every single moment. It doesn't make me live life in a rushed or panicked way, but rather in an intentional and meaningful way. Balanced. I don't want to squander or waste a single minute; nor do I want to live so hastily as to not appreciate and savor every moment either. Time, sweet time. We are each blessed with our very own moment in the vast endless time of eternity. We are a mere blip on this planet, in this solar system, this galaxy, and the entire universe, at this very moment in time. You don't control the beginning of your life. And with rare exception, neither do you control the end of your life. However, you do control your life in between. Out of all that eternity, how do you choose to spend the precious time you've been given? Will you be petty, hateful, and negative? Will you dwell on the racial/gender label you've given yourself? Obsess over a troll on unsocial media? Will you be a lazy Bumbling Dumbledorf? A rat in a wheel? A sheeple? Maybe you'll be content to scroll and double-click your life away. Not me, not a chance. I plan to live! Please don't waste your precious life – don't you dare. And after we're done living, who knows what's next. Are you beginning to see how our beliefs can affect our daily lives? Our beliefs about *beyond* this life also affect our spirituality.

Spirituality (Life Beyond)

I think most of us can agree (for now) that we're all going to die. That is to say our mortal life here on Earth will end. So, what then? As for me, I believe our spiritual energy (soul) continues on in some fashion. What does that look like and how does it happen? I don't know. That's the question of the hour, right? Before continuing into such a grand topic, keep some things in mind.

It's important to follow the logic on *why* this all matters. So far, this playbook has not only shown us *how* to prosper, but has also shared *why* we should do so. This includes the choice to build a strong and loving marriage. It includes the optional joy and heartfelt reward of raising children. And it culminates in the choice to live a rich, happy, and generous life. What a blessing. As wonderful as that all is, there's more. Our thoughts would be incomplete if we stopped there. After our brief mortal life here on Earth, what's next? That is the question at hand.

Over the course of my life, I *believed* many things only to find out they were far different than I originally thought. Maybe not better or worse, but certainly *different*. Perhaps you've experienced the same. For example, as a child, my beliefs about adulthood, relationships, and even Santa Claus turned out to be not so accurate. As an 18-year-old, my beliefs about the military turned out to be different from actually *serving*. And even as a grown adult, my beliefs about parenthood were different in many ways from actually *being* a parent.

Therefore, as I lay out my beliefs regarding life after death (life beyond), I remain humble and open-minded. My beliefs about things such as Santa Claus, the military, or parenthood were not exactly accurate. So, why in the world would I be so arrogant and so audacious to think my beliefs about *life beyond* would be any more accurate?! After all, I've never *actually* died! (At least not that I know of.) I must chuckle and shake my head at people who pound their fist with religious conviction that they are absolutely right! They proclaim anyone who disagrees is a sinner and will risk some horrible fate. Hmm, okay. How presumptuous.

As for the playbook up to this point, I've learned it, experienced it, and actually *lived* it. I'm positive there are many other paths to prosperity, but I speak with conviction that *this* path works. However, from this point forward, I must emphasize that I have not walked the walk in life *beyond*. Although I've shared my beliefs on death, I have not yet actually experienced it. The following concepts are only my opinion on possibilities and always open for discussion. That said, the beliefs that I share have certainly helped me in *this* life! (That's why I include them here.)

There are many possibilities, but regardless of how we carry on, we *do* carry on. Why do I believe that? Because all of the cosmos, infinite space, eternal time, endless energy, human soul, and countless other wonders are *too grand* and *too amazing* for our lives to simply just…end. It doesn't fit. It doesn't make sense. After all, are we not a form of energy?

There are many forms of energy all around us. Think about assorted types of invisible energy: ultraviolet rays, x-rays, gamma rays, electromagnetic waves, radio waves, microwaves, and many others. Although we can't see this energy with the naked eye, it is still very real. Here's a little thought exercise. Imagine you teleported back to the year 1500. You pulled out your smartphone and conducted a video call with a friend across the country. The image of you and that friend would fly invisibly through the air and display on your phone's screen – just like magic, right? If *that* wouldn't get you burned at the stake, I don't know what would. Today, we think nothing of it. And that's just *one* form of energy – there are countless *other* forms of energy in existence. Much of this energy is invisible. I'd argue there are many forms of energy we haven't yet discovered and/or don't yet fully understand.

It's my belief that one form of energy is that of our spirit (soul). Although it's not fully understood (yet), I believe we'll continue to learn more about our soul in due time. After all, we're already starting to discover how the brain sends electrical impulses to make the body move. Various brain imaging technology can also detect indicators or biomarkers of mood and perhaps thought. What will be possible 100 years from now? Or longer? Hold that thought for later. Right now, all of this reinforces my belief that our spiritual energy (soul) will somehow live on after we die. Once again, *how* that happens is currently unknown, but all good things come to those who ~~wait~~ keep learning and figure it out. Where does that leave my thoughts on life beyond?

Simply put, we all go to Heaven. However, my vision of Heaven doesn't consist of pearly white gates, fluffy clouds, and sounds of harps playing in the background. Actually, that might be kind of neat and I'm open to that! But I don't believe so. I view Heaven as a larger universal energy. I envision our body's spiritual energy transcending to (re)join the larger realm of universal energy. Spiritual consciousness is a deep dream-like state. My idea of Heaven is a universal realm of tranquility and eternal peace. There is no Earthly concern or suffering. However, there also remains movement (energy) and who knows, some of that energy may get recycled or re-used again in some fashion. As our spirit rejoins the larger pool of energy, the potential exists to reconnect or cross paths with other spiritual life, including past loved ones. It's almost like static, interference, or crosstalk on radio waves. My perspective also comes with a small degree of disappointment.

The disappointment I have with my idea of Heaven is that we *all* go there. (If it's true, then it's true all the way through.) Unfortunately, that includes good people, bad people, evil people, and everyone in between. Yes, good and evil are on a relative scale. In fact, my sincerest wish is that truly evil people go somewhere evil. I would like that to be true, but I don't think it is. I believe all mortal characteristics (including good and evil) get left behind with our remains and that only our cleansed *energy* transcends to Heaven. Our energy flows in its purest form – perhaps like the day we were born, neither good nor bad.

By the way, if your vision of Heaven differs from mine, that's perfectly okay. Yes, the word itself (and concept) is of religious origin. I like the word Heaven because it's relatable to many and it's nebulous enough to fit my beliefs about where our spirit goes after death. Plus, I'll be pleasantly surprised if there are "levels" of Heaven for good and evil. That would be an unexpected but welcome surprise. After all, no two people think exactly alike. Again, you have your beliefs and I have mine. Perhaps my views on this topic will evolve as I learn more about religion.

Whether this all proves true or not remains to be seen. Time will tell. Just like Santa Claus, the military, and parenthood, I eagerly anticipate discovering what Heaven is *actually* like one day. Until then, the idea of a spiritual Heaven gives me comfort in *this* life. I sincerely hope you've thought about your own spirituality. Don't be concerned with right or wrong – our beliefs should evolve as we learn and discover new information. After all, haven't your own beliefs evolved over the course of your life? I surely hope so. Our beliefs are a work in progress. We should hone them as we learn more and refine our ways of thinking. That's a sign of intelligence. So, where do these beliefs leave us?

I won't speak for you or anyone else. As for me? I plan to live like I mean it, pass my torch of life to the next generation, and then transcend to Heaven into the great *beyond*. I believe my spiritual energy will return to the larger universal pool in some fashion. Of that, I am convinced. And who knows, perhaps our paths will eventually cross in some way. But before I get ahead of myself, there's one last twist that may affect these thoughts.

Life As We Know It

Although we *currently* know we'll eventually die, here's a thought. One day, you may hear people ask, **"Remember when people used to die?"** Wait, what?! Yes, I warned you earlier that I have some wild and unconventional ideas about life in the future. Follow along with an open mind.

The human body (especially the brain) is highly complex. What precisely defines "life as we know it"? What makes us conscious and self-aware? What gives us our personality, hopes, dreams, emotions, and desires? In other words, what makes us uniquely...*us*? I believe all of this collectively refers to our soul, but what precisely *is* our soul? That's the million-dollar question.

I don't know about you, but I'm certainly no expert in the field of biotechnology, genetics, or medical science. However, just as people adjust to virtual reality without being IT experts, we must also adjust to medical advances in life and longevity without being doctors or scientists. Here, I simply refer to common knowledge – nothing complex or scientific. For better or worse, changes are coming fast. Life as we know it *is* evolving. That is fact. Precisely *how* it will evolve remains to be seen. So, why do we care and how does this affect generational prosperity?

Up to this point, *Part II* has revealed many reasons *why*. However, our very existence, our life itself (body & soul) is the very essence of prosperity. *Life* is the core of everything; without it, we have nothing and are nothing – we don't exist. As humans, our life and the lives of others is why we do anything at all. And it's the conjoining generations that string all of humanity together.

Consequently, a book on generational prosperity *must* include these vital concepts. Unlike my beliefs on spirituality, what follows are *not* my suggestions or desires, but rather *possibilities*. Don't burn me at the stake, because I'm neither for nor against any of these concepts. That said, I am *convinced* that many (all?) are inevitable to some degree. Living in denial will not change reality. You should incorporate your own thoughts and opinions about life along with your religious, spiritual, and personal beliefs.

Life as we know it is actually a moving target. This is because we (humanity) continue to learn progressively more about life with each passing year. Mind you, much of this is already happening. We have *already* altered life in various ways, and we continue doing so at an exponentially faster rate. Think about medical, biological, genetic, and scientific breakthroughs that have already occurred. Think about ongoing advances in…

- Increasing human life spans.
- Extending lives with antibiotics and vaccines.
- Organ and limb transplants.
- Animal cloning.
- De-extinction efforts.
- Brain-computer interfaces (or human-machine).
- Stem cell research.
- Genetic sequencing and decoding.
- Artificial and lab grown organs.
- Body and cellular imaging.
- Advanced pharmaceuticals.

These things are only the tip of the iceberg. If you follow the arc of what's already possible and what's currently in progress, who knows where this all leads. If you think compound interest is powerful, just imagine the power of compounding advances in genetics, science, computing, and biotechnology. What's next? What other medical advancements and scientific breakthroughs exist that haven't yet been publicly disclosed? When you merge current medical science with advancements in computing power, it's like pouring gas on the fire. Improvements to artificial intelligence may also help us synthesize information even faster. Where will all of this lead? By continuing down this road, will we inevitably reach a point of completely transforming life as we know it? If our body and mind can be manipulated by science, the sky's the limit, right?

*Humanity continues to ask, "**What if…**"*

Longevity

By extending life, we get to live longer. Conceivably, there are various ways to accomplish this. If you happen to be a professional scientist, geneticist, or similar, please forgive my primitive conjecture. I claim no specialized education, training, or expertise. So, let's explore just two ~~scientific theories~~ creative guesses…

Perhaps science will extend our life through **genetic editing**. Through genetic decoding and sequencing, we could decipher *why* cells age. After all, something cellular causes or allows aging to occur. Therefore, editing that genetic code could possibly reverse, slow, or stop the aging process. Even if aging can't be stopped completely, maybe it could be slowed considerably. If so, that would be one way to extend life. Is there another way?

A second option to increase longevity is to **regrow cells**. Instead of trying to slow or stop the aging process through genetically editing existing cells, we could simply regrow new ones. We'd regrow our entire body, one piece at a time. After all, certain lizards, starfish, and other organisms have regenerative abilities. This is not science-fiction. They can *actually* regrow limbs, skin, and other parts of their body. Did you know that whitetail deer regrow their antlers annually? Of course, human skin regrows over cuts and wounds. Our blood can also replenish itself. And so on.

Therefore, what if humans could regrow limbs, organs, bones, ligaments, tendons, and *all* body parts? It's not so far-fetched when you consider our bodies have already done it once; we all started as a fertilized egg and grew into adulthood. Imagine humans had full regenerative abilities. No brittle bones. No wrinkly skin. No gray hair. In theory, we could extend life considerably. I've read some amazing things about growing organs using stem cells. If this technology can be perfected, watch out!

So, if we could extend life in any way, how much longer could we live? Years, decades, or centuries? Aging as we know it would become a thing of the past. People would ask, "Remember when people used to get old?" Life (as we know it) would change considerably. And that is all still the tip of the same iceberg. Because what could happen next? Let's take our thoughts to the next level…

Redefining Life

It's one thing to extend life, but what if it were completely redefined? For simplicity, allow me to view this concept in two stages. The first stage is probably the most difficult, which is to capture, decode, and store brain waves (speech, thought, memories, emotion, etc) – let's call it **brain wave science**. The second is a little scary, so we'll hold that thought for the moment, but we'll call it **life redefined**. Let's look a bit deeper into these two stages…

Through **brain wave science**, certain brain waves (electrical signals) can already be *captured*. This is done primarily through an electro-encephalogram (EEG). If science can capture these brain waves or neural signals, would it be possible to fully *decode* them? And if so, how accurately? In other words, we could determine the brain wave's precise meaning (emotion, word, or thought). If the signals could be decoded and understood, it's logical they could also be *stored* in some fashion (electrically, digitally, etc). This requires an understanding of memory.

Engineers fully understand computer memory. But how does the human brain store and recall *its* memory? This is still an emerging science. Just like computers, we know the brain can be volatile. We've all heard of amnesia, right? (Wait, what did I just say?) If amnesia can occur, why can't the opposite? (Oh yeah, now I remember.) Our memories have been shown to come and go. There are others who have a so-called photographic memory. How does this all work? If we fully understood brain memory, could it be artificially duplicated? Where can this all lead?

Basic computer history shows how processing power has exploded over the past several decades. That's right, computers are mere babies, not even 100 years old – just imagine what the future holds! The same trajectory is very likely for advances in brain wave science. I'd argue that with today's evolving computing power, biotechnology, and artificial intelligence, it will occur even faster! Imagine a world where brain wave science could…

- Capture, decode, and store human memories at the speed of electrons.
- Decode signals with such specificity that we can type (or transmit) words and memories simply by thinking them.
- Transfer vast stores of knowledge to/from memory in seconds.
- Capture not only words, but thoughts, memories, knowledge, experience, and even emotions. (After all, are these not electrical or neural signals of some sort?)

Yes, this is complex and difficult. It may also take a while, but relatively speaking how long is a "a while" – decades, centuries? Nonetheless, if these capabilities evolved and matured, things could get scary.

This brings us to **life redefined**, the hypothetical second and final stage of redefining life as we know it. It also brings us back to the question of what comprises our soul. Mind you, achieving the first stage is an essential pre-requisite to this stage being possible. Just for fun, let's assume our soul is the sum total of our thoughts, memories, emotions, feelings, and desires. Let's include *all* of it, including whatever magical formula makes us **conscious** and **self-aware. Now**, *that* **would be scary!** Let's also imagine our body was only the *vehicle* that carried our soul. That would essentially decouple our soul from our physical body. (Similar to computer software from hardware.) Our soul could then be captured, decoded, stored, and transmitted. That certainly would redefine life as we know it. Yes, that would do it alright. If our soul (consciousness and self-awareness) could be copied, stored, or transmitted, what then? Yes, the thought is a bit overwhelming. Perhaps something out of a sci-fi movie…

- Could we copy our soul (including self-awareness)?
- Could there be more than one of us?
- Could we transmit ourself (soul) via satellite or the Internet?
- Could we create backup copies of ourself (in case one died)?
- Would we ever truly die? (our physical body may, but would our soul?)

Wow, my head is spinning. This gives new meaning to the term *unplug*! It sounds like virtual reality gone wild. We would *become* virtual reality. Should I cry now or later?!

Granted, achieving any of this is not exactly *easy*. If this all seems far-fetched, think about things today that were deemed impossible only 100 years ago! Think about that video phone call to a friend in the year 1500. Think about holograms. Think about satellites, microwaves, x-rays, Bluetooth, wi-fi, genetics, organ transplants, and various other technologies, with more to come. Just because it doesn't seem possible *at the moment*, doesn't mean it's impossible. I believe we're just getting warmed up.

These concepts will be researched and tested by experts well into the future. There are many brilliant minds on this planet and more are born each day. When you couple that brilliance with *exponential* advances in genetics, computing power, and medical science, humanity has the power and potential to shape its own destiny. Let's hope for the better.

As it applies here, the focus is on what defines life as we know it. Our concern is the impact to our hopes, beliefs, spirituality, and humanity as a whole.

Life as we know it *will* continue to change. That's a scary thought for many people. My guess is that life will change *significantly* by the year 2125. It will be *completely* and *forever* changed by 2225. Maybe I'm off by a few decades, but I think that's close. Even a century is nothing in the scope of time. And beyond that, there may even come a day in the far distant future, when people will ask, **"Remember when people used to die?"**

Consequences?

By the way, all of this comes with additional considerations. How will this affect our life and future generations? How will this affect broader humanity as we know it?

Just because you *can*, does it mean you *should*? If the human race develops the ability to drastically change life as we know it (which I'm convinced we will), we must also consider the implications. I can think of at least three major considerations...

First of all, we must weigh the moral, ethical, legal, and religious concerns. There are billions of people on the planet and therefore billions of differing viewpoints and opinions on life. To what extent are they each comfortable with redefining life so drastically? After all, we've *already* changed life as we know it and continue to do so, but how far do we go? Is there a line in the sand? Is there a point of no return? Who gets to decide the answers to these questions? What if some people *don't want* to live longer – or forever? What if things go against your religious beliefs? What if your thoughts could be read with a high degree of precision? Do we want others reading our minds? Who controls these medical procedures and who wields the power of extending life?

Second, we must think about the socioeconomical and practical things such as financial sustainability. Imagine people lived longer by decades, centuries, or more. How does that affect programs such as Social Security? How does it affect health insurance and life insurance actuarial tables? How is employment affected in general? Would the timeline for public and private education become completely upended? How is it all paid for and by whom? There are countless considerations.

Third and finally, how would extending life affect our planet? Would it lead to overpopulation? What is the maximum human population that Earth can sustain? Would we be forced to populate other planets, the moon, or long-term space stations? There's a myriad of questions that need asking and answering. What do *you* think about such matters? I'll end on one last note about life in general.

[Entire books are written on humanity and life as we know it. The ideas here are not my suggestions or wishes, but rather possibilities and objective thoughts to ponder. Our beliefs (and our lives) *will* be affected in some way as things inevitably evolve. I would be severely remiss to omit these powerful and pertinent subjects from a book on generational prosperity. We *will* continue to learn, discover, and adapt – for all of humanity's existence. That begs the question, how long will we exist?]

"Will our species prosper eternally or will humanity eventually become extinct?"

The Power of Hope

Big thoughts such as these bring us to our hopes and dreams. Spiritually, what hopes do people have for their lives (and souls)? What do they hope is beyond? I alluded to the power of hope earlier in this chapter. Hope is tremendously powerful. The opposite of hopeful is hopeless. Don't be hopeless. Hopeless people rarely prosper.

Your hopes and beliefs can unleash nearly superhuman feats and break the self-limiting shackles of despair. I believe Henry Ford once said, "Whether you think you *can* or think you *can't*, you're right." It's all about your beliefs. Imagine the scenarios…

- A horrified mother lifts a car with her bare hands to save her child trapped beneath.
- A professional athlete shatters a world record once deemed unbreakable.
- An abandoned child overcomes poverty to build a billion-dollar company.

Sure, there are many factors at play in these situations. Things such as environment, adrenaline, hard work, education, and even luck can affect outcomes such as these. However, *none* of them would happen without hope! People *hope* to win the lotto; therefore, they buy tickets. Humanity *hopes* to cure cancer; therefore, we fund, staff, and research treatments to eradicate cancer. Society *hopes* to end global war; therefore, we strengthen ties to allied nations, maintain deterrent forces, and forge peace agreements. We *hope* to end world hunger and famine; therefore, we solicit volunteers and strive to build sustainable food sources. *Hope* for a brighter future and the *belief* that it's possible are the sparks required for action. You never *would* if you didn't believe you *could*.

As you can see, hopes and beliefs are a powerful elixir. If you have no hope of achieving (anything), how will it ever happen? In order to execute, you must first believe. Beliefs matter – not only about tomorrow or next year, but right here, right now.

Accordingly, what you believe about death and *beyond* matters. So, how does hope fit in with my beliefs on religion, transcendentalism, infinity, eternity, spirituality, and life as we know it? How do these beliefs affect me? This all converges into my deep conviction that there's some form of life *beyond* death. I can't tell you *how* it occurs, but our soul (spiritual energy) lives on in some way beyond our mortal life. Ever get the feeling of déjà vu? (Perhaps life is recycling or reconnecting in some fashion.) The idea of that awesome, electric *next* life energizes me! Some people call this *hope* – hey, I'll take it!

Nobody can steal my hope or beliefs about life beyond. Nobody can dampen my life spirit…it's far too powerful. My mortal life will certainly end, but never my spirit. And my beliefs about *beyond* don't only affect my next life…they also affect *this* life! Knowing that my energy will somehow carry on lifts my spirit in this life. I'm happy, content, peaceful, and ever grateful for the next phase of eternal life, whatever form it may take. I'm also unafraid of death; my beliefs allow me to *accept* it and *anticipate* it. Surely, I'll miss my loved ones and all of the beauty that planet Earth offers. I'm not trying to expedite my death. I certainly plan to live each day to the fullest. However, I know that all good things must end and I'm prepared for that – I accept it and anticipate it. Eternal peace awaits. Higher-level spirituality awaits. Whatever form it may take, Heaven awaits.

And by the way, if there is no life after death, then 'oh well', I've lost nothing because I'll never know it, right? But if there *is* life beyond, then without belief, I've lost. I've lost in *this* life. I will have lived a hopeless mortal life believing that this is all there is to it. Believing the glass is half empty. So, we all get to choose our own beliefs about life after death. I don't know about you, but I've made *my* choice! Remember, the world was once flat. And whether you think your spirit *will* live on or whether you think it *won't*…you're right!

Closure

This all leaves one final thought on how this applies to humanity. I started this book with the concepts of intentionality and critical thought. It all comes full circle back to right here, right now. In other words, where are you headed? What's your direction in life? All the way through. People don't intentionally select a destination without the hope of arriving there – what is your destination *beyond?* Never lose your curiosity or sense of wonder. Think wide open. Dream big. *Belief and hope fuel intention and effort.* I encourage you to reflect on your personal beliefs, particularly about *beyond* this life. What hopes do you have for your own spirit and the spirits of your loved ones? Ultimately, those beliefs should fuel *this* life.

As we look to the future, advances in computing, artificial intelligence, biology, genetics, and other technologies will continue to converge and even synthesize. How will it change life as we know it? What will become of humanity?

Our spiritual energy (our soul) is the link between all generations, connecting one life to the next and all of humanity. In that vein, countless generations have come before me. I will honor their memory and carry their spirit. I will build upon their legacy. Likewise, many generations will follow me. I will contribute to their prosperity. I'm blessed to be alive right here, right now. I will die someday; but until then, I will live!

*P*ART *III* (*W*HAT *N*OW?)

CHAPTER 15

HERE'S WHAT!

So, this brings a close to your playbook for generational prosperity. Whew! You now have a treasure trove of time-tested principles, processes, values, and concepts that lead to prosperity. We've examined all of that across *14 key areas of life*. This is not only knowledge and theory, but also more than a half-century of real-life experience that my family and I (and many others) have personally lived. I told you it was big…but we're not done yet. Remember the one-two punch of lifelong learning? That's right, you gained all this knowledge on how and why to achieve prosperity, now it's time to *apply* it! Don't you dare finish this book and then let it (or your life) collect dust. As you now see, the path is simple. It's certainly not easy, but as you know, nothing worth doing is easy. Let's see what's next. But first, a mini synopsis of key takeaways. *Part I* was chock full of *how*.

Part I (How)
Convergent Summary

To achieve much of anything in life, start by being **intentional**. Cast a vision and set a destination for your future, your family, and yourself. Humans are blessed with the most powerful minds on Earth; use yours to apply **critical thinking** to all areas of your life.

Pride yourself on being a **lifelong learner**. Feed your mind for the rest of your life; plant seeds, not weeds. Continue to learn, grow, and mature for the benefit of yourself and your family. There are countless ways to learn – all 100% debt free!

You'll likely work for many decades, so do work that you love! Find the intersection of passion and prosperity. **Grow a rewarding career** that is both personally fulfilling and financially lucrative. Be a servant leader and work like a stallion, not a donkey. Your income is the engine of wealth building.

Choose to **build financial wealth**. And it *is* a choice. Break the back of poverty and financial struggle forever! Follow the six principles (in order) for financial security; as a bonus, you can become a multi-millionaire! You'll follow a written budget, always grow your income, live debt free, keep a 6-month emergency fund, invest 15% into retirement, and own your home. Also follow the three money behaviors: have a plan for your money, give generous hand-ups, and leave an inheritance.

You have one body so take care of it. That involves more than just diet and exercise. Your **health wealth** is the *most important thing* in life! Focus on your physical, mental, emotional, intellectual, spiritual, and relational health in the pursuit of *total* health.

Unplug! Break free from the obsessions and addictions of digital opioids; give yourself a digital detox. Keep yourself and your kids safe from the potential online dangers of scammers, predators, emotional isolation, depression, anxiety, comparison, and a host of other nasties. For your own benefit – *use* virtual reality, but *live* in actual reality!

Follow **life's universal principles**. These are the helpful external rules of the road.

- Always give *helpful hand-ups*, not *hurtful hand-outs*!
- A life of order is more prosperous than one of chaos (*order>chaos*).
- If you want different results in life, you must do things differently (*different input = different output*).
- You can (and should) *control the controllables*; while nothing's guaranteed, it stacks the odds in your favor.
- Remember *relativity*; keep perspective, avoid comparison, and don't put yourself or others in a self-limiting box.
- Exercise *balance* in life; with rare exception, extremes are unhealthy.
- The *cost of procrastination* is expensive; less work today equals more work tomorrow (and vice-versa)!
- *Where you focus, you prosper*; the power of the pen helps in all areas of your life.

Personal values are the internal beliefs that shape your character, guide your actions, and help to define who you are. Live these values. Your value system is dynamic, so adjust your repertoire over the course of your life. A starter set of values consists of *thoughtfulness, dependability, diligence, integrity, excellence, generosity, contentment, and gratitude.* Also, be sure to *respect* others and respect yourself. Ultimately, you should strive to *live and leave a legacy!*

Harness **the power of individualism.** Shatter the mold of normal and conventional ways of thinking. Lead the way. Don't follow sheeple. Don't self-label, self-stereotype, self-discriminate, or self-limit. Don't be sexist or racist. Treat people (including yourself) as individuals and give them the respect they deserve. Have a high-control mindset. Be a *victor*, not a victim!

Part II (Why)
Convergent Summary

In addition to learning *how*, it's even more important to keep perspective on *why* you should live like you mean it. There are many people who want to prosper – they just don't understand how. You now know how. But that's only the first step. Understanding *why* is just as critical. In fact, I'd argue it's the most important part of this entire book (and your life). Knowing *how* is simple, but knowing *why* is not. Humans are highly complex and life is different for everyone. Each person's *why* is as unique as they are. Find your purpose. Stop living in black and white and start living in color! Discover what gives you true meaning in life. What is your life about? As I recap below, reflect on your own personal *why* and ultimately, what life means to you.

To achieve *extra*ordinary happiness and fulfillment, seek **marriage (lasting love).** When you find that special someone, don't half-step it. *Go all in…get married.* Build a strong and healthy marriage through commitment, communication, shared values, selfless love, spontaneity, growth, and quality time. Enjoying life with a soul mate by your side is deeply satisfying.

Parenthood is the most rewarding job on the planet! Parents should provide three main things to their children. The first and most important thing parents should do is *protect* their children. Second, parents should provide *structure* in their children's lives. Lastly, parents should provide *guidance* to their children. Also remember to always love them. Don't *be* a parent (the noun); actively *parent* (the verb). Children are the very essence of generational prosperity!

You only get one life; **live with meaning and purpose.** Don't be a rat in the wheel or a Bumbling Dumbledorf. Choose a life that adds value to others and the world around you. Be generous, selfless, and help others. This is where it all comes together; right here, right now. Live in the present with an eye toward the future. And just in case you thought it's all work and no play, have fun like you mean it! Yes, it's worth it <wink>.

As it currently stands, all of us will die. **Death** is a part of life. You're likely to experience the death of one or more loved ones over your lifetime. You'll certainly experience your own death. The mindset of *acceptance* can help you reconcile death. In fact, take it to the next level and *anticipate* death – in the interest of discovering what's *beyond*. Death is what makes life so precious!

Your **beliefs** greatly impact your life. Your perspective on religion, infinite space, eternal time, spirituality, and life as we know it help shape who you are. Transcendentalism encompasses all that and more; allow yourself to *transcend* above it all. Open your mind as far and wide as possible. Be reminded that we're all a smaller part of something bigger. Life is about more than just us. After mortal death, our spirit will live on in some manner; exactly how still remains a mystery. A little mystery is good. Your own personal beliefs, religion, and spirituality will guide you to the *beyond*, whenever that day comes. Harness the power of hope – for your family, yourself, and life beyond. And remember, our beliefs help us in *this* life!

All of this is *why* you live a prosperous life; this is *why* you live like you mean it!

These principles are interconnected and interdependent on each other – the how *and* the why. Therefore, one supports another, and vice versa. So, the more areas that you work on, the better success you'll have. It can be hard to succeed if you work in silos (money, career, marriage, etc). These things work in sync with each other like the gears of a machine. That's exactly why *The Torch of Life* brings it all together! Now…

It's Game Time!

Many will want what you have, but few will do what you do. Do you want generational prosperity? If so, you must *do*. Now, you know *how* and now you know *why*. Therefore, it becomes a *decision*; you're at a fork in the road. Your actions will determine your degree of success. It has come full circle, right back to *intentionality*. What will you decide? It's your choice – excuses or results. Will you execute the plays or not? Regardless of age, demographic or circumstance, you can (and should) start right now!

Remember, this playbook is *a* way, not *the* way. Nothing is perfect or guaranteed in life, so do the best you can and adjust along the way. Start. Again, do the *best* that you can, not the least! I sincerely believe that any able-bodied person can do this. I know *you* can do it, too. Let nothing or no one stop you! The football coach has his playbook for success. You, too, now have *your* playbook for success and you can pass it down through the generations. Now that you have a path, let the fun begin! It's time to run the plays and execute!

I encourage you to assess yourself honestly against the key areas I've outlined. Measure your work and your progress. Jot down specific goals, milestones, and notes in a journal or on some index cards. Be clear and concise, not vague and ambiguous. Ask yourself how you're doing in each key area. Track your progress and if it helps – *write it down*! If it's helpful, go back and re-read that area. If you're struggling with specific action items, here are a few starter ideas…

Lifelong Learning

- What (specifically) are you going to learn in the next 6-12 months?
- Which college degree plan can accelerate your career (and life)? (Enroll now.)

- Which professional certifications can boost your earnings? (Earn them this year.)
- Learn a new hobby this year (musical instrument, new language, art, sport, etc).

Grow Your Career

- When's the last time you got a raise? (Earn one this year.)
- What's the last thing you've done to level-up? (certification, degree, training, etc.)
- Specifically, how can you add value to your organization or company? (Increase sales, gain customers, or boost revenue by X percent.)

Build Financial Wealth

- Have you developed a written budget? (Start today.)
- What *specifically* will you do in the next 6-12 months to increase your income?
- Are you debt free? (If not, start a debt pyramid today.)
- Do you have an emergency fund? (Once you reach principle 4, build one immediately.)
- Are you investing 15% into retirement? (Once you reach principle 5, start!)
- Do you own your own home? (Once you reach principle 6, consider buying one.)

You get the point. I won't go through every key area, but the above should give you an idea of what questions to ask yourself. In each case, it's vital to develop *action* items for the desired areas. You must write down something that you're going to get *done*. Make it as specific as possible: timeframe, cost, measurable, realistic, etc. For example, 'work harder' or 'save money' is not specific or measurable. If you're not as prosperous as you'd like to be, it's likely that you're not getting traction. Remember, the rat in the wheel works hard, but you must have a specific path and be productive.

There's no secret here; just accomplish one thing and then another. Weight loss occurs one pound at a time. You become a millionaire one dollar at a time. You achieve anything one step at a time. Make tomorrow better than today. Then repeat for the rest of your life; you're never done. Prosperity is a means, not an end; it's the *journey*.

Why do any of this? Too many people are struggling, in my opinion unnecessarily – struggling with money, career woes, mental wellness, relationships, toxic bosses, drama, addictions, and more. Dumbing down or numbing down their lives. Too many victims and not enough victors. Stressing, short-cutting, scrolling and clicking, chasing their tail, and running like a rat in a wheel. Bumbling Dumbledorfs. Digital zombies. No need for all that. How do I know? Because I used to struggle as well. I was a Bumbling Dumbledorf for too long. I've done plenty of stupid things when I was younger and spent my fair share of time in a rut. However, I've come to learn everything that I've just shared with you and I'm better because of it…much, much better. Life's too short to stay stuck in a rut; it's your time to break free! Surely, this book is not a magical solution or a Pollyanna fix-all for every problem. Also, unfortunately, it cannot help with the tragic uncontrollables in life. Sadly, bad things will happen. That is for certain. However, these principles have led me and my family to true prosperity and the beauty is, any able-bodied person can achieve the same (and more)! Who's next? I hope *you* decide to be next. Let it be *you*.

Conclusion

So, as I hand off *The Torch of Life*, this copy is now yours. I sincerely hope it serves you well. I hope you find these principles valuable and they motivate you to live an inspired and fruitful life. I hope you find the love of your life and raise a wonderful family, if that is your wish. Love others. Love yourself. Be a lifelong learner. Lend a caring and helpful hand-*up*. Be courteous and kind. Treasure your copy of *The Torch of Life*. Keep it on your nightstand and reference it often. But please don't stop there – be sure to pass along a copy to the next generation. Continue the chain. And as for me?

For over a half century, my torch has been a blazing inferno. I've lived and done more than I ever dreamed possible. I'm humbly blessed and truly grateful. However, time keeps ticking. There's more to do and

I'll surely keep doing the *best* that I can. I'll continue to learn, grow, mature, and improve my life in as many ways as possible while also helping others along the way. Pedal to the metal. As you've seen, helping others is a core mission of mine. More importantly, I'll surely love my wonderful wife and kids…you can bet on that! But I'll also have one eye towards the future. I plan to pass along generational prosperity to not only my own two kids but anyone else who may be interested. Step by step, day by day. In case you missed it, a common thread throughout this entire book is to be generous and lend helpful hand-ups. It's a small world, so who knows, maybe we'll cross paths someday. I hope to see you around, preferably in ~~virtual~~ *actual* reality. If you see me first, be sure to say "Hi".

It's my hope that *The Torch of Life* becomes a part of my legacy when I'm gone from this Earth. This book is a heartfelt reminder to live a kind and generous life and to help others do the same. Upon my passing, I hope my spirit lives on to help future generations in some way. Either way, I'm at peace. I've lived a full and prosperous life and my cup continues to run over. But as we know, all good things must end, including our time here on Earth. So, as the flame of my torch burns down and my life nears its end, I patiently anticipate discovering what's *beyond* this life one day. Until that time comes, remember…everybody dies, not everybody lives. Don't ever sell yourself short. As long as I have a single breath in my body, I intend to live – and I hope you too intend to live…**like you mean it!**

ABOUT THE AUTHOR

Dave's a proud military veteran. He retired from the U.S. Air Force in 2010 as a Senior Master Sergeant with over 21 years of distinguished service. While serving, he managed multi-million-dollar IT systems and led hundreds of world-class professionals in support of global military operations. While assigned as a military instructor, he taught senior leaders on topics such as decision analysis, project management, effective communication, personality assessment models, situational leadership, quality management, and more. After retiring from active duty, he worked as an IT Specialist for the Department of the Air Force and the U.S. Treasury Department. He earned a master's degree in management, a bachelor's degree in information systems management, and multiple professional certifications, two of which were the gold standard in their field. He has over a half century of life experience working, traveling, and volunteering thousands of hours in communities all over the world. He's traveled to at least 39 states and 9 other countries, living in many over the years. Dave is married to the most wonderful woman in the world, who's also a military veteran. Together, they've raised two amazing adult children – one son and one daughter.

Enjoyed this book? Please leave a 5-star Amazon review!